DIW BERLIN

3

Vierteljahrshefte zur Wirtschaftsforschung 3.2015

The Greek Crisis: A Greek Tragedy?

Duncker & Humblot · Berlin

DIW Berlin – Deutsches Institut
für Wirtschaftsforschung e. V.

Mohrenstraße 58, 10117 Berlin
Tel. +49-30-8 97 89-0
Fax +49-30-8 97 89-200
www.diw.de

MAIN PUBLISHERS
Prof. Marcel Fratzscher, Ph. D.
Prof. Dr. Dorothea Schäfer (Editor in chief)
Prof. Dr. Gert G. Wagner

PUBLISHERS
Prof. Dr. Pio Baake
Prof. Dr. Tomaso Duso
Dr. Ferdinand Fichtner
Prof. Dr. Peter Haan
Prof. Dr. Claudia Kemfert
Dr. Kati Krähnert
Prof. Dr. Lukas Menkhoff
Prof. Karsten Neuhoff, Ph. D.
Prof. Dr. Jürgen Schupp
Prof. Dr. C. Katharina Spieß

Responsible for the current issue
Prof. Dr. Christian Dreger
Prof. Dr. Alexander S. Kritikos

SALE AND DISTRIBUTION
VERLAG DUNCKER & HUMBLOT GMBH
Carl-Heinrich-Becker-Weg 9
12165 Berlin

DESIGN
Edenspiekermann

LAYOUT AND COMPOSITION
Alfred Gutzler
Ellen Müller-Gödtel

PRINT
2016 bei Das Druckteam Berlin
Gustav-Holzmann-Straße 6
10317 Berlin

Printed in Germany

Printed on FSC-certified paper

ISSN 0340-1707 (Print) / 1861-1559 (Online)
ISBN 978-3-428-14963-6

The Greek Crisis: A Greek Tragedy?

ALEXANDER S. KRITIKOS AND CHRISTIAN DREGER

Alexander S. Kritikos, DIW Berlin–German Institute for Economic Research, University of Potsdam, e-mail: akritikos@diw.de
Christian Dreger, DIW Berlin–German Institute for Economic Research, Europaen University Viadrina, Frankfurt (Oder), e-mail: cdreger@diw.de

Since the 2008 stock market crash, the Greek economy experienced a double-dip recession. While the Greek GDP is almost 30 percent below its level before the financial crisis, its economy appears to be still in dire straits.

The ongoing reform process to overcome the sovereign debt crisis is mainly driven by the Troika (European Union, European Central Bank and International Monetary Fund), which seeks to balance the country's public budget. The strategic focus on reducing the public debt resulted in a cataclysmal economic downturn, because Greece's structural weaknesses were not sufficiently addressed and because public and private investments into R&D, the Greek innovation system and its infrastructure as components of a strategy for growth were neglected. With austerity in place—with its massive reductions in pension payments, social expenditures, and wages—there is not much beyond tourism, agriculture, as well as some copper, aluminum and petroleum products that Greece can export in considerably higher amount after having enforced the list of austerity measures.

In contrast, innovative, future-oriented industries with high value added are almost absent from Greece. Instead we see a massive exodus of Greek entrepreneurs, scientists, managers, and highly skilled employees toward the northern EU-countries and the United States, i.e. of those who could create future industries, because they lack the needed economic, institutional and political support. While cost disadvantages have been reduced, the underlying, persistent structural problems are inhibiting higher investment, innovation, and prosperity.

This issue of the "Vierteljahrshefte zur Wirtschaftsforschung" is inspired by the format of a Greek tragedy. It discusses the status quo in Greece in the seventh year of the crisis and potential policy strategies and reform options that could be a step forward in resolving the Greek crisis. After the *prologue*, it not only considers in the *parodos* and in three *episodes* the immediate consequences that the economic policy of the last six years had, but through five *stasima* it takes into account a wide range of aspects inherent to the debate on reforms, such as the healthcare and education systems, as well as labor and product markets. It finishes with the *exodos* stating what needs to be done to end the crisis. The contributions to this volume were written by 20 authors from Greece, the Greek diaspora, and selected non-Greek authors with interest in the Greek cause. Their contributions examine the Greek crisis from different perspectives and present different possible resolutions. These represent the opinions of the respective authors, which sometimes rest upon contrarian concepts. Thus, potential reform options remain under discussion.

In the *prologue, Renate Neubäumer* sheds light on the underlying causes of the Greek crisis and shows that it is deeply rooted in the country's earlier economic development. Although Greece had made some effort to improve the state of its economy before the year 2001—to be able to join the Euro-zone—many of the country's weaknesses continued to persist or even worsened. Over-regulation of product and labor markets as well as corruption hampered business activities and discouraged investment, thus harming the country's competitiveness and productivity. In addition, disproportionately high unit labor costs contributed to weak exports.

The government relied on foreign capital to finance its ever-increasing expenditures, which were in large part due to the bloated public administration. At the same time consumers used credit cards and loans to live beyond their means, all contributing to a real estate bubble. When the inflow of foreign capital dried up in 2007, the real estate bubble burst and the economy entered a depression.

Since then, the austerity and institutional reforms stipulated by the Troika have not revitalized the sclerotic economy. The current course can lead to modest growth, should agriculture and tourism provide higher value added, but is not sufficient to fuel higher long-term growth. Under such a scenario the accumulated public debt is insurmountable. As *Klaus Schrader, David Benček* and *Claus-Friedrich Laaser* argue in their *parodos*, even if the Greek government recognizes the need to modernize its economic structure and drives forward the implementation of reforms, a further debt relief in the form of a haircut or debt restructuring of at least 30 percent might be necessary in order for the country to return to a debt level that is sustainable in the long term.

Unfortunately, currently the opposite is happening. The tangle of regulations in Greece paralyzes business activities with time- and cost-intensive procedures and uncertainty. It undermines competition with rigid pricing, entry restrictions, and closed professions, thus deterring investment and impeding economic development. Product market regulation prevents international companies from doing business in Greece. As *Kaspar Richter, Gabriele Giudice* and *Angela Cozzi* point out in the first *stasimo,* future growth depends on reforms that open product markets for investment and exports, as well as on making products and services more affordable for consumers, thus increasing consumption.

In addition, persistent structural weakness in Greece is strongly related to the inefficient and corrupt public administration. The business environment is still characterized by bureaucratic hurdles for companies, which makes Greece even more unattractive for investment. As *Vasiliki*

Bozani and *Nick Drydakis* show in the second *stasimo*, while previous governments had removed some of the obstacles companies were facing, there are still significant delays to the reforms and many of the changes are not being enforced properly. This is due in part to a lack of monitoring and enforcement by the Troika. Making matters worse, the current Greek government is rolling back some of the structural reforms that previous Greek parliaments had approved.

At the same time, some of the Troika imposed policies have had devastating effects on the economy. Austerity to cut government expenditure and ensure prompt repayment of debt, as specified in the bailout programs, has inflicted greater harm on the Greek economy than expected by Troika, in particular by the IMF. *Sebastian Gechert* and *Ansgar Rannenberg* describe in their *episode* that the austerity measures implemented while the economy was at rock bottom intensified the negative impact, deepening the GDP decline between 2010 and 2014.

Government expenditure cuts have not only distressed the Greek economy directly, but also affected many publicly provided goods and services; for instance in education and healthcare services. As explained in the third *stasimo* by *Xeni Dassiou* the education sector suffers from cost inefficiencies and is characterized by unequal opportunities. While the economic crisis has thwarted accessibility of education, some long overdue reforms have been implemented in different areas. For instance, recent restructuring of research institutes and university departments as well as management reforms, as stipulated by the 2011 bailout program and enforced under the Papademos government, shifted the universities' strategic focus towards innovative research. However, while Greece should have intensified these efforts and continued the reform process, the current government decided to roll these back.

Also the health sector operates inefficiently and the austerity measures have further worsened its service provision. *Platon Yfantopoulos* and *John Yfantopoulos* show in the fourth *stasimo* that the health status of individuals in Greece deteriorated during the crisis, which is especially pronounced for vulnerable groups with low income.

Another misguided bailout measure is the Wealth Tax on Real Estate, which seeks to increase government revenues. *Dimitis Christelis* shows in his *episode*, that it effectively froze the real estate market, severely harming the economy. This tax especially hurts less affluent people, for whom an owned house represents most of their savings, driving many into bankruptcy. As an alternative to the dysfunctional tax system in Greece, *Gregory T. Papanikos* explores in his *episode* the concept of a flat tax on wealth as the only form of government revenue and argues that this could be a more efficient and effective way of taxation that takes into account the specific challenges in Greece.

If Greece is to achieve both sustainable long-term growth and access to private capital markets in order to roll over its debt at reasonable costs, the country will need to make significant investments to enter innovative sectors and compete in international markets. Even though there are entrepreneurs with promising business plans, the lack of funding, the overregulation, and the bureaucratic hurdles are major impediments to the creation and growth of innovative companies. Instead the latest actions of the present government and the ongoing capital controls are causing Greek companies to closing down or move out of Greece. The Greek government needs to cut red tape and to direct financial resources to research institutions and universities, as well as to companies that are engaged in innovative activities. As *Christian Dreger* and *Hans-Eggert Reimers* show in the final *stasimo*, public investments will, in turn, attract and spur private investments.

The transition to an innovation driven economy through suitable institutional and structural reforms is a pre-condition for an economic recovery and long-term growth.

After all, six years of the Greek economic downturn and the consequential six years of debate about it have produced one clear insight: Greece will only succeed in turning around and become prosperous if it starts making better use of its comparative advantages and if it lays the foundation for the production of higher value-added goods. The real misery underlying the Greek crisis is that the country has hidden assets that are substantially underappreciated in the analysis of its economic prospects. The most prominent one is its well educated citizens: People who excel at research, entrepreneurship, finance, and business. Instead of providing incentives for these people to stay in Greece and increase its productivity, the country is exporting its talents with low returns—instead of exporting the goods and services these talents could have produced.

There is a five-point plan to growth strategy—the *exodos* from the Greek crisis put together by *Alexander S. Kritikos* and *Marian Hafenstein*—which can be derived from the contributions of this volume: (i) developing a reform agenda under Greek ownership aiming to substantially improve its regulatory and institutional environment; (ii) reorganizing public finances and gaining back the trust of the markets and the European partners in the Greek government; thus (iii) making the Greek public debt sustainable; (iv) reducing the bureaucratic hurdles in the everyday life of Greek citizen, entrepreneurs, business owners and managers, and, last but not least, (v) expanding Greece's industrial base and its modern sector by investing into a better innovation system as well as by creating a business friendly tax- and regulation system.

If Greece better capitalizes on its Eurozone membership and makes structural reforms under Greek ownership, it will attract talents and investments that add innovative sectors to its economic structure. No magic bullet is needed: Eastern European countries have blazed this trail. All it needs is a government, regardless of party, committed to a better future for all Greeks, instead of continuing the clientele approach which prevails until today.

Greece will only turnaround when its brain drain is turned into brain circulation. To that end, it needs supportive creditors who will shift from asking for further austerity measures to asking for a comprehensive strategy that combines structural reforms with an investment strategy. As of today, the Greek government has taken no concrete steps towards structural reforms or encouraging innovation and the Troika continues to insist upon austerity measures only, like in the past six years. Under these conditions the Greek crisis will likely go on. So, we still await for what a Greek tragedy aims for: *catharsis*.

The Prologue to the Greek Crisis

RENATE NEUBÄUMER

Renate Neubäumer, University of Landau, e-mail: neub@uni-landau.de

Summary: This paper analyzes the prologue to the Greek tragedy—in particular, the long period of slow growth after Greece joined the European Union and the short period of very strong growth following its adoption of the euro—and deduces reform proposals. Ultimately, a growth strategy should contain three interrelated bundles of measures: First, an improvement of the institutional environment, which currently makes it difficult to do business in Greece and thus leads to too little investment. Second, a reorganization of public finances and the creation of a leaner, more efficient administration, as well as a reform of the pensions system. Third, an expansion of the industrial basis and the modern sector in order to build a strong export basis. All of these measures entail comprehensive changes to Greece's economy and Greek society, and the majority of Greeks must therefore be in favor of them. The alternative is to opt for moderate reforms and to return to the old path of low growth and a lower living standard.

→ JEL Classification: O52, E02
→ Keywords: Greece, slow growth, growth strategy, economic measures

1 Introduction

When Greece passed the convergence criteria in 2000 and entered the euro zone, it was the start of what looked like a success story: The country's gross domestic product (GDP) rose by 4.5 percent that year and from 2001 to 2007, it continued to increase by an average of 4.2 percent per year.[1] In 2007, Greece's GDP was one-third higher than it was in 2000. Portugal, which has a similar economic structure, saw an increase of only 8 percent in the same time span; in Germany, then dubbed "the ailing man of Europe," the GDP rose by only 10.5 percent. (In Spain and Ireland, on the other hand, the development of the economic output was similarly successful to that of Greece, if not more so.) (Figure 1).

Before that period of growth, however, there had been a much longer phase of stagnation or very low growth after Greece became a member of the European Union (EU) in 1981.[2] Between 1981 and 1995, Greece's GDP rose by a total of 14 percent, i.e. by only 0.9 percent per year (Table 1, fifth column). What caused this very different growth post-accession and post-entry to the euro zone? Was the prosperity exhibited by the Greek economy between 2000 and 2007 sustainable? Focusing on these two questions will allow us to draw conclusions as to which policy options Greece has for the future of its economy and its society.

Figure 1

Development of real GDP in Greece, other GIPS countries, and Germany
2000–2007

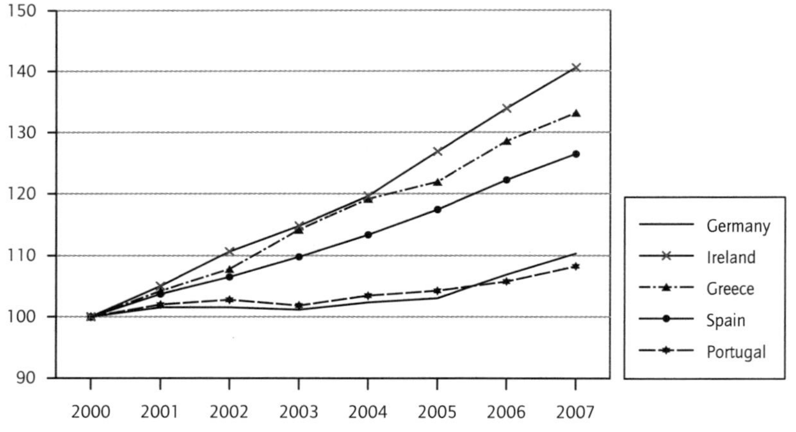

2000 = 100.
Source: Eurostat database (ESA 1995).

1 All numbers have been rounded to whole numbers (no decimal place), or to ½ (.5). One decimal place is given for very small figures and for the convergence criteria.

2 The European Union (EU) only came into being with the Maastricht Treaty; prior to that it had been called the European Community (EC). Like other authors, we use the term EU consistently.

2 Accession to the European Union in 1981

Greece's accession to the EU on 1 January 1981 was controversial right from the start, both among the Greeks and throughout the EU. Greece had only become a democracy in 1974, and the state was not considered stable yet; as well, its economy was much weaker than those of other EU countries (Axiopoulos 2010). Because Greece was largely agricultural and not able to compete economically, the EU Commission had initially advised against a quick accession. Moreover, Greece suffered from inflation, unemployment, and a trade deficit (Stergiou 2012). On the Greek side, both the pro-Soviet Communist party and the Panhellenic Socialist Movement (PASOK) were opposed to the accession (Trombetas 1983). In the 1981 election campaign, PASOK advocated Greece's immediate exit from the EU and NATO, using the slogan "Greece for the Greeks" (Stergiou 2012). Ten months after the accession to the EU, PASOK came to power, and although it remained in government for ten years, Greece still belongs to both the EU and the NATO to this day.

However, many of the reforms that had been agreed upon with the accession were never implemented in Greece (Bitros and Karayiannis 2013). Instead, PASOK carried out a series of "reforms" that ended up further weakening the country's public administration instead of improving it. Most crucially, competition for recruitment to the civil service was abolished and the emphasis shifted to social criteria over candidates' qualifications. In addition, General Directorates were abolished and the experienced top-grade civil servants were replaced with inexperienced political appointees. Furthermore, a large number of new government agencies, departments, and "institutes" were created, causing the number of state employees to multiply within only a few years (Valinakis 2012).

3 Low economic growth between 1981 and 1995 ...

In the 15 years following the accession to the EU, the Greek economy grew by an average of only 0.9 percent per year, whereas Spain's economic output grew by 2.5 percent, Portugal's by 2.7 percent, and Ireland's by 4 percent per year (Table 1, fifth column). This development in Greece was due to stagnation in the five years after its accession (Table 1, second column), which coincided with a general recession in all EU states. However, even in the ensuing economic upturn of 1986–1990, as well as in the subsequent five years, Greece's GDP rose by only a paltry 1.2 percent per year.

Table 1

Economic growth[1] in Greece, the other GIPS countries, and Germany
1981–2009

	1981[2]–1985	1986–1990	1991–1995[3]	1981–1995	1996–2000	2001–2007[4]	2008[5,6]	2009[6]
Greece	0.1	1.2	1.2	0.9	3.7	4.1	-0.4	-4.4
Ireland	2.5	4.7	4.6	4.0	9.6	5.5	-2.6	-6.4
Spain	1.4	4.5	1.5	2.5	4.1	3.8	1.1	-3.6
Portugal	0.9	5.7	1.7	2.7	4.1	1.5	0.2	-3.0
Germany	0.0	3.3	2.0	2.2	1.9	1.6	1.1	-5.6

1 Annual growth rate of real GDP in percent.
2 1981: Accession of Greece to the EU.
3 1994: Second stage of the Maastricht Treaty.
4 2001: Accession of Greece to the Euro zone; 2007: End of Greece's real estate boom.
5 October 2008: Escalation of the financial crisis.
6 2008 and 2009: Anticyclical fiscal policy in Greece and other industrial countries.

Source: World Bank database.

4 … due to low investment

One major reason for this was that investment showed a strong negative growth of 2.2 percent per year, i.e. that less and less capital was accumulated (Table 2, third column). Because of this, the capital per worker did not improve and labor productivity stagnated over a period of 15 years (Table 2, fourth column). In contrast, the other GIPS countries and other European countries saw a rise in labor productivity ranging from 1.5 percent in Portugal to 3 percent in Ireland. At the end of the 15-year period, these states' productivity therefore increased by almost 30 percent and 60 percent, respectively, enabling a much higher economic growth.

After profits "collapsed" due to a multitude of regulations, there was a lack of incentives for domestic and foreign companies to invest. For example, the rules governing dismissals were very restrictive, ranging from limitations on dismissals to large severance payments (Manessiotis and Reischauer 2001, Burtless 2001). In 1982, an automatic wage indexation system was introduced, under which low wages were fully indexed to past inflation at four-month intervals, while average and high wages were partially indexed (ibid.; Bryant, Garganas and Tavlas 2001). Accordingly, high inflation rates led to high pay rises, which combined with stagnating productivity resulted in a substantial rise in (nominal) unit labor costs in manufacturing amounting to 17.5 percent per year (Table 2, fifth column). Unit labor costs had multiplied more than tenfold in the space of 15 years, and had thus increased much more than in the other GIPS states. In addition, heavily regulated and inflexible product markets contributed to the low profit margins.

Table 2

Comparative economic performance of Greece
1980–1994[1]

	Annual growth of GDP	Annual growth of fixed investment[2]	Annual growth of productivity[3]	Annual percentage increase of unit labor costs in manufacturing
Greece	0.8	-2.2	-0.1	17.4
Ireland	3.5	0.3	3.2	1.7
Portugal	2.8	2.9	1.6	11.1
Spain	2.4	2.8	2.6	6.8
Total EU-15	2.0	1.7	1.8	3.1
	Annual consumer price inflation rate	**General government deficit as a percent of GDP**	**Current account balance as a percent of GDP**	**Annual unemployment rate**
Greece	18.3	-10.3	-3.5	7.3
Ireland	7.0	-7.2	-3.1	14.2
Portugal	14.6	-5.3	-2.6	6.9
Spain	8.6	-4.4	-1.5	18.0
Total EU-15	6.4	-4.6	-0.2	9.0

1 This looks at the time period 1980–1994, rather than, as in Table 1, 1981–1995 (though this does not lead to significant differences in growth rates).
2 The fixed investment includes equipment investment, housing construction and other construction, as well as other fixed investments.
3 GDP per person employed.

Sources: OECD, Historical Statistics 1970–1999 and Economic Outlook, cited after Bryant, Garganas, and Tavlas (2001: 4).

5 Strong increase in government activity and fiscal deficits

After Greece joined the EU, the Greek government increased its spending very quickly without increasing its receipts accordingly. Between 1980 and 1990 alone, the percentage of public spending in the GDP increased by 18.5 percentage points to a total of 48 percent of the GDP, while the percentage of public receipts only rose by 5 percentage points to 32 percent of the GDP (Table 3, 1990s column). This resulted in very high fiscal deficits—up to 16 percent of the GDP in 1990—leading to a rapidly increasing public debt and high interest payments.[3]

Consequently, the rapid increase in spending was largely caused by a strong expansion in debt service and public transfer payments to households (Table 3). In particular, there was an increase in health expenditure and pension payments without a matching increase in social security contributions. The backdrop for this was a highly fragmented social security system consisting of more than 300 separate funds that were poorly managed, as well. As a consequence, one must

3 The public debt increased from around 30 percent (1980) to 80 percent (1990), and then to 110 percent of the GDP (1995). The strong increase of the debt service from 2 percent (1980) to 11 percent of the GDP (1995) was not only due to the rising public debt, but also to higher interest rates (Manessiotis and Reischauer 2001: 119, 111). (Another contributing factor was that from 1988 onward, the public sector's borrowing requirement was increasingly financed by the sale of treasury bills to the non-bank public.)

Table 3

Government expenditure and receipts in Greece, the other GIPS countries, and Germany
1980–1995

	1980	1985	1990	1995[4]	1995 minus 1980
	as a percent of GDP				as a percentage point
Government Expenditure					
EU average	45.9	49.7	48.0	50.8	+4.9
Selected EU member states[1]	42.2	48.9	45.1	46.3	+4.1
Greece	*29.7*	*42.3*	*48.2*	*49.2*	*+19.5*
1. Government consumption	13.6	16.3	15.3	15.3	+1.7
Public employee compensation	9.5	11.6	12.7	11.3	+1.8
2. Transfers	11.5	16.8	16.2	16.8	+5.3
To households	9.4	14.3	15.2	15.1	+5.7
To enterprises	2.1	2.5	1.0	1.7	-0.4
3. Debt service[2]	2.0	4.9	10.2	11.1	+9.1
4. Gross fixed capital formation and other capital expenditure, including capital transfers received	2.6	4.3	6.6	6.0	+3.4
Government Receipts					
EU-14 average	42.5	45.2	44.9	45.1	+2.6
Selected EU member states[1]	33.8	38.5	38.9	39.5	+5.7
Greece	*27.0*	*30.6*	*32.1*	*39.1*	*+12.1*
1. Direct taxes	14.0	16.3	17.2	20.0	+6.0
Personal income and wealth + corporate income	4.6	4.6	5.5	7.4	+2.8
Social security contributions	9.4	11.7	11.7	12.6	+3.2
2. Indirect taxes (consumption taxes and other taxes)	11.1	12.6	13.2	13.5	+2.4
3. Other current resources	1.9	1.7	1.7	2.9	+1.0
4. Capital transfers received	–	–	–	2.7	–
Public Deficit[3]					
EU-14 average	-3.4	-4.5	-3.1	-5.7	-2.3
Selected EU member states[1]	-8.4	-10.4	-6.2	-6.8	+1.6
Greece	*-2.7*	*-11.7*	*-16.1*	*-10.1*	*-7,4*
For information: Net EU transfers[5]		1981–85	1986–90	1991–95	1981–95
(average of 5-/15-year-period)		1.5	3.2	4.3	3.0

1 Ireland, Italy, Portugal, and Spain.
2 Excluding amortisation payments.
3 Own calculation.
4 ESA 1995.
5 Gross inflow minus national contribution to EU budget (cited after Sparos, 2001, 282).
Of this: two thirds transfers to farmers and one third grants to the ordinary and the investment budget as well as grants to public enterprises (cited after Vassilios and Reischauer, 2001, 139).

Sources: Ministry of National Economy 1998 and 2000, and ESA 1979 and 1995 (cited after Manessiotis and Reischauer 2001: 112).

assume that many employees did not pay their full social security contributions, or paid none at all, and that many pensioners received multiple and/or excessively high pensions that they were not entitled to (OECD 1997). Government expenditure on civil servants increased strongly—their share in the GDP rose by 3 percentage points between 1980 and 1990—because their number increased strongly and they saw significantly larger increases in wages than did the private sector (Manessiotis and Reischauer 2001: 107). According to Stergiou (2012), the rapid increase in public spending and the resulting fiscal deficit must be seen in conjunction with the clientelism of PASOK (and later Nea Dimokratia).

The fiscal deficits contributed substantially to the high inflation rates in Greece, or at least hindered the restoration of price stability after the oil price shock of 1973/74 (Garganas und Tavlas 2001). Between 1980 and 1994, the average inflation rate amounted to over 18 percent, and was thus significantly higher than in the other GIPS states (Table 2, lower table, second column). Like other European central banks, the Bank of Greece adopted a policy of monetary targeting to tackle inflation, but often ended up exceeding its targets for M3. Consequently, monetary growth in the 1980s remained at rates that accommodated inflation.[4]

The need to finance the large fiscal deficits was a major reason for the high monetary growth rates. The public sector enjoyed preferential access to credit at subsidized rates in order to keep borrowing costs down. For example, until the mid-1980s the real rate of interest on twelve-month treasury bills was negative (ibid.). Additionally, the government exerted direct influence on monetary policy. Finally, the empirical results of Garganas and Tavlas (2001) strongly suggest that during the 1980s, the increase in the fiscal deficits caused the increase in M3. In effect, the money supply was not specified exogenously by the Bank of Greece, but was rendered endogenous (Garganas 1992).

6 Foreign trade did not profit from EU entry

Due to the above-mentioned structural weaknesses—overregulation of the economy, (too) low investment, and (too) high price and wage increases—Greek foreign trade did not profit from the common European market, in marked contrast to the foreign trade of the other GIPS countries. Consequently, Greece's openness in international trade—the sum of its export and import quota—decreased from about 45 percent to less than 35 percent of its GDP between 1981 and 1995. The decisive factor for this change was the marked decrease in the export quota (from around 19 percent to less than 9 percent of the GDP), while the import quota remained relatively stable. In addition, Greece saw a decline in its share of world trade, whereas Ireland, Spain, and Portugal managed to increase their shares (Tsaveas 2001).

The weak export quota was mainly due to low investment. For foreign firms especially, Greece was not considered an attractive location and thus drew significantly less foreign direct investment (FDI) than did Spain and Portugal, and much less than did Ireland (Bosworth and Kollintzas 2001). Among the causes were the rigidity of Greece's over-regulated labor markets and the lack

4 In the first seven years after the introduction of monetary targeting of M3 (1983-1989), the money supply grew by an average 24 percent per year (Garganas and Tavlas 2001: 52).

of transparency of its bureaucracy, which exacerbated uncertainty for firms and complicated their business activities (OECD 1993).[5] However, without the input from foreign firms, it was difficult for Greece to gain the funds and management skills needed to expand its small manufacturing base and make its export sector more competitive.

In addition to this, price and wage increases in the double figures led to a significant deterioration in Greek firms' monetary competitiveness. Between 1980 and 1994, the rise of the unit labor costs in manufacturing was seven times the EU average, and devaluations of the drachma did not fully compensate for this competitive disadvantage.

7 Reforms and the Maastricht Treaty

The Maastricht Treaty, which came into effect in November 1993, gave Greece the possibility of entering the future European Monetary Union (EMU), but also required reforms in order for the country to meet the convergence criteria.

A tightening of income and monetary policy had already lowered the inflation rate from over 20 percent to 11 percent between 1990 and 1994. It is important to note, however, that in 1989, inflation had been as low as 13 percent, and it was the second oil crisis in 1990, among other things, that induced the rapid increase. In connection with this, the public debt ratio had exceeded 16 percent of the GDP.

The government reacted with an extensive reform of collective bargaining. The automatic wage indexation, introduced in 1982, was repealed and collective bargaining was freed from direct government control through the abolition of compulsory arbitration panels (Burtless 2001).[6] As a result, the real wages of blue-collar workers in the manufacturing sector fell by 7.5 percent between 1991 and 1993 (Garganas und Tavlas 2001).

At the same time, a restrictive monetary policy was introduced. The monetary target for M3 was reduced by 11 percentage points in the space of only four years—after M3 growth had overshot its target range in 1992 and 1993—and 1994 saw an M3 increase of just 8.8 percent.

Between 1995 and 2000, the Bank of Greece continued its policy to attain price stability, while also pursuing a hard-drachma policy. In 1995, the bank announced a specific exchange rate target for the first time that limited the year-to-year devaluation of the drachma (against the ECU) to between 1 and 3 percent (1995 to 1997), and did not fully compensate for the inflation differentials between Greece and the other EU countries. In March 1998, Greece joined the European Exchange Rate Mechanism and devalued the drachma by 12.3 percent (ibid.).

In Greece, which has historically exhibited the EU's highest interest rates, long-term interest rates decreased especially strongly: from more than 20.5 percent in 1994 to 5.5 percent upon en-

5 The OECD study (1993) estimated that Greece saw less than two billion U.S dollars of direct investment in the 1980s, compared to 46 billion U.S. dollars in Spain, and 6.5 billion U.S. dollars in Portugal.

6 From 1975 to 1990, half of all collective bargaining agreements were imposed by compulsory arbitration panels.

Figure 2

Long-term interest rates[1] in Greece, other GIPS countries, and Germany
1994[2]-2002

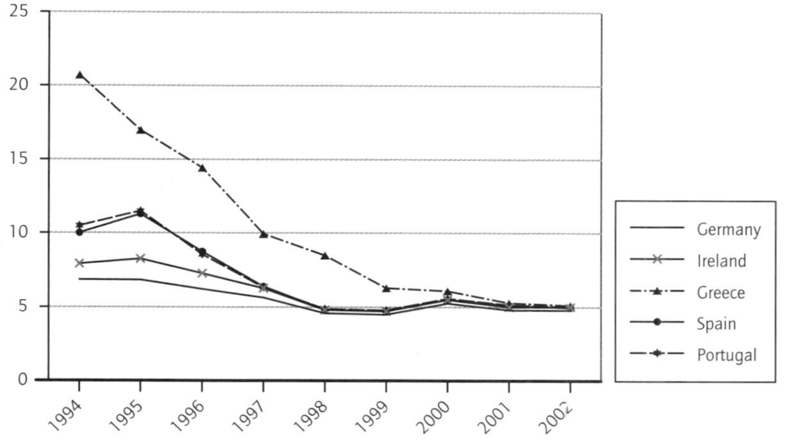

1 Long-term interest rates for assessing convergence in percent.
2 Start of the second stage of the European Monetary Union.

Source: Eurostat database (convergence criteria).

try to the euro (Figure 2). Combined with a public debt in excess of 100 percent of the GDP,[7] this led to a decrease of 6 percentage points in interest spending, to 6.5 percent of the GDP.[8] Consequently, hardly any reforms were necessary to reduce the budget deficit by 6 percentage points as well, down to 4.5 percent of the GDP. Only between 1997 and 1999, the reference period for entry to the euro, was the decrease of Greece's fiscal deficit higher than its interest savings. This decrease was reached exclusively by way of (temporarily) higher public revenue, rather than through savings. The public revenue rose from 41 percent of the GDP in 1995 to 46.5 percent in 1999, only to drop back to 41 percent of the GDP in 2001. However, other highly indebted European countries, first and foremost Italy, profited similarly from sinking interest rates in consolidating their budget and fulfilling the criteria of the Maastricht Treaty.

In 1998, when the first decisions were being made as to which countries would join the EMU, Greece was unable to fulfill any of the convergence criteria.[9] However, the country managed to

7 The public debt in Greece stood at 80 percent of the GDP in 1990, at 107 percent in 1994, and at 104 percent in 1999.

8 For the period from 1994/95 onwards, we are using (revised) Eurostat data, which are largely available from 1994 onwards. (For the interest expenditure, data is only available from 1995 onwards.) How strongly and how often the Greek statements about budget deficits have been revised can be seen in Table 1 in Bofinger (2011). In 2001, for instance, the deficit was revised three times, from 1.4 to 6.1 percent of the GDP; in 2003 it was revised six times, from 1.7 percent to 6.2 percent of the GDP.

9 In the reference period between February 1997 and January 1998, Greece had an HICP inflation of 5.0 percent (as opposed to the demanded reference value of 2.7 percent), and a long-term interest rate of 9.8 percent (as opposed to 7.8 percent). Its budget balance was -4 percent of its GDP (as opposed to -3 percent) and its public debt was at 108.7 percent of its GDP (as opposed to 60 percent) (EMI, 1998). In addition, Greece only became a member of the European Exchange Rate Mechanism in March 1998.

achieve such substantial progress that two years later, its inflation rate (at 2.0 percent) was lower than the reference value, as were its long-term interest rate (at 6.4 percent) and its budget balance (at 1.6 percent of its GDP) (ECB 2000).[10] Only its public debt, at 104.4 percent of the GDP, was significantly higher than the 60 percent demanded by the reference criteria (which, however, was also true for several other EU countries). In 2001, Greece became the twelfth member state of the euro zone.

In the 1990s, Greece implemented a series of reforms, not least with regard to its joining the euro: It deregulated collective bargaining, introduced a monetary policy aimed at more price stability, restructured its financial markets, and deregulated product markets formerly dominated by publicly owned companies.

However, as we will argue in the policy recommendations section, these reforms had to be continued in order to arrive at sustainable economic growth, and broadened to include other areas of the Greek economy. This is what our analysis of the long period of slow growth following Greece's EU entry shows. Firstly, the institutional framework that hindered investment, especially FDI, had to be improved. Increasing efficiency and transparency in public administration was especially important, as was continuing the deregulation of labor and product markets. Secondly, a reform of the public sector, which had grown a lot after the accession to the EU, had to be tackled in order to achieve "sustainability of the fiscal position" as demanded in the ECB's convergence report (2000). Thirdly, the Greek export sector had to be expanded and its competitiveness had to be improved. This was the only way to achieve sustainable economic growth.

8 Accession to euro zone and economic growth

Between 1996 and 2000, the GDP increased by an average of 3.7 percent per year, a significantly stronger growth than in the 15 years after accession to the EU (Table 1). Bryant, Garganas and Tavlas (2001) as well as Bosworth and Kollintzas (2001), see the reason for this development in the impending accession to the euro zone and the reforms carried out to facilitate it. The sinking interest rates, however, also played a major role, leading to a rising demand for real estate: During the period in question, housing investment increased by 80 percent; between 1996 and 1999, by 20.5 percent; and in 2000, once entry to the euro zone was secure, by a further 50 percent. (On the other hand, companies' investments in plants and equipment, i. e. all investment exclusive of housing investment, increased by only about 30 percent in the same period.)

The property boom continued after Greece's accession to the euro zone. Between 1999 and 2007, real estate investment nearly tripled, and its share in the GDP rose from 6 percent to 12.5 percent. There were several reasons for this: Interest rates for mortgage loans were at a historic low, and the Greek banks were generously giving out credit. They attracted a lot of capital from other European countries (Sinn 2014, Smeets and Schmid 2014), and securitization of mortgage loans allowed them to displace the risk to third parties (Neubäumer 2008, Erber 2011). Consequently, sub-prime borrowers also received mortgages. Finally, the Greek property market received

---

10 In 2004 it was revealed that the numbers for the budget deficits had been manipulated, and that Greece had not met the 3 percent criterion between 1997 and 1999.

Figure 3

Housing investment[1] in Greece, Spain, Ireland[2], and Germany
1995-2012

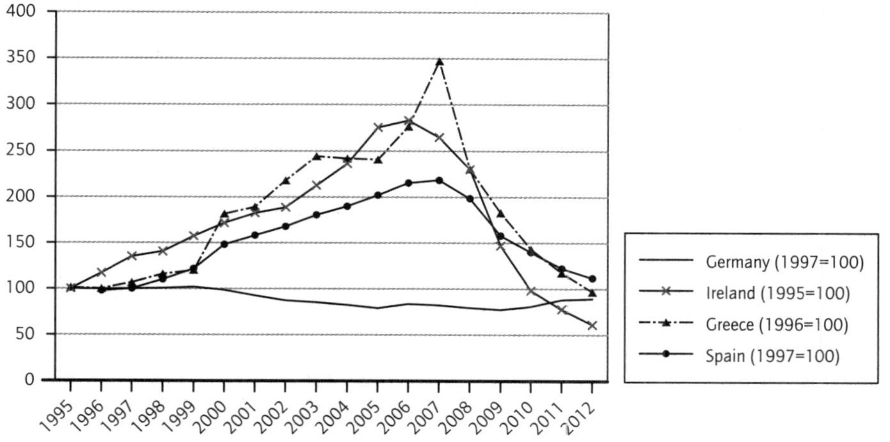

1 For Greece, housing investment from 2012 are estimates.
2 In Ireland, the share of housing investment in the GNP is about 2 percent higher. Due to high net payments to non-residents for earned and investment incomes, Ireland's GNP is roughly 15 percent lower than its GDP.

Source: Eurostat database (ESA 1995).

another boost through the housing buyers' tax legislation changes that were being discussed in the media and used as a sales argument by property agencies. Between 2005 and 2007, housing investment increased by another 44 percent (Triantafyllopoulos and Kandyla 2010) (Figure 3).

The result was that many new jobs were created in the building sector, with the number of gainfully employed individuals in this industry increasing by about 30 percent between 2000 and 2007. Combined with disproportionate wage increases, this led to a 90 percent rise in (nominal) incomes among building sector workers. This additional income led to multiplier processes, i.e. they incurred a rise in demand for the production of consumer goods.

Furthermore, Greek households financed additional consumption by credit card and consumer loans. This is evidenced by the fact that the consumption quota increased by 3 percentage points up until 2008, and thus 72 percent of the Greek GDP was spent on consumer goods (16.5 percentage points more than the average for euro zone countries). The "cause" was (once again) high capital inflows from other euro zone countries, which in turn led to Greek banks granting generous loans with low interest rates. There was "excessive lending" to the private sector (SVR 2011, Neubäumer 2011) to such an extent that in 2008, its debts were twice as high as those of the Greek state. As evidenced by the low aggregate saving ratios, which in 2007 and 2008 were negative, at –3 percent and –7 percent respectively (i. e. the sum of consumer spending exceeded the sum of the disposable incomes), private households were living "beyond their means."

9 Weakening pressure for reform—strong increase of the government share

After accession to the euro, easy access to cheap loans weakened the pressure to lower public spending and increase public revenue through reforms. For instance, the Greek government was unable to implement a plan for reforming the pension system (Vlachantoni 2005) that had been put forward as early as 2002, because members of the governing party refused their consent. They argued, instead of implementing steep cuts into the pension system, the government should take out more low-interest loans.

Consequently, the share of public spending in the GDP increased by a further 2 percentage points, to 47.5 percent, despite strong economic growth; in the stagnation year of 2008, the share further increased, to 50.5 percent. This was mainly due to the rising pension costs and the enlargement of public administration (Neubäumer 2015, 2016). After Greece joined the Euro, the already high number of public employees increased by almost a quarter, and their wages were raised substantially. This explains why expenditure on public administration rose by 75 percent between the time Greece joined the euro and 2008. Furthermore, with 130,000 soldiers Greece's armed forces were "inflated" (in comparison, Germany only had 200,000 soldiers), which led to defense expenditures of 3 percent of the GDP.

On the revenue side, the tax quota quickly fell again from 26 percent (1999) to 22.5 percent (2001) after entry to the euro zone had been achieved. High tax losses were (and are) caused by the extensive shadow economy (about a quarter of the economic output; estimated annual tax

Figure 4

Public balance[1] in Greece, other GIPS countries, and Germany
1999–2008

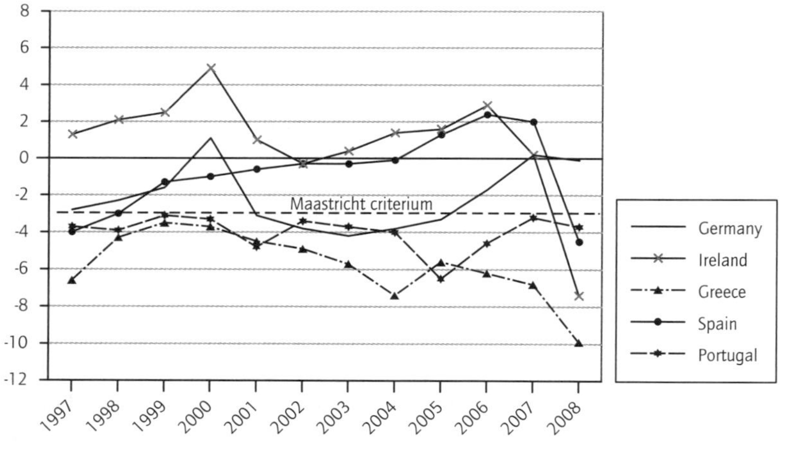

1 Public balances given in percent of the GDP.

Source: Eurostat database (ESA 1995).

loss of 30 billion euro), large-scale tax evasion and tax fraud, and failure to collect tax debts by an inefficient and corrupt financial administration (Landeszentrale 2015).

The consequence was a consistently high fiscal deficit: On average, the budget deficits stood at 6 percent of the GDP from 2000 to 2007, and exceeded the Maastricht criterion of 3 percent of the GDP (Figure 4). Therefore, the Greek government not only followed a pro-cyclical fiscal policy, but also lived "beyond its means."

10 Strong growth due to capital influx rather than investment

Greece's success story following its entry to the euro zone was based on a demand-side boom caused by high capital inflows from other euro countries: The strong economic growth was the result of the (foreign) credit-financed housing boom, additional credit-funded consumption, and a substantial increase in public expenditure (Neubäumer 2015).

The steep increase in GDP, however, did not result from innovations and firms' expansion of their capital stock. One indicator of this is that firms' fixed investment[11] averaged only 14.2 percent of GDP during the growth phase, and thus 0.7 percent percentage points less than it did in the year of the euro zone entry. Production capacities increased only relatively marginally.

Accordingly, Greece increasingly had to import goods and services in order to satisfy the rising demand. Between 2001 and 2007, the country's import quota rose from 36 percent to 38 percent, whereas its export quota stagnated at around 24 percent. In 2007, Greece's current account deficit reached 14.5 percent of the GDP—that is, domestic production was increasingly less able to meet the absorption. In addition, the strong economic growth was mainly due to higher production of non-tradable goods, such as housing construction and services for residents, rather than tradable goods that would have provided an alternative to importing, or an opportunity for exporting.

All in all, Greece did not achieve sustainable growth after its euro zone entry. Instead, its GDP was "inflated" in 2007 due to high capital inflows that led to a demand-side boom. Therefore, a sharp fall of its GDP was "preprogrammed" as soon as capital flows from other euro countries "dried up," resulting in this Greek tragedy: From 2007, the GDP fell as quickly as it had risen after the euro entry, dropping to the 2001 level by 2013.

We see the main cause of this development in the fact that many of the factors that had led to the low investment, minimal productivity progress, and very weak growth in the 15 years after the EU accession had not improved. Even though reform measures were started in the 1990s, they were insufficient, and were not continued after Greece joined the euro zone.

11 Firms' fixed investment is calculated by subtracting housing investment from the total fixed investment.

11 Sustainable growth only with fundamental reforms

For the future, the Greek economy "needs a growth strategy" (Brenke 2012)—which, as our analysis of the events preceding the "Greek tragedy" shows, should include three interdependent bundles of measures:

1. An improvement in the institutional environment, which is currently impeding business dealings in Greece and leading to too little investment,
2. reorganization of public finances and—in connection with this—a leaner, more efficient administration, as well as a reform of the complex and highly fragmented pensions system,
3. the expansion of the industrial base and the promotion of modern services and—in connection with this—the building of a broader export basis.

In order to make Greece an attractive business location, and thus an interesting asset for Greek and foreign investors, the institutional environment must first be improved, primarily in terms of the labor market and the efficiency of the public administration.

This is evidenced by the "Global Competiveness Index" by the World Economic Forum 2008/09 (Schwab and Porter 2009). Executives consider doing business in Greece problematic because of the high burden of government regulations and the non-transparency of policy-making and tax regulations, which has been accompanied by widespread corruption. This in particular has deterred new businesses and FDI. The high corruption in the public sector is evident in a corruption index of 3.8 (0 = very corrupt, 10 = high integrity) (Transparency International 2009).[12] Thus Greece was in last place among European countries, followed by Brazil and Colombia.

In the labor market, a lack of flexibility in wage determination as well as too-high wages and non-wage labor costs (relative to productivity) have weakened firms' competitiveness. Moreover, firms are now facing rigid hiring and firing regulations, inflexible employment conditions, and a lack of cooperation and trust between workers and employers.

Secondly, a cutback and restructuring of public expenses is necessary, not only to decrease the high fiscal deficit but also to open up opportunities for more productivity-oriented public expenditures, such as investment to improve the education system and public infrastructure.

It was first and foremost the high expenditures on public administration—which reached 10.5 percent of the GDP in 2007—that had to be lowered (compared to 6.5 percent in all EU countries and 6 percent in Germany). The background was an inflated public administration: Roughly one-fifth of Greece's employees worked in public service (compared to about 11 percent in Germany). In addition, civil servants received 40 percent higher salaries than did those employed in private companies (Landeszentrale 2015).

---

12 Along with Greece, Romania, Bulgaria, and Macedonia placed last among European countries. The Corruption Perceptions Index (CPI) measures the perceived levels of public sector corruption in 180 countries and territories. A composite index, the CPI is based on 13 different expert and business surveys.

Additionally, the high pension payments, which amounted to 12.5 percent of the GDP in 2008, had to be reduced. The extremely fragmented and badly managed pension system needed basic reforms—not only from a financial point of view, but also from a social and economic perspective (Börsch-Supan and Tinios 2001).[13] It is important to stress that the equivalence between contributions and benefits was distorted. The self-employed and those employed in the informal sector profited from this, whereas those working for mid-sized and large firms in the formal sector were disadvantaged. This pension system also provided an incentive for early retirement and thus a low labor force participation (ibid., Burtless 2001).

Thirdly, the extension of the industrial base and the promotion of modern services were necessary to achieve a broader export base. Only 12.5 percent of Greece's gross value added came from industry (compared to 20 percent in the rest of the euro zone and 26 percent in Germany), and modern services only accounted for 1.6 percent of gross value added (compared to 3.7 percent in all EU countries).[14]

This cannot be seen independently of Greece's special corporate landscape. A third of all employed persons were self-employed, and there were many family-based firms and few corporations. Among firms with dependent employees, small and very small firms dominated. In 2007, for instance, almost half of all jobs in the manufacturing industry were in firms with fewer than 10 employees (Brenke 2012).

Burtless (2001) sees a major reason for this in the fact that the legal framework favored (and still favours) job creation in microenterprises where the employment per euro invested is higher than it is in larger firms. In small and very small firms it was possible to minimize the burden of taxes and social security contributions, and they were not required to observe the rigid labor regulations regarding dismissals, work schedules, or limits in overtime work.

This has led to perverse incentives by discouraging the creation of capital-intensive medium-size or large firms, thus missing the opportunities of economies of scale and a higher productivity. It has also hindered innovation and technological progress, as only bigger firms can afford the high costs associated with research and development; as well, bigger firms invest (more) in employee training and usually adopt new technologies more quickly, and the overwhelming share of employment in the modern sector is wage and salary employment in medium-size and large firms (ibid.).

Therefore, a broadening of the industrial base and the modern sector could (and can) only work if the legal framework is changed and no longer discriminates against employment in medium-size and large firms. However, the building of bigger firms and thus the broadening of the export base take time.

---

13 Börsch-Supan and Tinios (2001) not only offer a comprehensive description of the Greek pension system, but also analyze its strengths and weaknesses and discuss reform alternatives.

14 Industry excluding building (data for 2008, Eurostat); modern services include services for the IT sector, technical and science-oriented services for firms, and research and development (data for 2009 taken from Brenke 2012).

12 Fundamental change in Greek society or weaker growth and a lower living standard

The implementation of such a comprehensive growth strategy would lead to a fundamental change not only in the Greek economy, but also in Greek society. The "omnipresent" state (and the widespread corruption connected with it) would be pushed back, the privileges of a number of social groups would be reduced, and employment in larger firms would increase (even at the expense of very small businesses). Such far-reaching reforms can only be implemented successfully if the majority of Greeks and their politicians not only accept them, but also actively pursue them.

The alternative is to implement only moderate reforms in order to return to the path of low growth. This would entail slow changes to increase the efficiency of the public sector, improve the institutional environment, and avoid a further rise in pension payments, and will only lead to slightly higher investment. Therefore, to opt for this alternative is to opt for a lower standard of living. Portugal can serve as an example: Its economic structure[15] was similar to Greece's, and in 2000, the country had the same per capita income as Greece (14,500 euros). Afterwards, however, the Portuguese economy grew at a rate of only 1.5 percent per year, so that by 2007, its per capita income of 15,100 euros was one-fifth lower than Greece's was.

Even if it opted for modest reforms, Greece would not be able to avoid cutting its public expenditure (and increasing taxes). This is due to the fact that its government activity was oriented towards a GDP that was "inflated" by a (foreign) credit-financed demand. This was also the case in Portugal; however, its GDP and its government expenditures had risen far less.

All in all, with low growth rates of 1.5 percent or 1.2 percent respectively, it would take Greece 16 or 20 years to arrive at the per capita income of 2007.

13 Summary

The low growth in Greece in the 15 years after its accession to the EU in 1981 was caused by (too) low investment from foreign and local firms and the resulting stagnation in productivity. The background to this situation comprised a large number of regulations that led to inflexible product and labor markets, and caused profits to "collapse." In addition, firms' business practice was hindered by the lack of transparency of the bureaucracy coupled with high corruption. As well, the expansion of government activity led to a steep rise in money supply and high inflation rates. Because of the automatic wage indexation system, this resulted in increasing pay rises and high unit labor costs. As a consequence of these structural weaknesses, foreign trade did not profit from the common market with the other EU countries; on the contrary, Greece's export quota and its share in world trade sank.

In the 1990s, Greece—not least with regard to its joining the euro—implemented a series of reforms: It deregulated collective bargaining, introduced a monetary policy aimed at more price

15 In Portugal, agriculture and tourism were of similar importance as they were in Greece. However, the country also manufactured low-price products ("extended work bench") and therefore its manufacturing industry had a somewhat higher share of the gross value added than did Greece's (12.7 percent compared to 10.5 percent; Brenke 2012).

stability, restructured its financial markets, and deregulated product markets formerly dominated by publicly owned companies. These measures led to a decrease in the high inflation rates, long-term interest rates, and the state's interest payments. This contributed to Greece being able to largely fulfill the convergence criteria for entry to the euro in 2000.

However, the reform processes were not continued after the euro entry. The strong economic growth from 2000 to 2007 was caused by capital inflows from other euro countries and historically low interest rates. Firstly, housing investment nearly tripled and, together with steep rises in wages in the building sector, caused multiplier processes. Private consumption received an additional boost from credit card and consumer loans. Secondly, the Greek government increased its expenditures significantly more than the GDP, not least due to access to low-interest state loans, accepting a steep rise in public debt and a high fiscal deficit. The result was a demand-side boom. The high growth was not due to innovation and a broadening of capital stock, and additional production was largely limited to non-tradable goods, such as housing construction and services for residents.

For these reasons, Greece did not achieve long-lasting growth after joining the euro zone. Instead, the substantial increase in the Greek GDP up until 2007 was the result of a real estate bubble and a large rise in government expenditures, both (mostly) financed by foreign loans. Therefore, a sharp fall in GDP was "preprogrammed" as soon as capital flows from other euro countries stayed out. This led to the Greek tragedy. From 2007, the GDP fell as quickly as it had risen after the euro entry, dropping to the 2001 level by 2013.

For the future, Greece has to decide whether it will choose a growth strategy containing three interrelated bundles of measures:

- an improvement of the institutional environment, which obstructs doing business in Greece and thus leads to too little investment;
- a reorganization of public finances and—in connection with this—a leaner, more efficient administration, as well as a reform of the highly fragmented pensions system;
- and an expansion of its industrial basis and its modern sector, thus building a broader export basis.

This strategy would entail comprehensive change to not only Greece's economy, but also to its society as well. Such a reform strategy can only succeed if the majority of Greeks and their politicians actively pursue it.

The alternative is to opt for moderate reforms, i. e. slow changes to increase the efficiency of the public sector, improve the institutional environment, and avoid a further rise in pension payments. This would mean a return to the old path of slow growth of 1.2 percent to 1.5 percent per year and would lead to a lower standard of living.

References

- Axiopoulos, Lukas (2010): Europäische Geschichte: Den Süden sichern. DIE ZEIT, June 10, 2010. www.zeit.de/2010/24/Griechenland-EG-Beitritt.
- Bitros, George C. and Anastasios D. Karayiannis (2013): Creative crisis in democracy and economy. Berlin, Springer.
- Bofinger, Peter (2011): Wie können sich die Mitgliedsländer des Euroraums aus dem Würgegriff der Finanzmärkte befreien? Wirtschaftsdienst, 91 (12), 811–816.
- Börsch-Supan, Axel and Platon Tinios (2001): The Greek pension system: Strategic framework for reform. In: Ralph C. Bryant, Nicholas C. Garganas and George S. Tavlas (eds.): Greece's economic performance and prospects. Athens, Washington, D. C., Bank of Greece Printing Work, 361–442.
- Bosworth, Barry and Tryphon Kollintzas (2001): Economic growth in Greece: Past performance and future prospects. In: Ralph C. Bryant, Nicholas C. Garganas and George S. Tavlas, (eds.): Greece's economic performance and prospects. Athens, Washington, D. C., Bank of Greece Printing Work, 153–192.
- Brenke, Karl (2012): Die griechische Wirtschaft braucht eine Wachstumsstrategie. DIW Wochenbericht Nr. 5/2012, 3–15.
- Bryant, Ralph C., Nicholas C. Garganas and George S. Tavlas, (eds.) (2001a): Greece's economic performance and prospects. Athens, Washington, D. C., Bank of Greece Printing Work. www.bankofgreece.gr/BogDocumentEn/Greece's_Economic_Performance_and_prospects.pdf.
- Bryant, Ralph C., Nicholas C. Garganas and George S. Tavlas (2001b): Introduction. In: id., (eds.): Greece's economic performance and prospects. Athens, Washington, D. C., Bank of Greece Printing Work, 1–42.
- Burtless, Gary (2001): The Greek labour market. In: Ralph C. Bryant, Nicholas C. Garganas and George S. Tavlas (eds.): Greece's economic performance and prospects. Athens, Washington, D. C., Bank of Greece Printing Work, 453–492.
- ECB – European Central Bank (2000): Convergence report, 2000. Frankfurt a. M.
- EMI – European Monetary Institute (1998): Convergence report, March 1998. Frankfurt a. M.
- Erber, Georg (2011): Verbriefungen sind tot – lang leben Verbriefungen? DIW Wochenbericht Nr. 35/2011, 3–11.
- Garganas, Nicholas C. (1992): Modelling the monetary system in Greece. Greek Economic Review 13, 11–50 [zitiert nach Garganas and Tavlas 2001: 94].
- Garganas, Nicholas C. and George S. Tavlas (2001): Monetary regimes and inflation performance: The case of Greece. In: Ralph C. Bryant, Nicholas C. Garganas and George S. Tavlas (eds.) (2001): Greece's economic performance and prospects. Athens, Washington, D. C., Bank of Greece Printing Work, 43–95.
- Landeszentrale für politische Bildung Baden-Württemberg (2015): Ursachen der Krise in Griechenland. www.lpb-bw.de/ursachen_krise_griechenland.html (January 7, 2015).
- Manessiotis, Vassilios G. and Robert D. Reischauer (2001): Greek fiscal and budget policy and EMU. In: Ralph C. Bryant, Nicholas C. Garganas and George S. Tavlas (eds.): Greece's economic performance and prospects. Athens, Washington, D. C., Bank of Greece Printing Work, 103–149.
- Mylonas, Paul and George Papaconstantinou (2001): Product market reform in Greece: Policy priorities and prospects. In: Ralph C. Bryant, Nicholas C. Garganas and George S.

Tavlas (eds.): Greece's economic performance and prospects. Athens, Washington, D.C., Bank of Greece Printing Work, 499–539.
— Neubäumer, Renate (2008): Ursachen und Wirkungen der Finanzkrise – eine ökonomische Analyse. Wirtschaftsdienst, 88 (11), 732–740.
— Neubäumer, Renate (2011): Eurokrise: Keine Staatsschuldenkrise, sondern Folge der Finanzkrise. Wirtschaftsdienst, 91 (12), 827–833.
— Neubäumer, Renate (2015): Eurokrise: Sparpolitik zweitrangig für den Einbruch der Wirtschaftsleistung in Griechenland? ifo Schnelldienst, 68 (18), 25–34.
— Neubäumer, Renate (2016): Inwieweit hat die Fiskalpolitik die Wirtschaftskrise in den GIPS-Staaten verursacht, verschärft oder mitbewältigt? – Eine Analyse aus keynesianischer Sicht (will be published 2016 in List Forum: Sonderheft zur Tagung des Wirtschaftspolitischen Ausschusses des Vereins für Socialpolitik).
— OECD (1993): Economic surveys: Greece. Organisation for Economic Cooperation and Development, Paris.
— OECD (1997): Economic surveys: Greece. Organisation for Economic Cooperation and Development, Paris.
— Schwab, Klaus and Michael E. Porter (eds.) (2009): The global competitiveness report 2008–09. World Economic Forum, Geneva.
— Sinn, Hans-Werner (2014): The Euro trap. On bursting bubbles, budgets, and beliefs. Oxford, Oxford University Press.
— Smeets, Heinz-Dieter and Anita Schmid (2014): Europäische Staatsschuldenkrise, Lender of last resort und Bankenunion. ORDO, Jahrbuch für Ordnung von Wirtschaft und Gesellschaft, 65, 47–73.
— Spraos, John (2001): EU transfers and Greece's real exchange rate: A naked eye view 281. In: Ralph C. Bryant, Nicholas C. Garganas and George S. Tavlas, (eds.): Greece's Economic Performance and Prospects. Athens, Washington, D.C., Bank of Greece Printing Work, 281–313.
— Stergiou, Andreas (2012): Anatomie eines Niedergangs? Griechenland und die Europäische Union. Bundeszentrale für politische Bildung. www.bpb.de/apuz/142837/griechenland-und-die-europaeische-union?p=all.
— Transparency International (2009): Corruption perceptions index 2009. www.transparency.org/research/cpi/cpi_2009.
— Triantafyllopoulos, Nikolaos and Thomai Kandyla (2010): Buyers' behaviour and the housing bubble in Greece. European Real Estate Society Conference 2010, 23 June to 26 June 2010. www.propertyfinance.it/sitoeres/contents/papers/id36.pdf.
— Trombetas, T.B. (1983): The political dimensions of Greece's accession to the EC: Commitment or retrogression? Australian Journal of Politics & History, 29 (1), 63–74. http://onlinelibrary.wiley.com/doi/10.1111/j.1467-8497.1983.tb00303.x/abstract.
— Tsaveas, Nicholas T. (2001): Greece's balance of payments and competitiveness. In: Ralph C. Bryant, Nicholas C. Garganas and George S. Tavlas (eds.): Greece's economic performance and prospects. Athens, Washington, D.C., Bank of Greece Printing Work, 323–360.
— Valinakis, Yannis (2012): Greece's European policy making. GreeSE Paper No. 63. October 2012. The London School of Economics and Political Science, London. http://eprints.lse.ac.uk/46660/1/GreeSE percent20No63.pdf.
— Vassilios, G. Manessiotis and Robert D. Reischauer (2001): Greek fiscal and budget policy and EMU. In: Ralph C. Bryant, Nicholas C. Garganas and George S. Tavlas (eds.): Greece's economic performance and prospects. Athens, Washington, D.C., Bank of Greece Printing Work, 103–149.

— Vlachantoni, Athina (2005): Greek pension reform and the change "from within". Paper prepared for the 2nd LSE PhD Symposium on "Modern Greece: Current Social Research on Greece", June 10, 2005. www.lse.ac.uk/europeanInstitute/research/hellenicObservatory/pdf/2nd_Symposium/Athina_Vlachantoni_paper.pdf.

Saving Greece once again: Have we Reached the Root of the Crisis?

KLAUS SCHRADER, DAVID BENČEK AND CLAUS-FRIEDRICH LAASER

Klaus Schrader, Kiel Institute for the World Economy (IfW), e-mail: Klaus.Schrader@ifw-kiel.de
David Benček, Kiel Institute for the World Economy (IfW), e-mail: David.Bencek@ifw-kiel.de
Claus-Friedrich Laaser, Kiel Institute for the World Economy (IfW), e-mail: Claus-Friedrich.Laaser@ifw-kiel.de

Summary: In 2010, the first economic adjustment program began offering a blueprint for economic recovery and a feasible way for Greece to emerge from the crisis. The authors show that Greece neither overcame its structural weaknesses nor developed export industries as a driver of growth in the course of reforms, and they conclude that Greece's sectoral structures still mirror a low level of industrial development as well as a service industry with a below-average growth performance compared to other EU countries. Greece's composition of exports exhibits a limited growth and value-added potential, and is similar to the export patterns of low-income countries due to a focus on raw materials and labor-intensive goods. The analysis also shows that without significant growth, the Greek debt will remain unsustainable. A haircut or a phasing out of the debt burden can only complement supply-oriented structural reforms, however. The reform agenda of August 2015 is a new attempt to implement the reforms that the creditors have been waiting on for the past five years.

→ JEL Classification: F15, F43, H63
→ Keywords: Structural change, foreign trade, unsustainable sovereign debt, structural reforms

1 A new attempt to overcome the Greek crisis

In August 2015, after two elections and a month-long struggle over debt relief, fresh money, and the future of the reform process, the EU Commission signed a Memorandum of Understanding for a three-year ESM program on behalf of the euro countries and the Tsipras government. A Grexit, which had already been considered by the creditors (see Frankfurter Allgemeine Zeitung 2015), is no longer being discussed as a policy option, and the same is true for a generous haircut claimed by the Greek party. However, it is crucial for the future of the political process that the Greek government does not try to suspend the reform process again and return to welfare and demand policies.

The reform stalemate has been worsening the economic climate since the end of last year, causing a fall in confidence on the part of domestic and foreign investors and fostering a large-scale capital outflow. The new Greek government needs to restore confidence in the reform process and accelerate the implementation of reforms that are still pending after so much time has been lost. Greek policymakers should be aware that reforms are necessary to reduce the structural deficiencies that continue to plague the Greek economy. In the past, these deficiencies prevented the Greek economy from attaining a path of sustainable growth that will also be needed to reduce the debt burden by Greece's own efforts. But after five years of failed bailout programs, the question arises whether the new reform agenda will be the final act of the Greek tragedy.

Five years ago, the first economic adjustment program was already offering a blueprint for economic recovery and a feasible way out of the crisis. The Papandreou government agreed to a three-year program that was designed to restore fiscal stability, reduce domestic demand, and increase supply and competitiveness. According to the program, cuts in benefits and wages as well as structural reforms should pave the path to an investment- and export-led growth model in Greece (IMF 2010: 8). This program reflected the idea of developing trade as a driver for long-term innovation and growth (e. g. Grossman and Helpman 1991: 237–257). The globalization process has created lots of opportunities to follow such a trade and growth strategy. In addition, the Greek economy, being part of the EU Common Market, could benefit from the openness of the European markets. But according to Krueger (1984, 1998: 1519–1520), for example, trade liberalization has to go along with liberal domestic economic policies, which promote structural change, competitiveness, and export capabilities.

Against this backdrop, our paper is organized as follows: In Chapter 2 we analyze whether the structural deficiencies of the Greek economy, which have been impeding a substantial catching-up beyond demand-driven boom periods, are still prevalent. In Chapter 3, we complement the structural analysis by examining what is keeping exports from becoming the driver of Greek growth. In Chapter 4, we explain why growth and economic reforms are also essential to achieving a sustainable level of public debt in Greece. In Chapter 5, we evaluate the suitability and feasibility of the commitments to structural reforms that are tied to the third bailout program and part of the Memorandum of Understanding from August 2015. Finally, in Chapter 6 we ultimately assess whether the new attempt to overcome the Greek crisis is more promising than are the failed attempts from before.

2 Structural weaknesses and insufficient productivity

When compared to other European countries, Greece suffers from both severe structural weaknesses as well as a low productivity across the various sectors of its economy—and both phenomena are not new. Despite minor adjustments, Greece's basic structural problems seem to be more or less persistent since the country joined, in 1981, what was at the time known as the "European Community" (see Laaser 1997: 90–98, 108–111, 115–118).

In an international comparison, manufacturing is usually a source of higher incomes for countries with a high share of manufacturing value added and employment. Although the share of manufacturing in value added and employment is shrinking globally, this sector has retained its position as a generator of income and as an important driver of economic growth (Manyika et al. 2012). According to the complexity theory put forward by Hausmann and Hidalgo, manufacturing still serves as the pivotal device for R&D, innovation, and economic growth.[1] Both authors emphasize that economic complexity—meaning the great variety of knowledge, skills, and capabilities available within a given country—is directly embodied in the manufacturing activities that occur in the course of producing individual commodities. The more a country is able to acquire these kinds of productive capabilities, the better its opportunities for future prosperity (Hausmann and Hidalgo 2012: 13). This view is corroborated by Tassey (2014: 28–29), who concludes that: (i) High-paying jobs are found primarily in manufacturing, particularly where R&D is performed, and that manufacturing (ii) still dominates exports; (iii) generates substantial forward- and backward-linking demand for high-income services; and (iv) provides high incomes when linked to high-tech activities.

The actual size of manufacturing in Greece gives the impression, however, that this sector is barely there: Only 8.5 percent of Greek value added was generated by manufacturing activities in 2014. The European average in the same period was—at more than 15 percent—nearly twice that share, while the figure in highly industrialized Germany was actually over 22 percent (Figure 1).

Around the year 2000, Greece's manufacturing sector was not much larger than it is today, contributing 10 percent to the gross value added. Since then, this share has shrunk a little bit less than has the same share in the EU-28 as a whole, while in heavily industrialized Germany, the manufacturing share has remained nearly constant. The insufficiency in the size of manufacturing in Greece that has yet to be overcome creates some kind of "déjà-vu" experience to an observer: The actual findings resemble the situation in the 1970s, when Greece still had a much smaller manufacturing sector (19 percent) than did the South European applicants Spain and Portugal (both 27 percent), and the situation after EU accession, when industrialization in Greece hardly evolved at all (Laaser 1997: 90, 109, 116).

A breakdown of the remaining Greek manufacturing activities reveals that labor-intensive industries account for about two-thirds of manufacturing jobs; important investment goods industries, such as the automotive industry, mechanical engeneering, and electrical engineering, only play a minor role. The Greek industry lacks a considerable productive capacity of investment goods

1 See Hidalgo and Hausmann (2009) and Hausmann and Hidalgo (2011a, 2011b, 2012) for a detailed elaboration of their theory. A brief summary of their reasoning as well as an evaluation of the consequences for future manufacturing can be found in Moavenzadeh et al. (2012).

Figure 1

Share of industry in Greece compared to EU-28 in 2014[1]

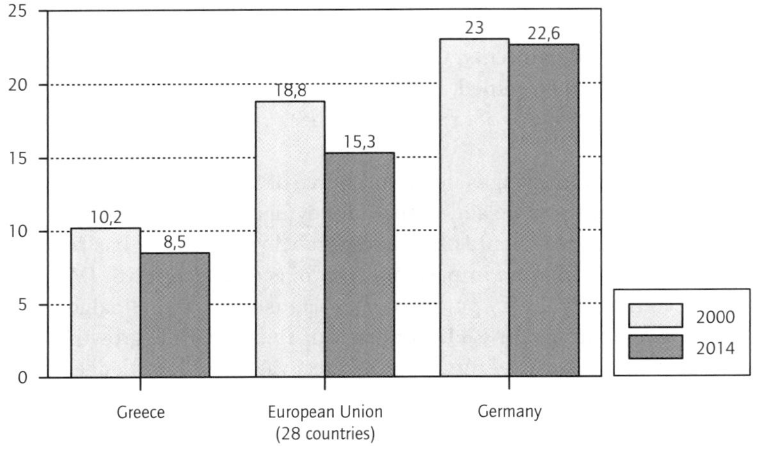

1 In per cent of aggregate gross value added.
Source: Eurostat (2015a): Database, Economy and finance, Annual national accounts, Basic breakdowns of main GDP aggregates and employment, Gross value added and income by A*10 industry breakdowns [nama_10_a10],

with a high value-added and a demand for highly qualified workers (Schrader, Benček, and Laaser 2013: 9–11).

With respect to service industries—which make up the largest share of the Greek economy at 83 percent of value added, a figure that is much larger than it is in the EU-28 or in Germany[2]—the situation does not seem to be much better. The 2014 upswing in tourism once again aggravated an old weakness of the Greek service sector, namely that low-income activities such as retail trade and tourism, which comprise jobs with low qualification requirements, account for more than a quarter of Greek value added. Along with activities connected to the public sector and to real estate—which each accounts for almost one-fifth of total value added—such activities dominate Greek service industries (see Schrader, Benček and Laaser 2015: 4–6). By contrast, activities in business and production-related services account for less than 5 percent of Greek value added, which is less than half the value in the EU-28 or in Germany.

The breakdown of the Greek value added already suggests that the country also suffers from insufficient productivity. Comparing Greece's labor productivity in manufacturing with the average of the EU-28 or Germany reveals that they are worlds apart (Figure 2).

In 2014, the Greek manufacturing productivity of 19.30 euro/hour did not account for more than 55 percent of the pertinent value in the EU-28. Since 2000, this relation has fluctuated somewhat

2 Numerical data in this paragraph are calculated from the data source of Figure 1. In 2014, service industries accounted for 74 percent of value added in the EU-28, and for 69 percent in Germany.

Figure 2

Productivity in Greece's manufacturing sector compared to that of the EU-28 and Germany, 2000–2014[1]

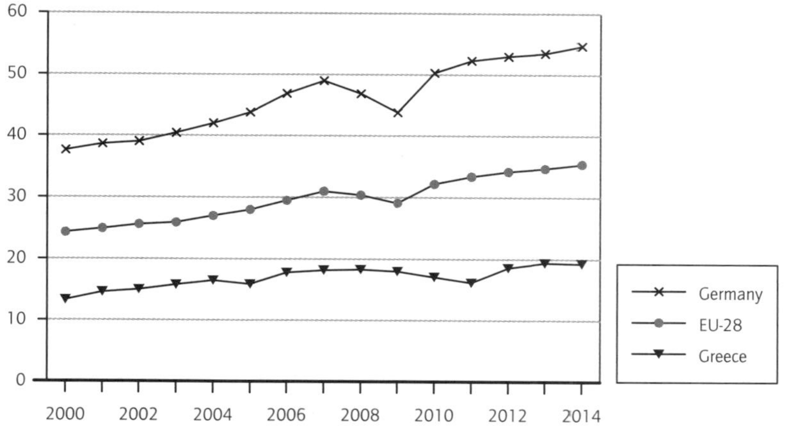

1 Value added in Euro, current prices, per working hour in manufacturing (Nace_R2 sect. C).
Source: Eurostat (2015a). Database, Economy and finance, Annual national accounts, Basic breakdowns of main GDP aggregates and employment, Gross value added and income by A*10 industry breakdowns [nama_10_a10], http://ec.europa.eu/eurostat/data/database; Eurostat (2015b). Database, Economy and finance, Annual national accounts, Basic breakdowns of main GDP aggregates and employment, Employment by A*10 industry breakdowns [nama_10_a10_e], http://ec.europa.eu/eurostat/data/database, own calculation and compilation.

in between 49 percent to 63 percent, but was virtually the same in the first and last reporting years. With respect to Germany, the relation did not exceed the threshold of one-third for the whole period very much, with the only exception being the crisis years of 2008 and 2009.

It can be concluded that Greece's sectoral structures mirror a low level of industrial development, as well as a service industry with a below-average growth performance in comparison to other EU countries. This situation has not substantially changed since Greece joined the Common Market in 1981. After accession, the country did not make use of the vast opportunities that the membership in the Common Market offers for penetrating other member states' markets. That, however, would have required substantial structural change—which did not take place. The need for structural change is also confirmed by the Hausmann-Hidalgo complexity model: At the beginning of the financial crisis in 2008, Greece only ranked 53rd on the economic complexity index scale, which depicts and ranks the amount of productive knowledge of countries around the world (Hausmann and Hidalgo 2011b: 62–66). This result reflects a "lost era" in Greece, with the consequence that a "big push forward" is less likely following the observation by Hausmann and Hidalgo (2011a: 340) for those countries which face the greatest scarcity of productive knowledge.

3 Can exports be the driver of Greek growth?

In their overview on trade and growth links in theory and evidence, Baldwin and Seghezza (1998: 379–381) find that trade affects growth via investment. In the case of a developing country like

Greece, it cannot be expected that openness encourage investments in product and process innovations, which is assumed in R&D based endogenous growth models. Rather, investment in industrial locations of production should have been expected, especially in the course of European integration. But Baldwin and Seghezza (1998: 390–396) empirically show that EU membership-induced, investment-led growth could not be observed for Greece as it could be for Ireland, Portugal, and Spain. According to their explanation, the effects of EU integration in Greece were not strong enough to overcome poor macroeconomic management and market rigidities.

The financial and economic crisis of 2008 meant the end of the demand-driven economic growth in Greece. However, exports did not become a driver of economic growth. With respect to trade in goods and services according to the national accounts statistics, it can be observed that from the beginning of the crisis in 2008 until the end of 2014, exports of goods and services recovered slightly, with an increase of 4.3 percent. At the same time, imports declined significantly, by about 12 percent (Eurostat 2015c). This correction of trade imbalances was accompanied by a shrinking current account deficit: from 35 billion euro in 2008 to about 4 billion euro in 2014, according to the Greek balance of payment statistics based on ELSTAT's trade statistics (Bank of Greece 2015). This correction of imbalances was primarily a reflex that had emerged from the crisis—a passive rehabilitation of the trade balance through shrinking imports due to a loss of purchasing power and remitted interest rate payments as well as increasing EU transfers.

In the past, Greece lost the chance to develop export-oriented industries. Accordingly, the Greek economy fares only slightly better than do the big EU economies like Italy, France, and the UK with respect to export intensity—exports of goods and services in percent of GDP—which amounted to 33 percent in 2014 (Figure 3). But Greece, as a country with only small markets, should be expected to trade much more intensively than these big economies would be. Therefore, more appropriate benchmark countries would be Hungary, Slovakia, and Ireland, which exhibit export intensities at a range between 89 and 114 percent—far beyond the Greek level. Moreover, Greece's rising export intensity did not signal an unprecedented export strength, but have resulted from the shrinking GDP since 2009. If the denominator for calculating the export intensity for the whole period from 2008 to 2014 is the GDP of 2008, the Greek export intensity attained merely 24 percent in 2014.

An investigation of Greece's past export performance makes it clear that the export of services was traditionally a Greek strength, accounting for an export share of about 56 percent in 2008 based on national accounts statistics (Figure 3). But until 2014, the export of services declined by 12 percent, and the service share only accounted for less than 48 percent. At least at the current edge, service exports increased again by 11.5 percent because the export of travel services remained on a growth path, and transportation also gathered momentum according to the balance of payments statistics (Bank of Greece 2015).

But in general, the focus on travel and transportation services brings along some disadvantages for the Greek recovery process. Sea transport, which dominates the export of transportation services, strongly depends on the global business cycle and cannot contribute crucially to a reduction of mass unemployment (IMF 2013: 22–24). The again-rising export of touristic services—benefiting from lower prices in the course of internal depreciation and tax cuts—has high potential, but due to a lack of investment, Greece's tourism industry is less competitive with respect to quality than are those of other Mediterranean countries, and it mainly offers low-wage jobs (McKinsey

Figure 3

Greek export performance, 2008–2014[1]

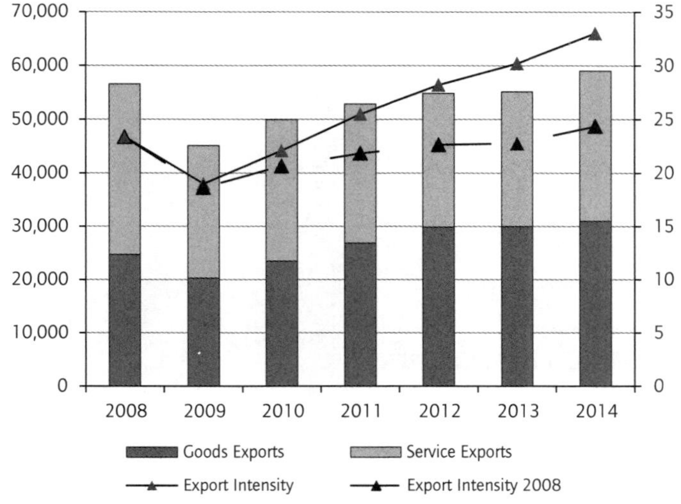

1 Goods and service exports in million euro; export intensity as total export in percent of GDP, export intensity 2008 as total export in percent of GDP of 2008.
Source: Eurostat (2015c). Statistics: National accounts, GDP and main components (output, expenditure and income) [nama_10_gdp]. http://ec.europa.eu/eurostat/web/national-accounts/data/database, Download 15.10.2015.

2011: 39–43). However, business-related services, which demand skilled labor and provide high earning potentials in return, are only exported to a minor degree.

In contrast to the gradual recovery of service exports, the export of goods increased rapidly, by 25 percent, between 2008 and 2014 (Figure 3). At first glance, these figures suggest that a new Greek business model is taking shape that is opening up the prospect of export-led growth in the near future. But a sectoral analysis reveals some deficiencies of Greece's commodity exports, which can be illustrated by the top ten export groups in 2014 (Figure 4). This ranking is dominated by the export of petroleum and products thereof, with a share of close to 40 percent—even though Greece is not an oil-producing, but rather an oil-importing country. Thus it is no surprise that oil imports dominate the Greek commodity import ranking. Far behind the exports of agricultural products are various metals, textiles, and fish. Even the medicinal and pharmaceutical products are less human capital-intensive than might be imagined, because the bulk of these exports comprises generics.

An earlier analysis by Schrader, Benček and Laaser (2013: 19–21) already concluded that the technology and human capital content of Greek exports were traditionally relatively low, and further decreased during the crisis years. Less than 17 percent of Greek commodity exports were more or less technology-intensive compared to, for instance, a share of 60 percent in Germany. This result is in line with figures from the OECD (2015), which uses an alternative method to measure

Figure 4

Top 10 commodity exports in Greece, 2014[1]

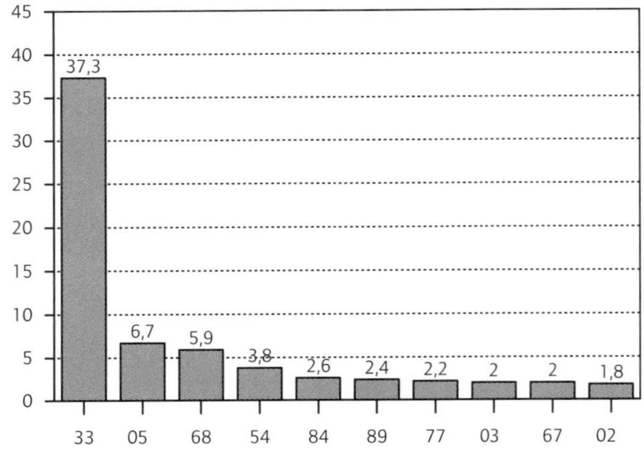

1 Exports in the 10 largest two digit commodity groups in percent of total export.

SITC codes:
33 Petroleum, petroleum products and related materials
05 Vegetables and fruit
68 Non-ferrous metals
54 Medicinal and pharmaceutical products
84 Articles of apparel and clothing accessories
89 Miscellaneous manufactured articles, N. E. S., electrical machinery, apparatus and appliances, N. E. S., and electrical parts thereof (including non-electrical counterparts, N. E. S., of electrical household-type equipment)
77 Fish (not marine mammals), crustaceans, molluscs and aquatic
03 Invertebrates and preparations thereof
67 Iron and steel
02 Dairy products and birds' eggs.
Source: Eurostat (2015d): Database: International Trade detailed data, http://ec.europa.eu/eurostat/web/international-trade/data/database (Download 05/07/2015).

the technology content of exports: In 2013, again less than 17 percent of Greek exports came from high- or medium-high technology industries.

Against this backdrop, the slight recovery of Greek exports indicates neither a stronger role of Greek exporters on growing global markets, nor of technology- or human capital-intensive contributions of Greek enterprises to international value-added chains of production. Instead, exports are focused on raw materials and products thereof, as well as on labor-intensive goods and agricultural products. They reveal Greece's technological gap compared to highly industrialized countries, as well as a growing number of emerging market economies in Asia and Eastern Europe. Greece's composition of commodity exports exhibits a limited growth and value-added potential, and is more comparable to the export patterns of low-income countries. Hence Greece's structural deficiencies also become obvious in its export industries. Both the present size and quality of the Greek export industries create doubt that Greece will overcome the present crisis in the short term through an export-led growth.

Figure 5

Development of debt trajectory projections for Greece
In percent

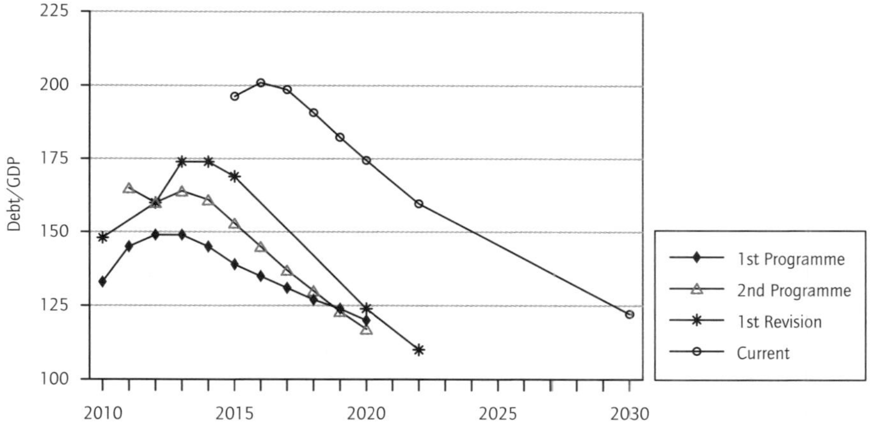

Source: IMF (2010), EU Commission (2012a, 2012b, 2015a), own compilation.

4 Debt sustainability

The previous sections have shown in detail the structural weaknesses still present in the Greek economy. They have also demonstrated that the potential for an export-led growth of Greece is highly limited. However, this has always been one of the major building blocks for the intended economic recovery, particularly in order to restore debt sustainability (IMF 2010: 8). As long as the economy grows at a fast pace, the high debt-to-GDP ratio would be negligible, and would cease to be an obstacle to capital market access.

This assumption also underlies the third economic adjustment program for Greece, which was constructed in August 2015 to provide the country with much-needed liquidity: Over the next three years, Greece will receive financial assistance of up to 86 billion euro. Although parts of the package are intended to repay existing loans, the total sum of public debt will have to rise sharply. Accordingly, the latest projection of the debt trajectory shows just how much the recent program falls short when compared to initial projections from the start of the Greek debt crisis in 2010 (Figure 5). By now, a formally sustainable debt level of around 120 percent of GDP will be reached a decade later than originally expected.

But given the lack of growth potential, other possible measures to reduce Greece's burden of debt seem to be necessary. During the past five years, two such targeted measures to increase or restore the sustainability of Greek debt have already been undertaken: A haircut on privately held government bonds in February 2012 as well as the debt buyback program that was agreed upon and executed in November/December 2012. The result was the large dent in the debt trajectory from the first revision of the second adjustment program depicted in Figure 5. However, an economy that continues to shrink and an additional need for loans have led to steady increases in Greece's debt-to-GDP ratio.

Figure 6

Harmonized long-term interest rates since 2009
In percent

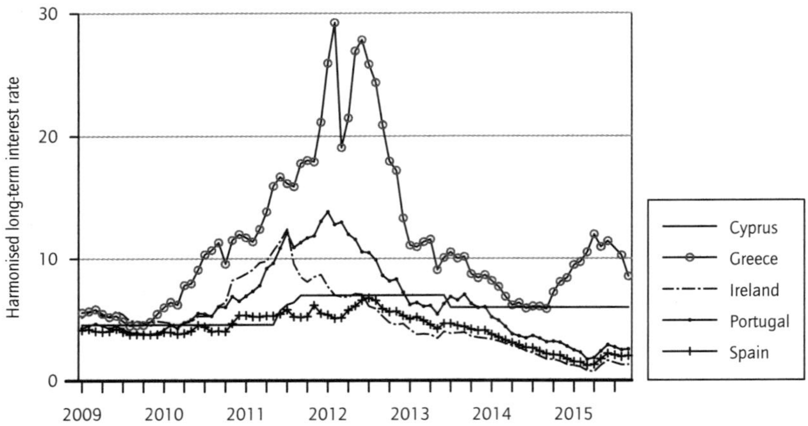

Source: ECB (2015), own compilation.

Of course, such high levels of debt do not pose a problem as long as the state can refinance them. But while both measures, the haircut and the debt buyback, strongly affected the secondary market interest rate of Greek government bonds and considerably reduced the excessive risk premium, a comparison with the rest of the program countries also illustrates how detrimental the final quarter of 2014 and the first six months of 2015 have been to the fragile Greek recovery (Figure 6): Political uncertainty, as well as a dwindling commitment to and even outright backtracking on previous reforms have caused interest rates to soar well above 10 percent again.

Against this backdrop, a targeted action to increase Greece's debt sustainability is required, as independent capital market financing is not feasible and the structural lack of growth potential prevents simply outgrowing public debt. The rest of this section will address this issue by first applying a general measure of sustainability and then using it to determine the extent to which Greek debt would need to be reduced.

Since neither solvency nor liquidity is a suitable criterion to assess the sustainability of public debt, the concept of a debt-stabilizing primary surplus has been adopted in the finance literature as an appropriate tool (see e.g. Buiter and Kletzer 1992, Buiter 1993, Wigger 2010). It identifies the primary surplus a country needs to achieve in order to hold its debt-to-GDP ratio constant. To derive it, the following relationship between current and future debt-to-GDP ratio (d_t and d_{t+1}) is used:

$$d_{t+1} = \frac{1+i}{1+g} d_t + c_t - \tau_t .$$

Where i denotes the nominal interest rate on government debt and g represents the nominal growth rate. The difference between government revenue and spending relative to GDP $\tau_t - c_t$ is by definition the primary surplus ratio p_t. Thus the change in debt-to-GDP between two periods can be expressed as

$$d_{t+1} - d_t = \frac{i-g}{1+g} d_t - p_t.$$

Assuming a constant debt-to-GDP ratio requires the left-hand side of this equation to be zero, and leads to the debt-stabilizing primary surplus

$$p^* = \frac{i+g}{1+g} d_t.$$

Determining p* for the case of Greece is then only a matter of plugging in the appropriate data: Taking the current secondary market interest rate of ten-year government bonds as the average interest rate i, and the current debt-to-GDP ratio as d_t, we can consider two conservative long-term nominal growth scenarios with g=2 percent and g=4 percent: The resulting debt-stabilizing primary surplus is 12.4 percent and 8.4 percent for both growth scenarios, respectively.

Greece's debt-stabilizing primary surplus has decreased significantly since its peak in February 2012—this should not, however, hide the fact that the current level is still far from being achievable: A p* of 5 percent can be considered the upper limit of a sustainable public debt in the long term (Benček and Klodt 2011). Values above this threshold cannot be expected for longer periods of time. Significant drops in Greece's debt-stabilizing primary surplus have only ever occurred with the help of extraordinary measures: debt restructuring, the ECB announcement of unlimited bond purchases, and the bond buyback program. Therefore, a similarly decisive external coping mechanism for the still-increasing level of debt seems inevitable. Whether a restructuring of Greek public debt takes place via an outright haircut, or by extending the life of the loans, postponing the amortization period, and reducing the average rate of interest, the required extent of debt relief is the same and can be calculated in the following way:

Using the critical level of p*=5 percent and solving the p*-equation for d_t, we can calculate the maximum sustainable debt-to-GDP ratio, and can therefore derive how much of a reduction in debt h is necessary to reach it:

$$(1-h)d_t = 0.05\frac{1+g}{1-g}$$

This crude measure would, however, neglect that the interest rate would react to a lower debt-to-GDP ratio, and the required reduction would be overstated. According to Baldacci and Kumar (2010) as well as Laubach (2009), a reaction of the interest rate between 3 to 7 basis points for each percentage point of debt reduction can be expected. The interest rate will thus become

$$i_h = i - hd_t \frac{x}{100}, x \in [3,7].$$

We can use this relationship in the p*-equation to arrive at a more dynamic expression for the required reduction in debt h:

Figure 7

Haircuts necessary for a sustainable level of debt, depending on nominal growth and market reaction

In percent

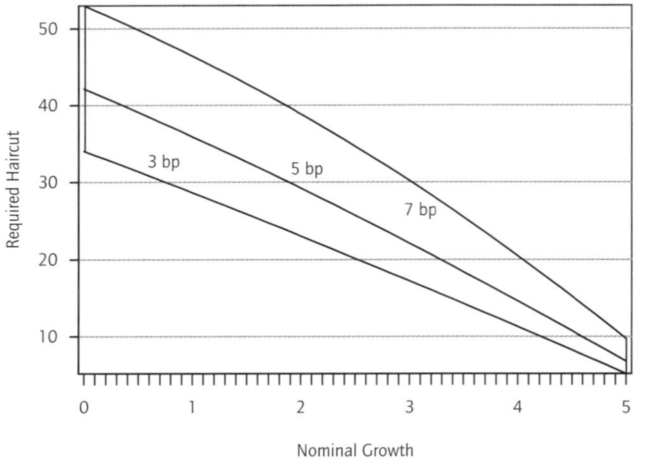

Source: Own compilation.

$$\frac{1}{1+g}(i-hd_t\frac{x}{100}-g)(1-h)d_t=0.05.$$

The solution is depicted in Figure 7 as a corridor of required haircuts subject to the underlying nominal growth rate. Assuming an average long-term growth of 3 percent, the cost of reducing Greece's public debt to a sustainable level would equal a haircut between 17 percent and 30 percent. Instead of an outright haircut, the politically more likely scenario is a restructuring of Greece's debt (see e.g. Darvas and Hüttl 2015). From a purely economic perspective, there is no difference between such a silent debt relief and an unconcealed haircut, since the costs incurred by the creditors are the same. But in any case, such a reduction in debt will not be sufficient without new growth impulses. While a sustainable level of debt can provide the fiscal stability Greece needs to regain capital market access, a haircut (or debt restructuring) can only serve an economic recovery if it is accompanied by continuing structural reforms. They are the necessary condition for future export-based growth.

5 A relaunch of structural reforms

Against the backdrop of its persistent structural weakness, the Greek economy needs supply-oriented structural reforms to initiate a process of investment- and export-led growth. Within the scope of a comprehensive analysis of the EU's Southern enlargement, Laaser (1997: 135–151) showed that in the course of European integration, Greece missed the opportunity to develop a properly functioning market economy and to catch up with the EU core members. In contrast to the other EU accession countries Portugal and Spain, it failed to remove market distortions and disincentives to invest. As Krueger (1998: 1519–1520) already concluded, growth-inhibiting policies can diminish the growth effects of trade liberalization. Baldwin and Seghezza (1998: 390–396) confirmed these insights empirically when analyzing European integration: They explained the absence of EU membership investment-led growth in Greece with the continued state control of the economy and political mismanagement—unlike in Ireland, Portugal, and Spain.

Structural reforms can take effect only in the medium and long term. In the short term, the reforms will result in a loss of income, wealth, and privileges, as well as of social security. Under these circumstances, it is agreed that no more time should be wasted accelerating the reform process. In view of the economic and political reform burden, it is reasonable for the creditor countries and institutions to support Greek reform efforts by all available means. Reforms that would stimulate the growth process and thereby pave the way to economic recovery are eventually a necessary condition to overcome the pending debt crisis.

The Memorandum of Understanding for a three-year ESM program that Greek representatives and the EU Commission signed in August 2015 (EU Commission 2015b) seems to imply the awareness that structural reforms matter for enhancing competitiveness and growth. Reforming the labor market, modernizing the educational system, liberalizing product markets, improving the business environment, better regulating the network industries, continuing the privatization process, and reorganizing public administration and other state institutions—no cornerstone of a comprehensive reform process is missing.

But this list of structural reforms negotiated with the Greek government raises a feeling of déjà vu. Since May 2010, the euro area countries have tied financial assistance for Greece to extensive structural reforms. The Second Economic Adjustment Programme for Greece included a detailed reform agenda with a time schedule for the implementation of single reform measures, supervised by the troika of the IMF, EU Commission, and ECB (EU Commission 2012a, 2012b). This process should have been completed within the duration of this program. That it has not been completed is made clear by the monitoring reports of the troika institutions (IMF 2014: 17–24) and the obvious necessity to include numerous familiar reform actions in the Memorandum of Understanding. It is more or a less a relaunch of the Greek reform process.

Therefore, it appears ambitious to implement the bulk of the reform agenda within roughly one year, with a lot of reform elements actually being subjected to prior action ahead of the next disbursement. As of August 14, the majority of the 58 prior actions the Greek government had been committed to were done or were scheduled to be completed by September to November 2015 (EU Commission 2015c: 15–18). In reference to structural reforms, at the very least, the improvements of the business environment and the market liberalization must be completed by December 2016 at latest, and the bulk of reforms even earlier.

But what does implementation mean? Is the Greek government also committed to enforcing the reforms and to supervising the compliance with the new rules? Again, the answer to these questions depends firstly on the political will of the Greek decision makers to support the application of the new rules in administrative practice, and secondly on the administrative capabilities in Greece. In the past, both requirements were not met: Evaluations by the OECD of previous reform efforts (OECD 2011) suggest that the Greek administration is unable to cope with the complex reform process in a professional manner. Moreover, in the course of 2015, the new and re-elected Greek government lacked ownership of the reform process and did not imply that it has the political will to carry through the reforms.

Doubts regarding a near-term completion of the reform process in particular remain in two major fields of structural reforms: labor market policy and privatization policy. In the case of labor market policy, the Memorandum of Understanding (EU Commission 2015b: 21–22) appears to be rather defensive. It postulates to balance flexibility and fairness for employees and employers, demands to refrain from returning to pre-reform policy settings, and announces a review process on labor market institutions. In contrast, only just one year ago the IMF (2014: 19, 23) complained about the delays in the field of labor markets reforms and the missing European best practice. But now, a speed-up of labor market reforms has become unlikely.

The same is true for the privatization process (EU Commission 2015b: 27–29). The relaunch of the privatization process, which has been stagnant since the beginning of 2015, promises at least the conclusion of projects initiated by the former government. But the newly established privatization fund, a centerpiece of the Memorandum of Understanding, is far from being established, its independence from the government is questionable, and the revenue target of 50 billion euro appears to be just as illusionary as it was in 2010.[3]

In view of Greece's limited administrative capability, technical assistance to carry through the reform process successfully seems indispensable. To speed up and improve the reform process, it makes sense to entrust external experts with the task of organizing and implementing reform measures. These external experts could be recruited from European institutions or from the public service of other EU countries. In addition, domestic and international consulting firms could be charged with the implementation of reform projects. The privatization of state property and state-owned enterprises in particular offers opportunities for professionalization. The outsourcing process could be coordinated by an EU institution together with an independent Greek deregulation agency with far-reaching competencies. The transfer of official competencies to external experts would mean a limitation of Greek sovereignty, but it should be acceptable within the scope of well-defined reform projects.

Unfortunately, the Memorandum of Understanding follows this idea of outsourced reform projects only halfway. In fact, it is explicitly written down that the Greek authorities intend to seek technical assistance from the OECD, World Bank, and EU Commission, as well as member state experts, other international organizations, and independent consultants (EU Commission 2015b: 25). But it is up to the Greek authorities on a project-by-project basis to decide whether and whose assistance they request—and the authorities that failed to complete the reform process successfully during the past five years are still in charge. Hence, technical assistance as intended by the Memorandum differs significantly from outsourcing as proposed.

But it is not only the better prospect of a successful completion of the reform process that suggests its outsourcing: The Greek authorities have to rely on a state and public administration that itself has to undergo a complex process of reorganization, rationalization, optimization etc. in the years ahead (EU Commission 2015b: 29–32). Needless to say that these reforms are long overdue;

3 The IMF has since lowered its 2010 projection of 50 billion euro to 22.4 billion euro (IMF 2014: 18).

however, they also mean that the public administration will become even less functional and a less effective tool for carrying out the reforms.

6 Conclusions

In 2014, there was evidence that Greece's economic situation would take a turn a turn for the better for the first time in a long while. A positive growth rate and a primary surplus of the Greek state budget seemed to signal that the reform and austerity policy would pay off. Meanwhile, the prospects in the current year 2015 are gloomy, and the economic recovery and the fiscal consolidation process have come to a standstill in the course of the political struggle between the Greek government and the creditors, as well as inside the ruling Syriza party.

The Memorandum of Understanding that was signed in August 2015 comprises a suitable reform agenda—as it already was with the last bailout program. In addition, a final haircut or a phasing-out of the Greek debt burden should be considered to make Greece's public debt sustainable. But again, it is crucial that the Tsipras government will take the ownership of the reforms. There is reasonable doubt that the Greek policymakers have understood that structural reforms are indispensable for economic recovery. And there is also reasonable doubt that the Greek administration can implement and enforce the reforms without external support—and for this reason, the outsourcing of reform projects is advisable despite a loss of sovereignty. Therefore, the Greek government should send appropriate signals that it supports the reform process without any qualification.

Greek policymakers should keep in mind that the reform process is essential for improving the conditions for doing business in Greece and attracting private investors who could initiate the kind of structural change Greece needs to generate economic growth in the long run. A dynamic investment process is indispensable for accelerating the modernization of the Greek economy. Greece needs private capital to develop competitive structures and to integrate the economy into international chains of production, preferably with high value added at Greek locations. Greece faces the problem that it can never win a wage race against low-income countries from Eastern Europe or Asia if it seeks to retain its prosperity level. To remain in the group of high-income countries, Greece has to increase its total factor productivity by modernizing its economic structures.

References

— Baldacci, E., and M. S. Kumar (2010): Fiscal Deficits, Public Debt, and Sovereign Bond Yields. IMF Working Papers 10/184.
— Baldwin, R., and E. Seghezza (1998): Regional Integration and Growth in Developing Nations. Journal of Economic Integration, 13 (3), 367–399.
— Bank of Greece (2015): Statistics: Balance of Payments. www.bankofgreece.gr/Pages/en/Statistics/externalsector/balance/basic.aspx (download 10/19/2015).
— Benček, D., and H. Klodt (2011): Fünf Prozent sind (zu) viel: Szenarien zu den benötigten Primärüberschüssen der Euroländer. Wirtschaftsdienst, 91 (9), 959–600.

— Buiter, W.H. (1993): Public debt in the USA. How much, how bad and who pays? NBER working paper 4362. Cambridge, MA.
— Buiter, W.H., and K.M. Kletzer (1992): Government Solvency, Ponzi Finance and the Redundancy and Usefulness of Public Debt. NBER working paper 4076. Cambridge, MA.
— Darvas, Z., and P. Hüttl (2015): How to reduce the Greek debt burden? Bruegel: Analyses, January 9. www.bruegel.org/nc/blog/detail/article/1533-how-to-reduce-thegreek-debt-burden/ (download 10/13/2015).
— ECB (European Central Bank) (2015): Long-term interest rate statistics for EU Member States. www.ecb.int/stats/money/long/html/index.en.html (download 10/13/2014).
— EU Commission (2012a): The Second Economic Adjustment Programme for Greece. Occasional Papers 94. March. Brussels.
— EU Commission (2012b): The Second Economic Adjustment Programme for Greece First Review. December. Brussels.
— EU Commission (2013): European Economic Forecast, Autumn 2013. European Economy 7/2013. November. Brussels.
— EU Commission (2015a): Debt Sustainability Analysis. Download 10/13/2015. http://ec.europa.eu/economy_finance/assistance_eu_ms/greek_loan_facility/pdf/debt_sustainability_analysis_en.pdf.
— EU Commission (2015b): Memorandum of Understanding between the European Commission Acting on behalf of the European Stability Mechanism and the Hellenic Republic and the Bank of Greece. Brussels.
— EU Commission (2015c): Report on Greece's compliance with the draft MOU commitments and the commitments in the Euro Summit statement of 12 July 2015. Brussels.
— Eurostat (2015a): Database, Economy and Finance, Annual National Accounts, Basic Breakdowns of Main GDP Aggregates and Employment, Gross Value Added and Income by A*10 Industry Breakdowns [nama_10_a10]. http://ec.europa.eu/eurostat/data/database (download 10/06/2015).
— Eurostat (2015b): Database, Economy and Finance, Annual National Accounts, Basic Breakdowns of main GDP Aggregates and Employment, Employment by A*10 Industry Breakdowns [nama_10_a10_e]. http://ec.europa.eu/eurostat/data/database (download 10/06/2015).
— Eurostat (2015c): Statistics: National accounts, GDP and main components (output, expenditure and income). http://ec.europa.eu/eurostat/web/national-accounts/data/database (download 10/15/2015).
— Eurostat (2015d): Database: International Trade detailed data. http://ec.europa.eu/eurostat/web/international-trade/data/database (download 05/07/2015).
— Frankfurter Allgemeine Zeitung (2015): Letzte Frist vor dem Grexit. 9.7.2015.
— Grossman, G.M., and E. Helpman (1991): Innovation and Growth in the Global economy. Cambridge, MA and London.
— Hausmann, R., and C.A. Hidalgo (2011a): The Network Structure of Economic Output. Journal of Economic Growth, 16, 309–342.
— Hausmann, R., and C.A. Hidalgo (2011b): The Atlas of Economic Complexity: Mapping Paths to Prosperity. Cambridge, MA, The MIT Press. www.cid.harvard.edu/documents/complexityatlas.pdf (download 11/25/2015).
— Hausmann, R., and C.A. Hidalgo (2012): Essay—Economic Complexity and The Future of Manufacturing. In: J. Moavenzadeh, P. Philip, C.A. Giffi, and A. Thakker (eds.): The Future of Manufacturing. Opportunities to Drive Economic Growth. A World Economic Forum Report in collaboration with Deloitte Touche Tohmatsu Limited. Cologny/Geneva.

www3.weforum.org/docs/WEF_MOB_FutureManufacturing_Report_2012.pdf (download 11/25/2015).
— Hidalgo, C. A., and R. Hausmann (2009): The Building Blocks of Economic Complexity. Proceedings of the National Academy of Sciences of the United States of America, 106 (26), 10570–10575.
— IMF (International Monetary Fund) (2010): IMF Country Report 10/110. Washington, D. C.
— IMF (International Monetary Fund) (2013): IMF Country Report 13/241. Washington, D. C.
— IMF (International Monetary Fund) (2014): Greece. IMF Country Report 14/151. Washington, D. C.
— Krueger, Anne O. (1984): Problems of Liberalization. In: A. C. Harberger (ed.): World Economic Growth. San Francisco, 403–423.
— Krueger, Anne O. (1998): Why Trade Liberalisation is Good for Growth. The Economic Journal, 108 (September), 1513–1522.
— Laaser, C.-F. (1997): Ordnungspolitik und Strukturwandel im Integrationsprozess: Das Beispiel Griechenlands, Portugals und Spaniens. Kieler Studien 287. Tübingen.
— Laubach, T. (2009): New Evidence on the Interest Rate Effects of Budget Deficits and Debt. Journal of the European Economic Association, 7 (4), 858–885.
— Manyika, J., J. Sinclair, R. Dobbs, G. Strube, L. Rassey, J. Mischke, J. Remes, C. Roxburgh, K. George, D. O'Halloran, and S. Ramaswamy (2012): Manufacturing the Future: The Next Era of Global Growth and Innovation. McKinsey Global Institute and McKinsey Operations Practice. www.mckinsey.com/insights/manufacturing/the_future_of_manufacturing. (download 11/25/2015).
— McKinsey & Company (2011): Greece 10 Years Ahead. Defining Greece's new growth model and strategy. Executive summary, September, Athens.
— Moavenzadeh, J., P. Philip, C. A. Giffi, and A. Thakker (2012): The Future of Manufacturing. Opportunities to Drive Economic Growth. A World Economic Forum Report in collaboration with Deloitte Touche Tohmatsu Limited. Cologny/Geneva. www3.weforum.org/docs/WEF_MOB_FutureManufacturing_Report_2012.pdf (download 11/25/2015).
— OECD (2011): Greece: Review of the Central Administration. OECD Public Governance Reviews. 2. December. Paris.
— OECD (2015): STAN Bilateral Trade in Goods by Industry and End-use (BTDIxE), ISIC Rev.3. Download 10/14/15.
— Schrader, K., D. Benček, and C.-F. Laaser (2013): IfW-Krisencheck: Alles wieder gut in Griechenland? Kieler Diskussionsbeiträge 522/523. Kiel Institute for the World Economy, Kiel.
— Schrader, K., D. Benček, and C.-F. Laaser (2015): Greece: How to Take a Turn for the Better. Kiel Policy Brief 83. Kiel Institute for the World Economy, January.
— Tassey, G. (2014): Competing in Advanced Manufacturing: The Need for Improved Growth Models and Policies. Journal of Economic Perspectives, 28 (1), 27–48.
— Wigger, B. U. (2010): Öffentliche Haushalte in der Krise. In: T. Theurl (ed.): Wirtschaftspolitische Konsequenzen der Finanz- und Wirtschaftskrise. Berlin, Schriften des Vereins für Socialpolitik, 85–103.

The Costs of Greece's Fiscal Consolidation

SEBASTIAN GECHERT AND ANSGAR RANNENBERG*

Sebastian Gechert (corresponding author), Macroeconomic Policy Institute (IMK), e-mail: Sebastian-Gechert@boeckler.de
Ansgar Rannenberg, Macroeconomic Policy Institute (IMK) and Central Bank cf Ireland

Summary: This policy brief reexamines the effects of the Greek austerity experiment on its economy via a counterfactual analysis. We combine the fiscal multipliers from the meta regression analysis in Gechert and Rannenberg (2014) to the fiscal consolidation measures that have been implemented in Greece between 2010 and 2014. We estimate that austerity explains almost the entire collapse of Greek GDP after 2009. This result suggests that—ceteris paribus—, in the absence of austerity, the Greek economy would have entered a prolonged period of stagnation, rather than a depression. At the same time the path of the government debt-to-GDP ratio would have been only somewhat higher. Furthermore, we estimate that if the consolidation would have been postponed until after the recovery of the Greek economy and implemented gradually, almost 80 percent of the cost in terms of lost output could have been avoided. Our results suggest that the period 2010-2014 was the wrong time to implement frontloaded spending cuts due to their strong multipliers in downturns. Implementing only the revenue components of the Greek fiscal consolidation would have strongly reduced the output contraction as compared to the actual path of GDP, but would have been much more effective at lowering the debt-to-GDP ratio than the actual fiscal consolidation. A more cautious consolidation would thus have been in the interest of international creditors as well.

→ JEL Classification: E27, E62, H30
→ Keywords: Fiscal multiplier, regime dependence, austerity

* The opinions expressed in this paper are those of the authors and do not necessarily represent the views of the Central Bank of Ireland. We would like to thank Andrew Watt, Fabian Lindner, Gustav Horn, Katja Rietzler, Matteo Salto, Peter Hohlfeld, Rudolf Zwiener, and Werner Röger for helpful discussions. All remaining errors are of course our own.

1 Introduction

The recent Greek elections resulted in a new government led by the Syriza party, whose original goal was to slow the pace of fiscal consolidation as well as the rollback of some of the austerity measures forming part of the "Memoranda of Understanding (MoUs)" between the Greek government and the European Commission, the ECB and the IMF. The attempt by the new government to change course has been met with strong resistance from euro area finance ministers. The latest negotiations on the third bailout program resulted in a list of further spending cuts and tax increases whose impact on macroeconomic performance remains to be seen.

Against this background, we reexamine the effects of the Greek austerity experiment during the years 2010 to 2014 on its economy. We estimate that austerity almost entirely explains the collapse of Greek GDP after 2009. This result suggests that ceteris paribus, in the absence of austerity the Greek economy would have entered a prolonged period of stagnation, rather than a depression. At the same time, the path of the government debt-to-GDP ratio would have been only somewhat higher in 2014. Furthermore, we estimate that if the consolidation had been postponed until after the recovery of the Greek economy and implemented gradually, about 80 percent of the cost in terms of lost output could have been avoided. To be sure, we do not argue that the Greek public finances were in good shape when the fiscal consolidation began. However, irrespective of whether the Greek budget was structurally unbalanced or not, as the economy was in particularly bad shape, our results suggest that the 2010–2014 period was the wrong time to implement spending cuts, and that any expenditure-based consolidation should have been phased in gradually after the recovery of the Greek economy. Implementing only the revenue components of the Greek fiscal consolidation from 2010 to 2014 would have strongly reduced the output contraction as compared to the actual path of GDP, but would have been much more effective at lowering the debt-to-GDP ratio than the actual fiscal consolidation was.

2 Estimating the value of fiscal multipliers

We employ the multiplier estimates of Gechert and Rannenberg (2014) to assess the impact of the fiscal consolidation in Greece over the period 2010–2014, following Gechert et al. (2015), who use them to assess the effects of the euro area's fiscal consolidation on aggregate euro area GDP. Gechert and Rannenberg (2014) conduct a meta-regression analysis of fiscal multiplier estimates based on a broad set of empirical reduced form models, which is extracted from 98 scientific papers. The meta-study aims to identify and quantify the dependence of individual fiscal instruments' fiscal multipliers on the economic circumstances in the period in which the multiplier was estimated, controlling for model uncertainty and sample uncertainty. Taking averages across all other independent variables, the authors report multiplier estimates for a range of expenditure categories as well as for taxes, and for three economic regimes, which are reported in Figure 1. The regimes are an "upper regime" (above average economic circumstances), an "average regime" (average economic circumstances), and a "lower regime" (below-average economic circumstances). The lower regime clearly corresponds to the post-2007 state the Greek economy.

Figure 1

Cumulative multipliers of fiscal impulses for different regimes, full sample

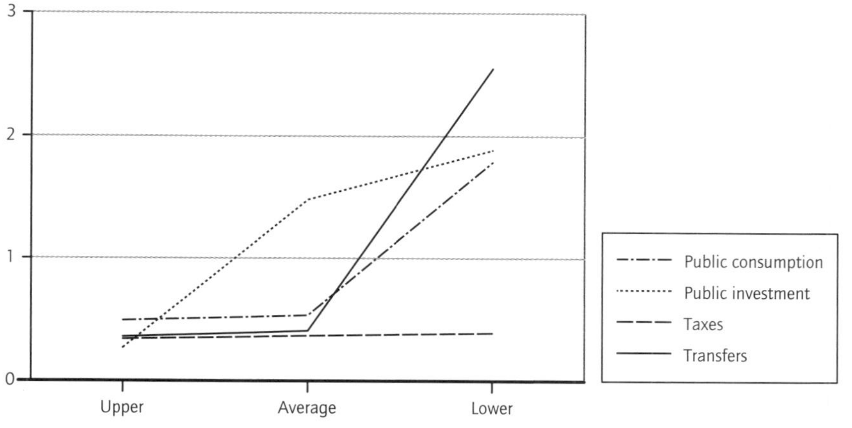

Upper: above-average economic circumstances, Average: average economic circumstances, Lower: below=average economic circumstances.

Source: AMECO, own calculations.

For all expenditure categories, the cumulative multipliers always exceed one in a downturn. By contrast, tax-impulse multipliers are substantially below one across all regimes.[1]

Are these multiplier estimates valid in the case of the fiscal contraction that occurred in Greece? Basically, the multipliers are roughly in line with a recent estimation of regime-dependent multipliers for Greek time series (Monokroussos and Thomakos 2013). However, a common argument is that when embarking on fiscal consolidation, financial markets had severe doubts regarding the sustainability of Greek public finances. By helping to restore investor confidence and thus lowering sovereign bond yields, fiscal consolidation measures would support private expenditure, implying lower fiscal multipliers than would be the case in the absence of fiscal stress (Trichet 2010, Corsetti et al. 2012). However, recent empirical evidence suggests that the effect of cuts to government consumption expenditure on GDP is actually higher in the presence of fiscal stress than in its absence (Born et al. 2015), which is perhaps related to the fact that the effect on the sovereign risk spreads is ambiguous (Born et al. 2015, Cottarelli and Jaramillo 2012).

We do stress, however, that applying the fiscal multipliers estimated by Gechert and Rannenberg (2014) to the Greek fiscal consolidation to gauge its effects requires the assumption that under the alternate fiscal policies we explore below, everything else would stay the same. In particular,

1 Some authors, e. g. Alesina and Ardagna (2010, 2013) argue that tax-based consolidations have bigger adverse GDP effects than do spending based consolidations. Their findings are included in the fiscal multiplier database Gechert and Rannenberg (2014). However, their finding is an outlier in the literature on empirically estimated tax and spending multipliers, which mostly finds tax multipliers to be smaller than spending multipliers, unlike what is sometimes alleged. Therefore, the impact of their estimate on the point estimate of the meta-regression analysis of Gechert and Rannenberg (2014) is small. Simulations of structural models also lend support to the finding that, especially during downturns, tax multipliers are much smaller than are expenditure multipliers (e. g. Erceg and Lindé 2013, Coenen et al. 2012).

Greek does not exit the euro. The Greek fiscal bailout and the associated bailout of the Greek banks do take place and the Greek banks still receive funding via the ECB's unconventional measures, etc. Whether such alternative scenarios would have been realistic given the politics of the Eurogroup is beyond the scope of this article. The value added of our analysis lies in exploring how GDP might have evolved if alternative strategies had been given a chance.

Another caveat is that the path of the expenditure or tax impulse for which the multipliers in the multiplier database are estimated will in general not equal the changes implemented over the 2010–2014 period in Greece. However, given that any assessment of the effects of fiscal consolidation is bound to suffer from uncertainties, and that the multipliers reported here are based on a substantial amount of estimates generated by a range of different methodologies, we believe the following exercise to be useful nevertheless.

3 Measuring the consolidation effort

For the exercise conducted below, we would ideally like to use data on the discretionary, exogenous policy changes to government consumption, government investment, transfers to households, and taxes as caused by the implementation of the Memoranda of Understanding (MoUs) between the Greek government and the Troika. As we are not aware of such detailed data on the Greek fiscal effort, we take the following route. For changes in government consumption, government investment, and transfers, we use AMECO series "Final consumption expenditure of general government," "Gross Fixed Capital Formation: General Government," and "Social Benefits other than social transfers in kind: General government," and deflate them using the GDP deflator. These three categories comprise more than 90 percent of non-interest government expenditure in Greece. Note that we are not able to perform any cyclical adjustment on these measures.[2] This should not pose a big problem with respect to government consumption and investment, whose magnitudes are arguably directly determined by fiscal policy. However, the available figures for transfers are likely to underestimate the discretionary consolidation effort as they are affected by both fiscal policy and economic developments. Benefit claims would be expected to increase when unemployment is on the rise, as observed in Greece from 2008 to 2013, thus countering the discretionary cuts in transfers.

To measure the discretionary increases in taxes and social security contributions, we used the AMECO series "Discretionary Measures Current Revenue." This measure is held to be superior to the changes in cyclically adjusted revenue, which tend to understate the true discretionary fiscal effort due to imperfections of the cyclical adjustment procedure and the fact that the Greek economy was in a severe downturn (European Commission 2013, Gechert et al. 2016).[3]

2 There is a time series on "discretionary measures current and capital revenue" in AMECO. However, the series does not distinguish the different expenditure components, which arguably have distinct multipliers.

3 This measure is generated by the country desks of the Directorate General for Economic and Financial Affairs of the European Commission following the so-called "bottom-up approach," which cumulates the budgetary effects of changes to tax laws holding the tax base constant.

Table 1

Consolidation actions in Greece

a) Cumulative revenue increases and expenditure cuts, 2010 Billion Euro

	2010	2011	2012	2013	2014
Total revenue	10.0	19.6	25.2	28.4	28.9
Transfers	1.5	1.2	2.7	7.3	7.1
Government consumption expenditure	5.5	11.2	14.5	18.2	18.7
Government gross fixed capital formation	2.1	3.3	3.2	2.2	1.7
Total expenditure	9.1	15.7	20.5	27.8	27.5
All measures	19.1	35.3	45.7	56.3	56.4

b) Cumulative revenue increases and expenditure cuts, percent of 2009 GDP

	2010	2011	2012	2013	2014
Total revenue	4.2	8.2	10.5	11.9	12.1
Transfers	0.6	0.5	1.1	3.1	3.0
Government consumption expenditure	2.3	4.7	6.1	7.6	7.8
Government gross fixed capital formation	0.9	1.4	1.4	0.9	0.7
Total expenditure	3.8	6.6	8.6	11.6	11.5
All measures	8.0	14.7	19.1	23.5	23.6

Source: AMECO, own calculations.

Table 1a and 1b present our estimate of the cumulative consolidation effort expressed in billions of 2010 euros and as a percentage of 2009 real GDP. The table illustrates the biblical scale of austerity in Greece. By 2014, total government expenditure is expected to have been cut by 27.5 billion euros, the equivalent of 11.5 percent of the 2009 GDP. As pointed out above, the discretionary cut we would ideally like to observe will likely exceed the decline of actual transfers reported in the table and used in our calculation below, so that to this extent our estimations must be considered conservative.

Estimated discretionary revenue increases are of essentially the same magnitude. By 2014, our measure of combined revenue and expenditure cuts accumulated to 56.4 billion euros, equivalent to 23.6 percent of Greece's 2009 GDP. This is above the change in cyclically adjusted net lending as measured by the European Commission (16.9 percent) and in the underlying primary balance as measured by the OECD (18.4 percent) over the same period, which should be due to the different assessment of discretionary changes on the revenue side. However, the broad time profile of our estimated fiscal consolidation effort—a very big initial impulse in 2010, followed by smaller efforts in subsequent years—is roughly in line with the profile of these measures of the fiscal stance.

4 Gauging the effect of Greece's fiscal consolidation

We now combine the changes of the fiscal instruments reported in Table 1 with the multipliers reported in Figure 1. We account for the fact that the Greek share of imports is somewhat higher than the average in the fiscal multiplier database on which the Gechert and Rannenberg's (2014) estimates are based, implying that the actual multipliers are somewhat below the values reported in Figure 1.[4] Table 2 shows the impact on GDP.

We find that the fiscal consolidation in Greece reduced GDP by almost 7.5 percent in 2010, with the cumulative GDP decline increasing to more than 21 percent in 2013, after which it decreases to about 20 percent in 2014, as—according to our estimates—fiscal austerity was relaxed somewhat on the expenditure side in 2014. Thus the austerity measures came at a huge cost.[5] By far the biggest contribution to the GDP decline comes from cuts to government consumption, which is driven by its high share in the overall consolidation effort and its high multipliers. By contrast, the contribution of tax increases to the GDP decline is much lower due to the lower tax multipliers.[6]

We can use our estimates of the GDP decline induced by fiscal austerity to gauge the path of Greek GDP in the absence of the austerity measures as displayed in Table 1. Figure 2 compares this scenario of no austerity to several benchmarks, including the actual path of Greek GDP. According to our estimate, in the absence of fiscal consolidation Greek GDP would be only about 2 percent lower in 2014 than in 2009, instead of suffering a decline of more than 25 percent. This result is driven by the aforementioned scale of austerity in Greece, and our fiscal multipliers. The average multiplier of the cumulated spending reduction and revenue increases amounts to 0.9.

We also report an estimate of the path of the Greek primary budget balance and the government debt-to-GDP ratio in the absence of fiscal consolidation. This exercise requires further assumptions. First, we have to estimate the feedback of the GDP contraction caused by the fiscal consolidation on the primary balance. This feedback effect partly offsets the direct effect of the discretionary fiscal measures summarized in Table 1 by reducing tax revenues and increasing benefit claims. To capture this automatic stabilizer effect, we assume a semi-elasticity of the primary budget balance with respect to GDP of 0.47, as estimated by Girouard and André (2005) for the Greek economy. Furthermore, we assume that the average interest rate on the outstanding stock of government debt equals its actual value over the 2010 to 2014 period in all scenarios considered below.

Finally, we have to assume a path for the GDP deflator, which is relevant in shaping the dynamics of the government debt-to-GDP ratio. As can be obtained from Figure 3, the change in the Greek

---

4 The share of imports in GDP ranges from 30.7 percent in 2010 to 35.1 percent in 2014. By contrast, the sample average equaled 22.8 percent. Multipliers are accordingly reduced by between 0.24 and 0.31.

5 This finding is consistent with Wren-Lewis (2015), who argues, based on some alternative fiscal measures, that changes in the underlying primary balance since 2009 explain all of the change in the output gap.

6 There is evidence that in response to tax increases, Greek firms shift economic activity from the formal to the informal sector in a quantitatively significant way (Pappadà and Zylberberg 2014). Such shifting could imply that the effect of the policy change on "true" overall economic activity (the sum of formal and informal activity) is smaller in Greece than it is in countries with more vigorous tax law enforcement. Thus applying the multiplier estimates of Gechert and Rannenberg (2014) to revenue increases in Greece might overstate their effect on "true" economic activity. Therefore the GDP effect of the revenue increases over the 2010-2014 period might be even smaller than what we estimate. We thank an anonymous referee for drawing our attention to this issue.

Table 2

Estimated cumulative GDP effect of Greece's fiscal consolidation

a) Billion Euro

	2010	2011	2012	2013	2014
Total revenue	-1.9	-3.0	-3.3	-3.6	-2.3
Transfers	-3.5	-2.8	-6.3	-16.8	-15.8
Government consumption expenditure	-8.8	-17.3	-22.2	-27.8	-27.7
Government gross fixed capital formation	-3.5	-5.5	-5.3	-3.6	-2.6
Total expenditure	-15.7	-25.6	-33.8	-48.2	-46.1
All measures	-17.6	-28.5	-37.1	-51.7	-48.4

b) Percent of 2009 GDP

	2010	2011	2012	2013	2014
Total revenue	-0.8	-1.2	-1.4	-1.5	-1.0
Transfers	-1.4	-1.2	-2.6	-7.0	-6.6
Government consumption expenditure	-3.7	-7.2	-9.3	-11.6	-11.6
Government gross fixed capital formation	-1.5	-2.3	-2.2	-1.5	-1.1
Total expenditure	-6.6	-10.7	-14.1	-20.1	-19.3
All measures	-7.4	-11.9	-15.5	-21.6	-20.2

Source: AMECO, own calculations.

GDP deflator decelerated substantially after 2008 and turned negative in 2013. This development is most likely caused by the collapse of GDP and the associated emergence of big spare capacities and mass unemployment, which reduced wage and price pressures. It appears likely that under the essentially flat GDP path in the scenario of no fiscal consolidation, the annual change in the GDP deflator would have avoided negative territory. As austerity explains almost all of the difference in the post-2009 GDP path between Greece and the euro area, we assume that in the absence of austerity, starting in 2010, the Greek GDP deflator would have grown at the same pace as the Euro Area GDP deflator.

Figure 4 shows that in the absence of austerity, although the primary deficit would have deteriorated somewhat further over the 2010–2014 period, the 2014 debt-to-GDP ratio would actually be only slightly above its value in the presence of fiscal consolidation, chiefly as a consequence of the more favorable path of real GDP.

Figure 2

Greek real GDP under various scenarios
2007 = 100

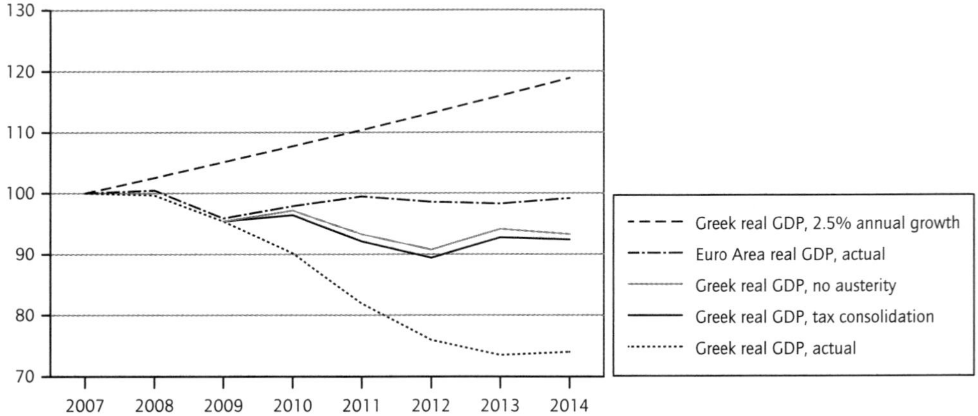

Source: AMECO, own calculations.

Figure 3

GDP Deflator, annual change
In percent

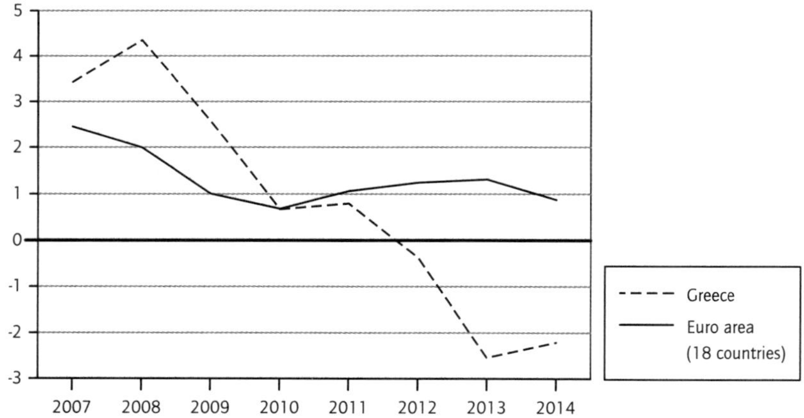

Source: Eurostat, own calculations.

Figure 4

Greek path of primary balances and debt-to-GDP ration for actual and counterfactual scenarios, percent of GDP

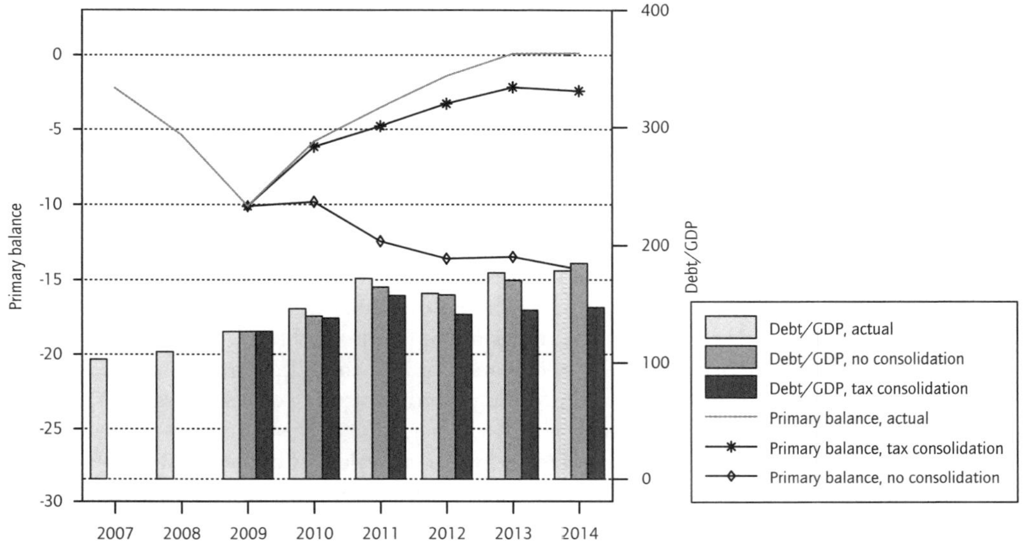

Note: The paths of primary balances exclude one-off measures, while the paths of government debt-to-GDP ratios include one-off measures and stock-flow adjustments. Excluding or including these measures would affect all scenarios in the same manner.
Source: AMECO, Eurostat, own calculations.

5 Alternative consolidation scenarios

According to the multiplier estimates reported in Figure 1, spending cuts have much smaller adverse effects on GDP during average economic circumstances than they do during economic downturns. We therefore also consider a scenario in which Greece would have backloaded its fiscal consolidation until after the recovery of its economy—a situation that could be classified as average economic circumstances. In this case, the cumulative negative GDP effects would have amounted to only 3.5 percent of GDP. That is to say, about 80 percent of the negative impact on GDP are due to the frontloading of measures, and could have been avoided by postponing and gradually implementing fiscal consolidation. The effect on the primary balance would also be more favorable: Under average economic circumstances, the measures displayed in Table 1 would cause a cumulative improvement in the primary budget balance of about 22 percentage points. As the overall contractionary fiscal impulse is rather big, even in average economic circumstances, a fiscal consolidation of Greek proportions would have preferably been spread over a number years, in order to avoid a return to recession. Our finding that, ceteris paribus, backloading the fiscal consolidation would have had strongly beneficial effects is in line with findings of other authors, using different models and empirical methods (Batini et al. 2012, ECLM, IMK and OFCE 2012).

Interestingly, the overall multiplier in the backloading scenario is not too far away from the value which was used by the IMF and other international institutions at the start of the financial crisis and after to quantify the effects of fiscal consolidation (Blanchard and Leigh 2013). This coincidence suggests that the Troika did not adequately take into account the prevailing crisis conditions causing higher-than-average multipliers when designing the Greek structural adjustment program. In doing so, it was ignoring some of the latest research (see for instance Eggertsson 2009 and Christiano, Eichenbaum, and Rebelo 2011, which was first circulated in 2009 as well).

Furthermore, Figure 1 shows that during economic downturns, estimated tax multipliers are much smaller than spending multipliers. We therefore investigate the effect of implementing only the tax increases but not the spending reductions listed in Table 1. As illustrated by Figure 1, the path of GDP would be somewhat lower than under the "no consolidation" scenario, but still a lot more favorable than the actual path. To estimate the implied paths of the primary balance and the debt-to-GDP ratio, we assume that with a tax-only consolidation, the GDP deflator would have remained at its 2009 level until 2014, as the economy would have been weaker still. The much-lower estimated decline in GDP allows an improvement in the primary balance almost as big as under the actual consolidation, illustrating that the spending cuts displayed in Table 1 contribute very little to fiscal consolidation, as their consolidation effects are almost self-defeating. At the same time, the lower GDP decline directly lowers the trajectory of the debt-to-GDP ratio, implying that the 2014 estimated debt-to-GDP ratio would be about 30 percentage points below its actual level if only the revenue increases listed in Table 1 had been implemented. These findings are in line with Erceg and Lindé (2013), who show in the context of a New Keynesian model that during a deep downturn, front loaded tax hikes are more effective for reducing government debt quickly than are expenditure cuts due to the smaller adverse effect on GDP.

To be sure, backloading the Greek fiscal consolidation would have faced considerable political and institutional challenges. In 2010, the Greek political establishment was not considered trustworthy by its European partners as a consequence of the persistent misreporting of the Greek government debt and deficits revealed in the previous year. Establishing mechanisms ensuring that the Greek government would eventually consolidate after having been granted financial assistance would have been difficult. Euro area governments might also have resisted focusing the consolidation on the revenue side to the extent that they discounted the Greeks' ability to reform its tax collection system. However, these challenges must be weighed against the cost of frontloaded consolidation based on spending cuts. Our estimates suggest that this cost was very high. Frontloading fiscal consolidation has thus made the repayment of the Greek government debt more difficult, which—if nothing else—should have been of concern to euro area governments keen on recuperating their domestic taxpayers' money.

6 On the plausibility of the Greek GDP path under the no-austerity scenario

Regarding the scenario that abstains from any consolidation effort, the fact that our estimate attributes almost the entire decline in Greek GDP since 2009 to fiscal consolidation may seem surprising. At the time the fiscal consolidation began, the Greek economy was widely held to suffer from severe problems, most notably a big decline in price competitiveness during pre-crisis years, a massive current account deficit, and private capital outflows driven by fear about the solvency of the government and the Greek financial system.

However, we believe the GDP path implied by our counterfactual scenario to be plausible on the following grounds. First, it is important to recall that in our hypothetical scenario, everything stays the same, except for the fiscal policy changes reported in Tables 1a and 1b. In particular, Greek does not exit the Euro. The Greek fiscal bailout and the associated bailout of the Greek banks do take place, and the Greek banks still receive funding via the ECB's unconventional measures. These helped to replace the flight of private capital and thus allowed for a more gradual current account adjustment, and with that a more gradual adjustment of private expenditure, than in the absence of such support.

What is more, the performance of the Greek economy under the counterfactual scenario of no austerity is by no means stellar, but amounts to a prolonged period of stagnation. In 2014, Greek GDP would still be more than 6 percent below the pre-crisis peak of 2007. Thus the Greek economy in the absence of domestic austerity would have fared worse than the euro area, whose fiscal consolidation over the period 2010–2014 cumulated to between 3.3 percent and 4.8 percent of the 2009 real GDP.[7] The Greek performance in the absence of austerity would also have been dismal by past Greek standards. From 2001 to 2007, the average annual growth rate of the Greek economy amounted to 4.1 percent. While the high growth observed during this period might be related to high capital inflows associated with Greece's accession to the Euro and thus might be considered unsustainable, during the preceding decade (1991–2000), average GDP growth still equaled 2.5 percent. Furthermore, in 2007, Greece was still the third poorest member of the euro area, with GDP per capita measured at purchasing power standards falling 17 percent short of the euro area average, thus suggesting the possibility of growth rates above the euro area average. As Figure 2 shows, if the Greek economy had grown at its average growth rate of the 1990s in the time since, its 2014 GDP would have exceeded the 2007 figure by almost 19 percent, rather than falling short by over 6 percent as in the no-austerity scenario. All in all, the no-austerity scenario appears consistent with an economy correcting past excesses and undergoing a process of current account adjustment, and thus does not appear excessively optimistic.

7 Conclusion

The debate on Greek economic policy since the outbreak of the European sovereign debt crisis as well as its future is set to continue over the coming months and years. We contribute to the assessment of the former by estimating the effect of the Greek tax increases and expenditure cuts during the years 2010 to 2014. We find that austerity in Greece almost exclusively explains the decline of Greek GDP since 2009 and only slightly lowered the government debt-to-GDP ratio as compared to a no-austerity scenario. We also estimate that most of the costs of fiscal consolidation could have been avoided by postponing and gradually implementing it after the recovery

7 If measured as the real change in cyclically adjusted net lending excluding interest, calculated by multiplying its share in potential GDP with real potential GDP as estimated by the European Commission, the consolidation effort cumulated to 3.3 percent of real GDP in 2009. The estimated magnitude of the effort would amount to 4.8 percent of 2009 real GDP if calculated as the sum of discretionary revenue and expenditure measures cumulated over the 2010 to 2014 period and deflated using the GDP deflator, also reported by the European Commission.

of the Greek economy, due to the lower expenditure multipliers during normal times. Finally, a much lower path of the Greek debt-to-GDP ratio could have been achieved by implementing only the revenue increases but not the expenditure cuts that were part of the consolidation package. It appears that those who warned against the Greek austerity experiment early on (e.g. Horn et al. 2011) were right.

To be sure, we do not argue that the Greek public finances were in good shape when the fiscal consolidation began. However, irrespective of whether the Greek budget was structurally unbalanced or not, as the economy was in particularly bad shape, our results suggest that the 2010–2014 period was the wrong time to implement spending cuts, and that any expenditure-based consolidation should have been phased in gradually after the recovery of the Greek economy.

References

— Alesina, A., and S. Ardagna (2010): Large changes in fiscal policy: taxes versus spending. NBER/Tax Policy & the Economy, 24 (1), 35–68.
— Alesina, A., and S. Ardagna (2013): The Design of Fiscal Adjustments. In: J. R. Brown (ed.): Tax Policy and the Economy, Volume 27. Chicago, University of Chicago Press.
— Batini, N., G. Callegari, G., and G. Melina (2012): Successful Austerity in the United States, Europe and Japan. IMF Working Paper, Nr. WP/12/190.
— Blanchard, O., and D. Leigh (2013): Growth Forecast Errors and Fiscal Multipliers. IMF Working Paper Nr. WP/13/1.
— Born, B., G. Müller, G., and J. Pfeiffer (2015): Does austerity pay off? CEPR Discussion Paper, Nr. 10425.
— Christiano, L. J., M. Eichenbaum, and S. Rebelo. (2011): When is the Government Spending Multiplier Large? Journal of Political Economy, 119 (1), 78–121.
— Coenen, G., C. J. Erceg, C. Freedman, D. Furceri, M. Kumhof, R. Lalonde, D. Laxton, J. Lindé, A. Mourougane, D. Muir, S. Mursula, C. d. Resende, J. Roberts, W. Roeger, S. Snudden, M. Trabandt, and J. in 't Veld (2012): Effects of Fiscal Stimulus in Structural Models. American Economic Journal: Macroeconomics, 4 (1), 22–68.
— Corsetti, G., K. Kuester, A. Meier, and G. J. Müller (2013): Sovereign risk, fiscal policy, and macroeconomic stability. The Economic Journal, 123, F99–F132.
— Cottarelli, C., and L. Jaramillo (2012): Walking hand in hand: Fiscal policy and growth in advanced economies. IMF Working Paper Nr. WP/12/137.
— ECLM, IMK and OFCE (2012): Independent Annual Growth Survey 2013. Failed austerity in Europe. The way out.
— Eggertsson, G. B. (2009): What Fiscal Policy Is Effective at Zero Interest Rates? Federal Reserve Bank of New York Staff Reports, Nr. 402.
— Erceg, C. J., and J. Lindé (2013): Fiscal consolidation in a currency union: Spending cuts vs. tax hikes. Journal of Economic Dynamics and Control, 37 (2), 422–445.
— European Commission (2013): Report on Public Finances in EMU 2013. European Economy, No. 4/2013.
— Gechert, S., and A. Rannenberg (2014): Are Fiscal Multipliers Regime-Dependent? A Meta Regression Analysis. IMK working paper, Nr. 139.
— Gechert, S., K. Rietzler, and S. Tober (2014): The European Commission's New NAIRU: Does it Deliver? IMK working paper, Nr. 142.

— Gechert, S., A. Hughes Hallett, and A. Rannenberg (2016): Fiscal multipliers in downturns and the effects of Eurozone consolidation. Applied Economics Letters (early access), doi 10.1080/13504851.2015.1137545.
— Girouard, N., and C. André (2005): Measuring cyclically adjusted budget balances for OECD Economies. Economics Department Working Papers, Nr. 434.
— Horn, G., F. Lindner, T. Niechoj, A. Truger, und H. Will (2011): Voraussetzungen einer erfolgreichen Konsolidierung Griechenlands. IMK report Nr. 66.
— Monokroussos, P., and D. Thomakos (2013): Greek fiscal multipliers revisited. Eurobank Research Economy & Markets, 8 (3), 1–29.
— Pappadà, F., and Y. Zylberberg (2014): Austerity Plans and Tax Evasion: Theory and Evidence from Greece. Mimeo. www.hec.unil.ch/deep/textes/14.01.pdf
— Trichet, J.-C. (2010): Stimulate no more—it is now time for all to tighten. Opinion piece in the Financial Times, July 22.
— Wren-Lewis, S. (2015): Greece and primary surpluses. Mainly macro blogspot. February 24. http://mainlymacro.blogspot.co.uk/2015/02/greece-and-primary-surpluses.html.

Wealth Taxation of Real Estate during the Greek Crisis: The Perils of Ignoring Market Signals*

DIMITRIS CHRISTELIS

Dimitris Christelis, University of Naples Federico II, CSEF, CFS, CEPAR and NETSPAR, e-mail: dimitris.christelis@gmail.com

Summary: During the Greek crisis the wealth tax on real estate (WTRE) was increased four-fold as a percentage of GDP in order to boost fiscal revenues. This increase contributed to an essentially complete freeze of the real estate market, a considerable drop in real estate prices, and a substantial deepening of the recession. Using conservative assumptions, we calculate that the WTRE increases unemployment by 70,000–100,000 persons yearly. Perversely, the net effect of the WTRE increase on fiscal revenues has been, at best, slightly positive if not quite negative, as the WTRE induces large tax losses by lowering household spending and housing investment. Moreover, the real estate market freeze prevents households from accessing their savings embodied in real estate in order to counter the recession's negative effects, and pay taxes and other debts. Reasons for this policy failure include flawed economic analysis, failure to monitor the real estate market, and cognitive biases.

→ JEL Classification: H20, H31, D14, E21, E22, E62
→ Keywords: Wealth tax, real estate, market collapse, liquidity constraints, multiplier, Greek crisis

* We would like to thank, without implicating, Calliope Akantziliotou, Dimitris Georgarakos, Heather Gibson, Michael Haliassos, and Theodoros Mitrakos for helpful discussions.

1 Introduction

Among the various measures that policymakers[1] have taken in order to address the severe budgetary crisis that is plaguing Greece, one that stands out is the very large increase of the wealth tax on real estate (WTRE). In this paper we analyse not just the features of the tax, but also its effects on public finances and the Greek economy.

As Haliassos (2015) notes, real estate holdings are by the far the most important part of Greek households' assets. Household-level data from the 2013 Household Finance and Consumption Survey,[2] conducted in 15 Eurozone countries and coordinated by the European Central Bank (ECB), indicate that the vast majority of households' assets consist of real estate, and that the median household has very limited liquid assets. In particular, the median ratio across households of the value of real estate holdings to total gross assets is about 88 percent; at the 25th percentile it is still very large at about 62 percent. The total value of real estate is about 84 percent of all gross household assets. Moreover, the prevalence of real estate ownership beyond the principal residence is about 38 percent, the second highest in the Eurozone after the one in Cyprus which is at 51 percent (the corresponding figures for France and Germany are 25 percent and 18 percent, respectively). All these figures point to the fact that, over time, the largest share of Greek households' savings by far has been invested in real estate.

There are various reasons for this strong preference to invest in real estate, which, incidentally, is common to all Southern European countries. Real estate is traditionally viewed as a relatively safe investment that protected a family's savings from the high inflation, currency devaluations, government defaults, stock market shenanigans, wars, and political upheavals that have plagued Greece throughout its modern history better than liquid assets. In addition, parents have traditionally given their children real estate as a gift or an inheritance in order to help them set up a new household.

Given the prevalence of real estate holdings in Greece, it is no surprise that the large increase in WTRE has had correspondingly large effects. We find, using very conservative assumptions, that it has deepened and prolonged the already deep recession, roughly costing between 70,000 and 100,000 jobs each year, and causing a corresponding annual drop in GDP of between 6 and 9 billion euro. Crucially, its impact on tax revenues has been at best insignificant if not quite negative. This fiscal outcome, which is the exact opposite of what policymakers had in mind, is due to tax losses induced by the WTRE, as the latter: i) lowers consumption, due to its negative impact on disposable income and real estate wealth; ii) lowers housing investment; and iii) contributes (partly due to its extreme progressivity) to the freezing of the real estate market that prevents households from accessing their savings embodied in real estate. As a result, they are unable to increase their spending so as to smooth consumption and absorb the recession's negative economic shocks. They are also unable to use these savings to pay their outstanding taxes and debts, thus reducing tax receipts and increasing the amount of non-performing loans, which in turn necessitates an increase in the financial support of banks by the government.

---

1 We include among the policymakers the Greek governments (past and present), the International Monetary Fund, the European Commission, and the European Central Bank. Following established practice, we refer to the latter three as the Troika.

2 For more details on the Household Finance and Consumption Survey, see Household Finance and Consumption Network (2013a, 2013b).

Overall, the enormous increase in the WTRE is an appalling policy failure that has devastated the Greek economy and considerably worsened the already severe economic problems faced by millions of Greek households. There are multiple reasons for this policy failure, including deeply flawed economic analysis, failure to monitor the state of the real estate market, cognitive biases, and various prejudices.

In Section 2 we discuss the WTRE. In Section 3 we look at the state of the Greek real estate market, while in Section 4 we examine how the WTRE affects tax revenue. In Section 5 we discuss various arguments proposed in favour of the WTRE. Section 6 concludes.

2 The WTRE and the state of the Greek real estate market

Recurrent taxes on immovable property have progressively increased from about 0.41 percent of GDP in 2007 to about 1.78 percent of GDP in 2014, i. e. more than four times relative to the size of the economy.[3] The increase in absolute values has been roughly a three-fold one (from about 1 billion euro to about 3.15 billion euro). This increase in recurrent taxes on immovable property is quite simply enormous, especially if one takes into account the fact that it has taken place in the midst of the most severe economic crisis ever seen in an industrialized country since World War II. It has been brought about almost entirely by the various incarnations of the WTRE,[4] as local taxes have not changed in the last few years.

The Troika has strongly favoured the WTRE, and its experts have been closely involved with its design. This policy view is evidenced in an article in the August 2015 Memorandum of Understanding agreed between the Troika and the Greek government, which stipulates that proceeds from the WTRE must remain stable at 2.65 billion euro, irrespective of what happens to cadastral values (see below for further discussion of this point).

---

3 We include in the definition of recurrent taxes on immovable property items D29AA, D29AB, D59AA, D59AB, D59FA in the National Tax Lists file compiled by Eurostat (2015), which contains data up to 2012. For data on 2014, we use the Greek government's announcements concerning the most recent version of the WTRE, namely the Unified Tax on the Ownership of Real Estate (Ενιαίος Φόρος Ιδιοκτησίας Ακινήτων in Greek or (ΕΝΦΙΑ)). The Greek government announced that ΕΝΦΙΑ brought in about 2.65 billion euro. To maintain comparability over time, we add to this figure the value of recurrent taxes on immovable property levied by local authorities, for which no data are available on a consistent basis. We estimate these taxes to be equal to at least 500 million euro. The details of our calculations are as follows: i) one of the local taxes (Τέλος Ακίνητης Περιουσίας) has a rate of 0.035 percent, which on an estimated value of real estate of about 600 billion euro (or two-thirds, after taking out the value of agricultural land, of the total value of real estate of about 900 billion euro calculated using 2007 cadastral values, as reported below), should generate proceeds of about 200 million euro; and ii) additional fees (δημοτικά τέλη) that are levied to finance local public services, which are typically much larger than the tax in i), and hence we conservatively estimate them to be equal to 300 million euro Our calculation of 3.15 billion euro in recurrent property taxes for 2014 may be an underestimate if one uses OECD data. In OECD (2015a), recurrent property taxes (item 4100) for 2013, i.e. the last year for which complete data are available, are about 3 billion euro. One likely needs to add to this sum at least part of item 4200 (recurrent taxes on net wealth), which is equal to about 1.1 billion euro. Taxes on sales of property, on gifts in the form of real estate, and on inheritance are not considered recurrent property taxes, and are thus excluded from our discussion.

4 The WTRE has had various incarnations over the years. It existed in 2007 and was levied on the total value of one's property, using a progressive rate schedule. The rates at which it was levied were increased in 2008 and even more in 2009. In 2010 there was a further very large increase of the rates, while a new additional tax was introduced in 2011 through 2013 and was levied on each property separately. Remarkably, policymakers decided to tie payments of this new tax to the electricity bill corresponding to each property, so as to make these payments harder to avoid. Finally, the latest version of the tax, the Unified Tax on the Ownership of Real Estate (ΕΝΦΙΑ) was introduced in 2014.

Policymakers have implemented these increases in the WTRE because they wanted to quickly increase tax revenue for the general government; this tax is unrelated to the needs or characteristics of local governments (who get a very small part of it), and all its incarnations have included a component (and in years prior to 2011 it was the only component) that calculates the tax on the accumulated value of all properties owned by an individual. Therefore, this tax can only be considered to be a wealth tax that is assessed exclusively on real estate holdings. Remarkably, this tax is assessed on the gross (i. e. the cadastral) value of real estate, i. e. it does not take into account any loans linked to it (e. g. mortgages); obviously, this feature makes it much more onerous for the taxpayer to bear.

As the WTRE is levied using cadastral values, it is important to discuss how these are related to actual market prices. The first thing to note is that dwellings' prices have fallen by about 40 percent between 2007 and the 2nd quarter of 2015 (Bank of Greece (BoG) 2015a). Given that consumer prices (as measured by the Harmonized Index of Consumer Prices) have increased by about 13 percent during the same period, the real drop in dwellings' prices is about 53 percent. Furthermore, the drop in commercial real estate prices in Athens between 2007 and 2014 is equal to about 34 percent (BoG 2015b, 2015c).[5] Given this massive drop in real estate prices, it is remarkable that policymakers have refused to adjust cadastral values, which have stayed constant at the 2007 levels. This refusal is due to their desire to get as much revenue out of the WTRE as possible, with inflated cadastral values serving this purpose quite well. In 2015 the Council of State (the top Greek civil court) has deemed this practice unconstitutional, ordering the government to assess the WTRE using updated cadastral values. The decision by the Council of State is most probably the reason why the Troika insisted on the aforementioned Memorandum article that emphasizes the need to keep tax proceeds from the WTRE constant, irrespective of what happens to cadastral values.

Policymakers, however, have quite simply refused to comply with the court's decision and have instead assessed the 2015 WTRE using the 2007 cadastral values. Even if they eventually decide to adjust the cadastral values downwards, it is likely that this adjustment will be small, in order to keep the assessed value of the WTRE as high as possible. It is also likely that, should cadastral values be adjusted downwards in the future, the tax rates of the WTRE will increase and/or the already very stringent conditions under which relief from the WTRE is currently provided will be further tightened.

The latest incarnation of the WTRE is the Unified Tax on Ownership of Real Estate (ΕΝΦΙΑ in Greek). It has two components: the first one (the basic tax) is applied using a tax amount per square meter, and it is roughly equal to 0.3–0.35 percent of the cadastral values, depending on the value of the real estate and other features like the age of the building, the number of façades, and the floor on which an apartment is located, etc. The second component (the supplementary tax) is a tax levied on the total value of someone's property. Taxation starts at a rate of 0.1 percent for values above 300,000 euro and up to 400,000 euro, and then is equal to 0.2 percent for values between 400,000 euro and 500,000 euro, to 0.3 percent for values between 500,000 euro and 600,000 euro, to 0.6 percent for values between 600,000 euro and 700,000 euro, to 0.7 percent for values between 700,000 euro and 800,000 euro, to 0.8 percent for values between 800,000

5 There are no corresponding series for other parts of the country, as the relevant price indices have been compiled from 2010 on. However, the path of prices has been broadly similar from 2010 on between Athens and the rest of the country.

euro and 800,000 euro, to 0.9 percent for values between 900,000 euro and 1,000,000 euro, and to 1 percent for values above 1,000,000 euro.

The first thing to observe is the very steep progressivity of the supplementary tax schedule, which imposes a ten-fold increase in the marginal tax rate going from 300,000 euro to 1,000,000 euro in cadastral value. We are not aware of another example of a wealth tax that entails such steep progressivity for changes in value of the order of 700,000 euro. Thus, it is clear that the policymakers' objective is to transfer the burden of the tax as much as possible to the relatively few owners who have properties valued beyond 600,000 euro, as the jump of the marginal rate above this level is a steep 0.3 percent.

Putting a disproportionately high tax burden on those who have large real estate holdings has a variety of negative consequences. First, it makes the tax less likely to be paid. In fact, the assessed value of ENΦIA is 3.3 billion euro, while the aim is to bring in 2.65 billion euro, meaning that 20 percent of the assessed tax is predicted to go unpaid. The burden to owners increases if one considers that cadastral values are much higher than market ones. Furthermore, a property owner has to pay various local taxes and fees. Things become worse if one considers that, as discussed above, the tax is assessed without accounting for any loans on the property. One should also keep in mind that the owner has no right to any tax relief unless a set of very stringent conditions are satisfied.[6] The worse part comes, however, from the fact that, as discussed below, it is currently practically impossible for owners to sell any real estate in order to reduce their tax liability, as the real estate market in Greece has essentially ceased to function. This is especially true for high-valued properties. Hence many owners are trapped owing a high WTRE for the foreseeable future on properties that cannot be sold.

It is instructive to compare the levels of the Greek WTRE to similar wealth taxes levied in two other Southern EU countries, namely Italy and Spain. In both countries these taxes were introduced in 2012 in order to increase revenue during the Eurozone crisis. In Italy the wealth tax on real estate (IMU) has a rate equal to 0.76 percent on average, while for an owner-occupied house the rate falls to 0.4 percent. Significantly, the Italian cadastral values are much lower than market ones. In Spain, there is a wealth tax (Patrimonio) assessed on the values of all assets, both real and financial. There is an allowance of 700,000 euro per person, plus an allowance of 300,000 euro for the main home. The values of all debts are deducted from the tax basis. Hence is someone has assets equal valued at 1,200,000 euro and a mortgage loan of 200,000 euro on a house in which she lives and is valued at 300,000 euro, then she pays no wealth tax.

Let us now consider two cases: one in which the market value of the property is 200,000 euro and one in which it is equal to 800,000 euro. In Greece and assuming that cadastral values are about 30 percent higher than market ones, the values on which the WTRE will be assessed are about 285,000 euro and 1,150,000 euro, respectively. Assuming a basic tax rate of 0.32 percent, the total amount of WTRE due in Greece (equal to the sum of the basic and the supplementary tax) will be 912 euro and 8,780 euro, respectively. We thus see that a four-fold increase in the val-

6 The conditions for obtaining a 50 percent relief from the WTRE, all of which must be satisfied, are: i) a taxable income of at most 9,000 euro for a single person or 12,000 euro for a couple; ii) a total property value of at most 85,000 euro for a single and 150,000 euro for a couple, and one's properties should include no structures that have a surface of more than 150 square meters in total; and iii) there should be no unpaid overdue taxes to the government, for which the taxpayer has not agreed with the tax authorities on a payment schedule.

ue of the property leads to an almost ten-fold increase in the tax liability. This very large increase is due to the very steep progressivity of the supplementary tax schedule. In Italy, on the other hand, assuming that part of the property refers to an own-occupied home and thus applying a rate of 0.5 percent, the amounts due would be 1,000 euro and 4,000 euro, respectively. In fact, given that Italian cadastral values are typically much lower than market prices, the actual amounts due are likely to be much lower than the ones calculated here. In Spain, there would be no wealth tax due in either case, assuming a value of an own-occupied home of at least 100,000 euro.

Hence, the WTRE exerts a much higher burden in Greece than Italy or Spain. We note that this happens in the midst of an unprecedented shrinkage of the Greek economy; between 2007 and 2014 GDP shrunk by 25 percent, which has led to large reductions in Greek households' disposable income. In this regard, it is instructive to compare the average wage (gross of employee social insurance contributions and income taxes) between Greece and the other two countries, as reported by the Organization of Economic Cooperation and Development (OECD 2015b): 20,168 euro in Greece, 30,463 euro in Italy and 26,162 euro in Spain. Hence, Greeks have to pay much higher wealth taxes while earning much less than their Italian and Spanish counterparts.

The very steep progressivity of the WTRE in Greece has likely an additional very pernicious effect: it discourages real estate acquisition. The vast majority of prospective real estate buyers in Greece must currently rely on their own funds to acquire real estate, as Greek banks have essentially stopped providing loans to the household sector (e. g. mortgage credit outstanding has been shrinking rapidly since the onset of the financial crisis). It is likely that individuals who have enough liquid assets to buy property have already invested some of their wealth in real estate (as already noted, an overwhelming share of Greek households' wealth is invested in real estate). Hence, if they buy some additional real estate, they must pay a considerably larger WTRE due to the steeply progressive supplemental tax schedule. In other words, real estate to be acquired carries a very large tax burden that is partly due to the existing real estate holdings of the prospective buyer. In contrast, these taxes are not imposed on investments in bonds, mutual funds, or on savings kept in bank accounts.

One may argue that prospective real estate buyers fully capitalize these large future tax payments and thus make low offers to sellers; in this case, they might still be able to buy the property. However, this view ignores the crucial fact that liquidity is at a premium at a time when nobody lends to households; hence, it is very dangerous to be burdened with very high tax payments for the foreseeable future, as they might be hard to honour in case of a negative shock. In addition, these large tax payments are unlikely to decrease in the future, given policymakers' attachment to the WTRE; rather, these taxes are much more likely to increase further due to Greece's dismal fiscal situation. Finally, what is even worse for any prospective buyer is the complete freeze of the market; nobody wants to buy an asset only to have no possibility to re-sell it. Hence the freezing of the market creates a vicious circle: it discourages prospective investors, who thus stay away from the market, and this in turn solidifies the market freeze.

Overall, the WTRE most likely acts as a powerful deterrent for the acquisition of any further property, especially if it is a large-valued one. In the next Section we discuss in greater detail the implications of a reduced volume of real estate transactions.

3 The freezing of the real estate market and its implications

To the best of our knowledge, what has happened to the Greek real estate market is unprecedented in the recent economic history of advanced economies: the volume, and especially the value, of transactions have been reduced to a startlingly large extent. In other words, the Greek real estate market is currently essentially frozen.

Data from the Bank of Greece (BoG 2015d) suggest that from 2007 to 2012 the number of real estate transactions in Athens, as compiled by the Athens Bar Association (a lawyer's presence was mandatory for all such transactions up to 2012), declined by 79 percent while the value of such transactions by 83 percent. To get an idea on developments beyond 2012, one can use data from the Hellenic Cadastral Registry, which indicate that transactions in Athens declined from 2012 to 2014 by another 70 percent. This implies that both the number and the value of transactions have declined by well above 90 percent compared to 2007. In other words, the real estate market in the greater Athens area, in which about 40 percent of the Greek population resides, has been annihilated.

For the whole country, the Hellenic Statistical Authority (HSA) reports that transactions reflecting buying and selling of real estate fell by about 71 percent from 2007 to 2013, while the drop from 2005 (the peak year for transactions) is about 77 percent (HSA 2015a). If one adds a drop in appraisals-related transactions by banks in 2014, as recorded by the BoG (2015d), then the overall drop in transactions from 2007 to 2014 is about 80 percent. The value of these appraisals (which can be linked to transfer of ownership, mortgage origination and renegotiation, or other real-estate related transactions) has fallen by about 92 percent in value from 2007 to 2014.

Before discussing the implications of the freezing of the Greek real estate market, it is important to point out the pervasive problem of liquidity-constrained households, as indicated by the large value of various unpaid obligations by the private sector. First of all, overdue taxes are about 80 billion euro (about 45 percent of GDP). The number of entities (the overwhelming majority of which are individuals) that owe these taxes is more than 3 million, when the adult Greek population is about 9.1 million. The value of non-performing loans in Greek banks' balance sheet is a bit larger than 100 billion euro (i. e. about 55 percent of GDP; BoG 2015e: p. 14). Finally, about 2.1 million connections to the electricity network (the overwhelming majority of which are linked to individuals) are associated with overdue bills.[7]

The presence of all this unpaid debt is a very strong indicator of a large prevalence of households that have problems making ends meet. Hence, they are likely to be liquidity-constrained, i. e. they have no or no access to savings, and thus must live a hand-to-mouth existence, leaving many of their obligations unpaid.

The freezing of the real estate market, when combined with the presence of liquidity-constrained households, is simply a devastating blow to the Greek economy. One must consider that real estate is the predominant vehicle in which the saving of Greek households (both past and present) is stored. Hence, a frozen real estate market implies that households have practically lost access to their savings. It is difficult to find words that can adequately describe how devastating this

7 According to the 2011 Population and Housing Census, the number of dwellings was about 6.37 million (HSA 2014).

blow is to households' welfare; savings are put aside at times of prosperity so as to have access to them during times of need. As a result, negative shocks to households' finances can at least be partially absorbed by drawing on these savings, and thus fluctuations in households' living standards are moderated. If households cannot access their savings by selling their real estate due to the freezing of the market, then they can only rely on their current incomes, which are likely much reduced due to the crisis. Hence, they are likely to considerably reduce their spending, thus having a much lower standard of living. The vital importance of the process of building up and drawing down savings, known as consumption smoothing, is generally accepted by virtually all schools of economic thought, whatever their other differences might be.

Furthermore, it is important to consider that a large number of households that want to sell real estate in the midst of the current recession likely want to do so not only to maintain their living standards, but also to pay debts to banks or taxes to the government. Hence, the freezing of the real estate market not only lowers their living standards, but also lowers the tax proceeds to the Government, and keeps banks in dire shape as loans remain unpaid. In contrast, those who buy real estate are only making a shift in their portfolio by using their savings in the form of liquid assets (or others' savings if they manage to obtain a bank loan) to finance their purchase of real estate. Hence, a change in property ownership is likely to lead to a net increase in aggregate demand in the economy due to the increased spending by the seller, as well as to higher tax receipts and fewer non-performing loans.

The enormous increase in the WTRE is obviously not the only adverse shock to hit the Greek economy during the crisis. Greece also experienced a severe drop in economic activity, a tightening of bank credit and considerable political uncertainty during this period. All these factors contribute to a drop in the demand for real estate. On the other hand, they are likely to lead to an increase in the supply, as owners have difficulties making ends meet, paying the increased WTRE, or just want to have more liquid assets so as to weather the economic storm. Both an increase in supply and a drop in demand unambiguously lead to a drop in prices, which is what has happened in Greece, as already discussed. The overall effect on the volume of transactions is less clear *a priori*, as the higher supply would tend to increase it, while the lower demand decrease it. Obviously, given the aforementioned very severe drop in real estate transactions, the effect of the drop in demand has been much stronger than that of the increase in supply. To put things plainly, there are currently very few individuals buying real estate in Greece.

While it is not easy to precisely determine the contribution of the WTRE to the freezing of the real estate market and the associated problems that it creates, one should keep in mind the enormity of its increase, as well as its steep progressivity that, combined by the unrealistically high cadastral values, severely discourages any prospective buyers. Hence, there is very little doubt that the WTRE has contributed significantly to the lack of interest in Greek real estate.

Unfortunately, there is no indication that policymakers have realized the implications of the frozen real estate market. In fact, there is one clear indication that they do not fully understand what is going on, as shown by the sad tale of the capital gains tax. This tax was included in a law passed in 2013 with the prospect of being first implemented in 2014. During the first four months of 2014, the Greek government and the Troika debated the details of implementing this tax. As a result, there were essentially no real estate transactions during those four months, as all market participants were waiting for the dust to settle, while the tax authorities would allow virtually no real estate transactions to go through. After policymakers reached an agreement, the tax was implemented. Predictably, its proceeds were trivially small; after all, its tax basis consists of transactions, and there are currently very few of these in Greece. Hence, in late 2014 policymakers decided to suspend the tax until 2017.

To recap, policymakers introduced a major new tax levied on a non-existent tax basis, then blocked the real estate market completely for four months before reaching an agreement on how to implement this new tax (in the process making Greece the only country in which virtually no real estate transactions took place in that period, other than North Korea and war zones), only to suspend the tax a year after its introduction due to its utter failure to generate significant revenue. Unfortunately, a necessary condition for such a woeful policy debacle is the failure of policymakers to adequately monitor the state of the Greek real estate market.

It is quite hard to understand the reasons behind this failure. After all, policymakers were not dealing with an opaque financial product whose properties are difficult to grasp, but rather with ordinary real estate, whose market is the second, after the labour market, most important in any economy, and which constitutes the most common household asset in industrialized countries. Furthermore, detailed statistics on the real estate market are made freely and widely available by the Bank of Greece and the Hellenic Statistical Authority.

The policymakers' failure to understand the implications of the enormous increase of the WTRE can be examined also through another angle, namely using a thought experiment involving banks. Let us suppose that all banks have one asset in their balance sheet, which is very illiquid. Let us also suppose that the market for this asset is essentially frozen, that banks are losing money, and thus desperately need to sell some of their holdings of this asset in order to fund their balance sheet. Let us further suppose that banks have no access to a lender of last resort, thus making their dependence on the sale of this asset even more critical. If in this situation someone proposed a four-fold increase in taxes on this asset as a way to make things better, it would be fair to say that her suggestion would not be treated kindly. Instead, policymakers would most likely try to relieve the banks' stress by taking all the necessary measures to restore liquidity in the market in order to facilitate transactions. If this asset were taxed, then such measures would almost surely include a considerable reduction of the associated taxes. Policymakers would act this way because the importance of financial market liquidity is by now well understood, as is the general importance of a healthy financial system.

Unfortunately, policymakers acted in exactly the opposite direction in the case of the household sector and its real estate holdings, at a time when households are unable to borrow and the real estate market is completely frozen. Policymakers should have realized that this situation is a real emergency, and that the frozen market has extremely negative implications for aggregate demand in the economy, government tax receipts, and the financial system, as there is simply no way financial intermediation can work properly when there is no market for the collateral asset behind most loans. Regrettably, policymakers insisted on administering the worst possible remedy, namely a four-fold increase in the WTRE, with predictably disastrous consequences for both households and the financial system.

4 The effect of the WTRE on tax revenues

The main reason for the introduction of the WTRE was clearly to increase tax revenues. Given the very strong insistence of the Troika on the continued imposition of this tax, it would be fair to say that it believes that this tax has indeed succeeded in its main aim. Some policymakers have been known to wonder how the 2.65 billion euro that the WTRE (ENΦIA) ostensibly collects would be replaced, should the WTRE be abolished. We call the belief that a tax's gross receipts are roughly equal to the net ones the doctrine of immaculate taxation (DIT). This section examines whether adherence to the DIT is justifiable.

To assess the fiscal implications of the WTRE we use the notion of the multiplier, which indicates how much a country's GDP changes due to a fiscal measure. For example, a multiplier of 1.2 implies that an increase in taxes of 1 euro leads to a decrease in a country's GDP of 1.2 euro.[8] Given that economics is far from a precise science, the size of multipliers is the object of considerable discussion and disagreement. A watershed moment in this discussion was provided by the by now famous paper by Blanchard and Leigh (2013),[9] which concluded that multipliers were been generally underestimated, and that they were likely to be between 0.9 and 1.7 during a recession. Similarly, Perotti (2012) finds that discretionary taxation (an instance of which is provided by the WTRE) has a multiplier of 1.5. Large fiscal multipliers are also found by Auerbach and Gorodnichenko (2012, 2013). Importantly, the size of the multiplier tends to increase in situations in which there is a high prevalence of liquidity-constrained households and in countries in which external transactions are relatively small. Greece amply fulfils both these requirements.

Clearly, a large multiplier invalidates the DIT. The WTRE is an autonomous tax (i. e. it does not depend on income) that has its own multiplier. Hence, an increase in the WTRE reduces economic output in a variety of ways, which in turn lead to reduced tax proceeds. As a result, the net receipts from the WTRE could be much smaller than the gross ones. We examine the fiscal impact of the WTRE under two scenarios: one in which the multiplier is equal to 1 and another in which it is equal to 1.5.

The first negative effect of the WTRE on tax revenues is due to its negative direct impact on households' disposable income. If the multiplier is equal to 1 (1.5) then GDP decreases by 2.65 (4) billion euro. Given that government revenues, including social insurance contributions (which depend on GDP), are equal to about 35 percent of GDP (excluding receipts from the WTRE),[10] this decrease in GDP implies that tax proceeds decrease in turn by about 0.93 (1.39) billion euro.[11]

---

8 We adopt the convention of using the absolute value of the multiplier. The sign of the tax multiplier is almost always negative because in almost all circumstances a rise in taxes reduces economic output.

9 Blanchard was the chief economist at the IMF at the time the paper was written.

10 Government revenue, including recurrent property taxes, was about 37.6 percent of GDP in 2013, the last year for which complete data are available (OECD 2015a,c).

11 The above calculation assumes that the share of taxes in Greek GDP is constant, i. e. that the elasticity of tax receipts with respect to GDP is about 1. Mourre et al. (2013: Table A.3, p. 32) estimate the tax elasticity in Greece to be equal to 0.92. On the other hand, the share of taxes in Greek GDP has steadily increased from 32.9 percent in 2007 to 37.6 percent in 2013 (OECD 2015a, c), due both to large increases in taxes and more stringent enforcement of tax laws. This increase in revenues as a share of GDP points to an elasticity that is larger than 1. Overall, we believe that a value of 1 for the tax elasticity is reasonable.

The second negative effect of the WTRE comes through its effect on real estate wealth. The WTRE negatively affects real estate wealth, just as a tax on any asset (e.g. an increase in the dividend tax reduces the value of shares). A drop in real estate wealth reduces final consumption, as households feel less secure about their economic position due to their reduced wealth. This is a decrease in autonomous consumption, thus independent of what happens to disposable income, as it is exclusively due to a drop in real estate wealth. To determine the size of this drop in autonomous consumption one must estimate by how much real estate wealth declined due to the WTRE, and what is the propensity to consume out of real estate wealth.

To the best of our knowledge, there is no official estimate of the aggregate value of real estate in Greece at market prices. An unofficial calculation by the Bank of Greece put its value close to 1 trillion euro at the peak of the real estate market in 2007.[12] Given that real estate prices have fallen about 35–40 percent since then, the total value of real estate should be about 600 billion euro, with the drop in real estate wealth equal to about 350 billion euro. One then must determine how much of this drop is due to the WTRE. A rough estimate can be computed by noting that if one were to increase the tax on a piece of real estate by an amount equal to 0.3 percent (the average rate of the basic tax) of its value, and if this tax is applied in perpetuity, then with a discount rate of 2 percent (which is a rather large value given the current environment of very low interest rates) the drop in the value of real estate is about 15 percent. If one assumes a new tax equal to 0.7 percent of the real estate's value (so as to incorporate the extremely progressive supplementary part of the WTRE), then the asset's value drops by about 35 percent. If a drop in real estate prices of 35–40 percent is equal to about 350 billion euro in real estate wealth losses, then a drop of 15 percent due to the WTRE represents a drop in wealth of about 130 billion euro. Another way to arrive at a loss of a similar order of magnitude is to simply discount in perpetuity the increase in the WTRE of 2.8 billion euro (from about 500 million euro in 2007, after excluding local taxes, to about 3.3 euro billion, which is the assessed value of ENΦIA). This calculation gives a real estate wealth loss of about 140 billion euro. In our calculations, and to bias our results against our premise, we conservatively assume as a benchmark a drop of 100 billion euro in aggregate real estate wealth due to the WTRE. Given the enormity of the increase of the WTRE, the extreme progressivity of its supplementary part, and the essentially complete freezing of the real estate market, this estimate is most likely very conservative.

The second magnitude needed is the marginal propensity to consume out of real estate wealth. While there is considerable disagreement about its magnitude in the related literature, a very conservative estimate would be about 1 percent.[13] In other words, for every 1 euro of a drop in real estate wealth, households reduce their spending by 0.01 euro. Hence, a 100 euro billion loss in real estate wealth leads to a 1 billion euro drop in autonomous consumption. Given that autonomous consumption is part of private spending, a multiplier of even 1.5 seems like a large underestimate. Be that as it may, if the multiplier is 1 (1.5), then GDP drops by 1 (1.5) billion euro, and taxes are thus reduced by 350 (525) million euro.

A third negative effect of the WTRE on tax revenue is due to the negative impact of this tax on housing investment. As the WTRE reduces the rate of return on housing investment, it should

12 We are grateful to C. Akantziliotou and T. Mitrakos for providing us with this information.

13 Several studies estimate marginal propensities to consume out of housing wealth that are much larger than 1 percent. See, e.g., Case et al. (2005), Campbell and Cocco (2007) and Carroll et al. (2011).

make investment less attractive, as it becomes less profitable. A negative association between a tax on investment returns and investment demand is a plausible assumption for every asset class. In order to evaluate quantitatively this channel one must calculate the user cost of capital, which is equal to

$$\left(P_H / P_O\right)\cdot\left(i+\delta+\tau-\left(\dot{P}_H / P_H\right)\right),$$ [14]

where P_H denotes the price of housing, P_O the price of output, i the nominal interest rate, δ the depreciation rate allowed in the tax code (which is typically larger than the true economic depreciation rate), τ the property tax rate, and $\dot{P}_H / P_H$ the rate of price appreciation of the house. Plugging in plausible values for these magnitudes,[15] one estimates the increase in the cost of capital due to the WTRE to be a little more than 40 percent. Investment is generally considered not very sensitive to the cost of capital, and hence we assume an elasticity of only –0.4 (Gilchrist and Zakrajsek 2007: Table 9, estimate it to be about –0.45 in the short run, and about –1 in the long run (Table 8)). This implies that the WTRE-induced increase in the cost of capital of 40 percent reduces housing investment by about 16 percent.

A value of –0.4 is likely to be an underestimate of the elasticity of housing investment, as housing is generally considered more elastic than other investment goods (Brayton and Clark 1988). One reason for this is that housing investment is typically small-scale and requires shorter periods of planning and execution than most other types of investment. Hence, its response to changes in economic conditions can be quicker and larger.

Investment in dwellings has fallen in constant prices from about 24.8 billion euro in 2007 to about 2 billion euro in 2014, a drop of 22.8 billion euro. The figure for 2014 represents an astonishingly low share of GDP of about 1.1 percent (investment in dwellings in the Eurozone was about 5 percent of GDP in 2014). If we assume that the aggregate value of dwellings is about 400 billion euro (i. e. about two-thirds of the total value of real estate assumed above),[16] and an economic depreciation rate of 2 percent per year, then the Greek economy needs to generate housing investment of 8 billion euro just to replenish its housing stock. Given that the actual amount invested in dwellings is about 2 billion euro, the stock of housing is reduced by about 1.5 percent (= 6/400) per year, which is an absolutely remarkable pace if sustained over time.

---

14 The formula for the user cost of capital is a standard one, first derived by Hall and Jorgenson (1967). We do not include in the cost of capital the present value of the tax reductions due to housing depreciation because most households are not entitled to such deductions. We also exclude any mortgage interest tax credits, as they have been abolished since 2013.

15 We assume a long term interest rate before the WTRE of 5 percent, which is the average long term interest rate in Greece up to 2007. We further assume that the WTRE increased this interest rate to 6 percent, which is a very conservative assumption because banks essentially stopped lending to the real estate sector, as the market is completely frozen. We also assume that the depreciation allowed in the tax code is 5 percent and constant throughout, while the property tax rate increases from 0.1 percent to 0.4 percent due to the WTRE. Moreover, we assume that the change in house prices was about 2 percent per year up to 2007 so as to keep the real price of housing constant, while after 2007 and due to the WTRE the overall price decrease has been about 15 percent through 2015 as already discussed, which translates to a house price drop of about 2 percent per year due to the WTRE. Finally, we assume that the price of housing has dropped by 15 percent due to the WTRE, as discussed earlier in this section, while the general price level has increased by about 13 percent (as measured by the Harmonized Index of Consumer Prices). If one substitutes these figures in the formula for the cost of capital, then its increase post-2007 that can be attributed to the WTRE is about 40 percent.

16 In the US, the ratio of the value of residential structures to the total value of real estate held by households is about 71 percent. This ratio should be somewhat lower in Greece given that land in the US is relatively abundant; hence, we assume that in Greece it is equal to about 2/3.

If 16 percent of the drop from a level of housing investment of 24.8 billion euro in 2007 is due to the increased cost of capital due to the WTRE, then this implies that the WTRE is responsible for about 4 billion euro out of the total drop in investment of 22.8 billion euro. One might counter that the 24.8 billion euro in housing investment in 2007 is an abnormally large amount, as it was equal to about 10 percent of GDP, while the Eurozone average was about 6.5 percent of its GDP in that year. To address this concern, one could apply to Greece the Eurozone share of housing investment in GDP and get an amount that is closer to the Eurozone average, and equal to 16.3 billion euro (instead of the actual 24.8 billion euro). In this case, a WTRE-induced investment drop of 16 percent amounts to about 2.6 billion euro.

One can try to estimate the effect of the WTRE on housing investment by also examining the price elasticity of such investment. Topel and Rosen (1988) estimate this elasticity to be about 1 in the short run, and about 2.7 in the longer run. This latter response, however, is reached in only about one year, which implies a quick and large response of housing investment to the business cycle. Using the smaller short-run price elasticity estimate of 1, a WTRE-induced 15 percent drop in house prices as (discussed above) should reduce housing investment also by 15 percent. Hence, using again very conservative assumptions, we arrive at about the same conclusion as when using the user cost of capital approach.

Assuming a multiplier of 1 (1.5), a drop in housing investment of about 2.6 billion euro implies a drop in GDP of 2.6 (3.9) billion euro, which in turn implies that tax revenues that smaller by about 0.9 (1.35) billion euro. Once more, this is a drop in GDP due to lower housing investment and has nothing to do with the multiplier effect that operates through disposable income.

We note that in all these calculations we have not included the effect that the WTRE-induced drop in GDP has on housing investment. The latter is much more volatile than GDP; hence, it would be reasonable to assume that its elasticity with respect to GDP is at least 1. Hence, the WTRE should have a further negative impact on housing investment that we are not capturing through its effect on the cost of capital.

If we add the drop in taxes due to the WTRE-induced drops in disposable income, real estate wealth and investment, then we come up with a total of about 2.2 billion euro and 3.3 billion euro for multiplier values of 1 and 1.5, respectively. As a reminder, actual gross receipts from the WTRE are about 2.65 billion euro. Hence, the WTRE has at best a marginal positive impact on government finances, but much more likely a considerably negative one. This is quite simply an disastrous outcome that stands in complete contrast to what policymakers were aiming for when they increased the WTRE.

Obviously, all the above calculations are approximate, given also the scope of this paper. Hence, we try to be conservative in many of our assumptions (e. g. with respect to the aggregate drop in real estate wealth due to the WTRE, the marginal propensity to consume out of real estate wealth, the multipliers corresponding to autonomous private consumption and investment that could well be much larger than 1.5, the increase due to the WTRE in the lending interest rate for housing investment, the elasticities of housing investment with respect to the user cost of capital and house prices, the neglect of the effect of the WTRE-induced drop in GDP on housing investment). Even under these conservative assumptions, however, it is very clear that the DIT should be summarily dismissed, and that the WTRE is an utterly ineffective tax from the point of view of its net impact on tax revenues.

Furthermore, there is an additional channel through which the WTRE can reduce fiscal revenue, namely by supressing tax receipts due to the freeze in the real estate market. As a result, liquidity-constrained households spend less and are unable to liquidate real estate in order to pay overdue taxes. This channel is independent of the multiplier effect; even if the multiplier were zero, tax receipts could increase (due to increased consumption and payment of overdue taxes) if the real estate market functioned normally again, thus providing households access to their savings stored in the form of real estate.

Once more, it is not easy to calculate this effect, but we will try to make an educated guess. Mitrakos et al. (2014: p. 9) calculate that the ratio of real estate transactions to the number of real estate properties (i. e. the turnover ratio) dropped from about 2.6 percent in 2007 to about 0.75 percent in 2014, i. e. a drop of about 1.85 percentage points. Let us first assume that the same drop is applied to the ratio of values, and take as given a total value of real estate of about 600 billion euro, as previously discussed. Then, if the WTRE-induced drop in turnover is equal to 0.5 percentage points out of the total drop of 1.85 percentage points, it reduces transactions by about 3 billion euro. If only 20 percent of this amount could be used to pay overdue taxes (which increase at the rate of 10–12 billion euro per year in recent years), then tax receipts would increase by another 600 million euro. One could apply similar calculations by positing another plausible percentage of these 3 billion euro in freed savings which would go toward increased consumption by liquidity-constrained households.

In addition, an increase in transactions would make it easier for property owners to repay their debts to banks, thus decreasing the need of the government to provide further support. Finally the Greek government is hoping to finance part of its debt repayment by selling assets, with a large part being real estate. A rebound in the real estate market would help the government sell its real estate for better prices. We are not able to quantify these additional two factors, but given the enormous magnitude of the non-performing loans in Greece and the large drop in real estate prices, they are likely to be quantitatively quite important.

Finally, the reinvigoration of the real estate market would make it easier for banks to decide to lend to households and firms because there would be a market for the by far most important collateral asset underlying loans. The increased lending activity would in turn increase economic activity, and thus government tax receipts. Once more, it is not possible for us to quantify this effect, but it should be economically significant, as financial intermediation is simply not feasible without a market for collateral, and an economy cannot function without financial intermediation.

The overall conclusion from the all the above is that the WTRE has been a disastrous policy failure that has devastated the Greek economy. Hence, it should be immediately abolished, as it is completely ineffective and causes considerable pain to large segments of the Greek population. Let us just look at its effect on unemployment. Using the above calculations, a multiplier of 1 (1.5) implies that the drop in a calendar year's GDP due to the drop in disposable income, real estate wealth and investment is equal to at least 6 (9) billion euro, as discussed earlier in this section. Greek GDP has dropped, in constant prices, from about 250.7 billion euro in 2007 to about 185.65 billion euro in 2014, i. e. by about 65 billion euro. Over the same period unemployment has increased by about 750,000 individuals. Hence, applying a simple proportional calculation, a drop in GDP of 6 (9) billion euro due to the WTRE results in about 69,000 (104,000) individuals losing their job a result of this tax each year. This quite simply represents an immense cost both in human misery and in lost output, made all the more unbearable by the fact that this tax is completely ineffective in achieving its principal aim, i. e. to increase fiscal revenues.

5 Arguments in favour of the Greek WTRE

In this section we examine various arguments put forward in favour of imposing a WTRE in general, and in Greece specifically. Given that we are not privy to the internal debate among policymakers regarding the implementation of the WTRE in Greece, and that, to the best of our knowledge, they have not made public their analyses of this issue, some parts of the discussion necessarily contain an element of speculation.

We start with the argument that an advantage of the WTRE is that it is difficult to avoid, as real estate is immovable. This is indeed borne out by the fact that the Greek government has met the target of receiving about 80 percent of the assessed value of the WTRE in its coffers. However, a limited possibility of tax avoidance has little to do with whether the WTRE increases net fiscal receipts overall. In fact, as noted in Section 4, net receipts from the WTRE are likely negative due to its severely detrimental side-effects. In addition, a limited possibility of tax avoidance has nothing to do with whether the WTRE is desirable from the point of view of economic welfare. After all, there are ways to raise revenue through other taxes that are difficult to avoid (e. g. a poll tax, or a tax based on being connected to the sewage system or on having a cell phone number), but for various reasons (economic, legal and ethical) such taxes are generally not implemented. Actually, if the WTRE is detrimental to a country's economy, the fact that it cannot be avoided easily is a cause for grave concern because it implies that its deleterious effects actually take place.

In addition, the readily available tax receipts from the WTRE likely distort policymakers' views about its effectiveness and desirability. A well-known cognitive bias in decision-making is the availability heuristic (Tversky and Kahneman 1973), which states that when making a decision individuals put a lot of weight on factors that are readily observable and tend to ignore those that are less so but may still be quite relevant for the decision. Let us now think how the multiplier effect operates: there are several hundred millions of spending decision that are cancelled due to the WTRE's negative effect on disposable income, real estate wealth and investment, as well as to the lack of access to one's savings due to the freezing of the real estate market. All this foregone spending entails taxes lost to the government. One can think of this mechanism as the proverbial death by a thousand cuts. Importantly, these cancelled transactions and associated lost taxes are not readily observable by the policymakers; those who reduce their spending do not announce publicly that they have done so because of the WTRE. Hence, policymakers are likely to underestimate this WTRE-induced spending drop and focus instead only on the observed tax receipts from the WTRE; in other words, they are more likely to believe in the DIT. In order to overcome this availability bias policymakers have to go beyond observed tax receipts and think of the likely economic implications of the WTRE; unfortunately, and to the best of our knowledge, there is no indication that policymakers have done so in any systematic way.

The availability bias also makes it more difficult to understand the plight of those who are prisoners of their own real estate property. Let us consider, for example, the people who were queuing in front of banks in the summer of 2015 due to the capital controls imposed in Greece by policymakers, and whose plight received very prominent attention in the various media. Many of these people were understandably desperate because they could not withdraw their money, even though they could make electronic payments within Greece without any issues. Let us now think about the plight of a property owner who might own a piece of real estate 20 or 50 times larger in value than the typical amount found in a bank account, and who can neither use this real estate to make any payments whatsoever (due to the frozen real estate market) nor to obtain any loan using it as a collateral. However, she may well have to pay very onerous property taxes on it, without being necessarily able to afford them. As a result, her plight is at least as serious as it is for most of those queueing outside the banks, but it is not immediately apparent to policymakers because it gathers relatively little attention in the media. It is likely known only to her family and her real estate agent.

Another argument put forward in favour of the WTRE is its presumed small welfare cost compared to other taxes. The welfare cost of any tax stems from the fact that it changes economic decisions; the smaller this change the more preferable the tax. While a WTRE does not distort the decision to work (since it is not generally related to one's income), it can seriously distort economic behaviour in several other ways: i) given that it reduces the rate of return on households' saving, it affects their saving decisions; ii) for the same reason, it affects the decision to invest in real estate. Even if taxing a piece of unoccupied land does not create a distortion, a WTRE affects the decision to build on it; iii) a WTRE makes more households liquidity-constrained, and thus it considerably changes their consumption decisions and reduces their economic welfare; iv) by decreasing the value of collateral, the WTRE changes the lending behaviour of financial institutions, thus impacting the possibility of households and entrepreneurs to borrow; v) as real estate is lumpy and indivisible, its owners do not have the ability to marginally adjust their decisions in the face of a WTRE. Given that such flexibility limits welfare losses, a WTRE is likely to be much more costly in terms of economic welfare than a tax on a perfectly divisible good.

One encounters often, however, the claim that recurrent property taxes are among the least detrimental to growth (see e.g. Johanesson et al. 2008, European Commission 2011, 2012, 2013). As far as we can tell there is no such theoretical result, especially one that is derived from of a realistic theoretical model that takes into account the considerable complications introduced by the presence of liquidity constraints, the lumpiness and irreversibility of real estate, as well as the potential market freeze due to high taxation. On the other hand there are some empirical results in Arnold (2008) and Arnold et al. (2011),[17] which suggest that increasing the role of recurrent property taxation can enhance economic growth. While Arnold (2008) offers some insights into the empirical modelling of the effects of various types of taxes on growth, one should bear in mind that results therein are based only on panel data regressions, which leave unaddressed many of the issues that hinder their causal interpretation.[18] Furthermore, Xing (2012) finds that the results in Arnold et al. (2011) are not robust to alternative specifications, and that the ranking of taxes in terms of their impact on economic output disappears completely after some crucial assumptions are relaxed. Crucially, when tested empirically, these assumptions are rejected. Moreover, the results in Xing (2012), have been corroborated by Acosta-Ormaechea and Yoo

17 Arnold et al. (2011), as well as Johanesson et al. (2008), use the methodology developed in Arnold (2008).

18 While panel regressions solve the issue of inconsistent estimation due to time-invariant unobservables, they do not solve the problems due to time-varying unobservables. Candidates for such unobservables in the context of taxes and growth abound: investor sentiment, investment incentives, political considerations, land zoning restrictions at the local level etc. Using as instrumental variables lagged values of endogenous regressors as in Arnold (2008) is unlikely to address these problems, as these regressors can affect growth for a long time.

(2012: p. 32), who find that recurrent property taxes cannot be considered as the least detrimental taxes to economic output.

Hence, to the best of our knowledge, there is currently no empirically credible ranking of taxes in terms of their effects on growth. Overall, a priori, it is not clear whether a WTRE is preferable to other taxes on either economic welfare or any other grounds. Furthermore, important factors affecting these issues (e.g. the availability of liquid savings, or the functioning of real estate and financial markets) are likely to differ across countries or different points in time, thus making conclusions likely country- and time-dependent.

Consequently, it is very difficult to understand why institutions like the European Commission repeatedly proclaim that recurrent property taxes are beneficial to growth. It is quite unjustifiable to make such strong statements, let alone to push hard for important policy changes like increases in recurrent property taxes throughout the European Union, as the European Commission has repeatedly done (see e.g. European Commission 2011: p. 5).[19] There are quite simply no unambiguous theoretical or empirical results that warrant such definite and bold positions. On the contrary, the current inconclusive state of the debate on this issue strongly points to the need to proceed with caution and implement any policy changes only incrementally, so as to be better able to gauge their effects. Hence, any policy recommendations should be guarded. In the case of Greece, however, all caution has been thrown to the wind, with policymakers implementing a radical four-fold increase in recurrent property taxes with respect to the size of the economy. Thus, it is no wonder that such ill-conceived experiments, with no solid theoretical or empirical foundations, have caused such devastation in the Greek economy.

Another argument in favour of the Greek WTRE that has been proposed in some quarters is that it retroactively taxes people who historically have evaded taxes, instead investing their spoils in real estate (rightly or wrongly, the prevalence of these people is presumed to be higher in Greece compared to most other European countries). However, this argument is completely illogical: not all real estate owners are tax dodgers, nor have all tax dodgers invested in real estate. Hence, it makes no logical sense to punish the investment good instead of the tax dodger. Importantly, this argument accepts the possibility that those who have played by the rules are punished in the same way as those who have evaded them. Thus it is a morally unacceptable argument, as it represents a form of collective punishment that has no place in modern societies. If some people living in a village have committed a crime, it would not be deemed acceptable that the police arrest all the village inhabitants in order to catch the criminals.

In a similar fashion, some claim that a big reason for the Greek debt crisis is the low amount of taxes paid by Greeks; hence, the WTRE is a legitimate way to raise tax revenue. First, as discussed in Section 4, the WTRE has only a slightly positive if not negative effect on tax revenues. Second, a rebuttal to the claim that the Greek crisis was due to weak tax collection is given by the IMF's own ex-post evaluation of the Greek stabilization program (2013: pp. 21, 23), which states:

19 The European Commission's very strong views on the alleged optimality of recurrent property taxes were once more in evidence when the Italian prime minister announced in August 2015 his government's plans to abolish property taxes on the main house (the aforementioned IMU), with the exception of very luxurious residences. The European Commission took strong exception to this policy change, through both unofficial and official channels.

> *39. More importantly, a flatter adjustment path would have required more than 110 billion euro in financing. [emphasis in the original] The Greek Stand-By Arrangement was already the highest access loan in Fund history. While the euro partners could have provided more than 80 billion euro in funding (although this was already more than 35 percent of Greek GDP), this would have been politically difficult. Debt restructuring could also have provided the authorities with some leeway, but as discussed below, this option was not politically feasible. ... 46. The adjustment mix seems revenue heavy given that the fiscal crisis was expenditure driven. [emphasis in the original] As discussed earlier, the ballooning of the fiscal deficit in the 2000s was almost entirely due to increased expenditure. The large dose of revenue measures in the Stand-By Arrangement-supported program can therefore be questioned, particularly since tax changes constituted almost half of the measures targeted for the first two years of the program.*

In other words, what led to the Greek fiscal crisis was increased expenditure and not insufficient tax collection. However, a large part of the fiscal adjustment entailed tax increases (including the WTRE) because there was neither enough financing available nor a debt haircut at the inception of the Greek stabilization program in 2010.

Importantly, the WTRE is a crucial reason why the stabilization program devised by the Troika has so clearly failed to reduce the size of Greece's public debt. As is now universally acknowledged, and as admitted by the IMF in its evaluation of the Greek stabilization program discussed above (IMF 2013), the growth rates assumed at the start of the program were quite unrealistic. To put things bluntly, they were utterly incompatible with the fiscal consolidation measures implemented during the course of the program. The enormous increase in the WTRE, a tax that achieves the unique feat of reducing tax revenues (or at best leaving them essentially unchanged), while also reducing GDP by at least 6–9 billion euro per year, goes a long way towards explaining what happened. In other words, the increased WTRE worked completely against the policymakers' objectives, as it raised considerably the public debt-to-GDP ratio, thus making the Greek public debt progressively less and less sustainable.

Policy makers have also favoured recurrent taxes on immovable property over transaction taxes, maintaining that the latter create market frictions (see e.g. European Commission 2013: p. 26). Another reason for the policymakers' interest in a liquid property market is its presumed enhancement of labour mobility. These views are in congruence with what happened in Greece: while the WTRE was dramatically increased, transaction taxes were reduced in 2014 from 12 percent-14 percent to 3 percent. However, one should always keep in mind the obvious fact that potential buyers of real estate are by definition also potential future owners, and thus weigh not only transactions taxes in their calculations, but also their future property taxes. Hence, raising the latter inordinately, as has happened in Greece, can very well negate the benefit from the reduced transaction taxes, thus driving prospective buyers away. As a result, the transaction never takes place and the market is frozen. This situation is the polar opposite of what policymakers intended when they lowered transaction taxes and increased recurrent property taxes.

The insistent focus on gross tax receipts from a WTRE without any regard to any tax shortfalls is also congruent with the mentality of someone who acts as if primarily interested in enforcing a court judgement against a delinquent borrower. In this case, there is no concern about the wider implications of any confiscatory measure on the debtor's property: the focus is squarely on how to get back as much as possible from the debtor. It is hoped that this mentality is not very strong in the Troika, as going after the property of a whole country's population is fundamentally different from what happens in the single-debtor paradigm. The freezing of the real estate market and the significant tax losses due to the WTRE discussed in Section 4 are examples of the aggregate WTRE implications, which make it ineffective as a source of revenue.

A WTRE is also advocated in some quarters as a progressive policy measure that affects primarily the wealthy. This argument is fundamentally flawed because it overlooks the fact that income (a flow) is a concept that is totally different from wealth (a stock, created by an accumulation of savings flows and price changes). Hence, someone who over time has invested her savings primarily in real estate can be cash-poor in any given year if she has low income or no income at all, due, e. g., to unemployment. In addition, individuals have typically low incomes in old age, while having accumulated wealth during their working years. Importantly, the tension between high wealth and low income is aggravated by the freeze in the real estate market, which makes savings in the form of real estate inaccessible. To put things bluntly, it is oxymoronic to consider someone wealthy when the market for her assets has ceased to function. Finally, one should also keep in mind that, as discussed in Section 2, it is very difficult to have the WTRE payments reduced due to a low income, which makes the plight of cash-poor real estate owners all the more onerous.

There is also a perception that high real estate taxes affect relatively few individuals, given the very pronounced progressivity of the WTRE discussed in Section 2. However, a frozen real estate market has implications for the whole economy, given the crucial importance of real estate as a vehicle for saving, investment and collateral. It is simply not possible to contain the implications of the annihilation of the market of the most important material asset in any economy to a small set of individuals. The fact that the WTRE has aggravated the Greek crisis implies that it is the economically weakest who suffer the most, as is the case in virtually all economic downturns. Furthermore, the concentration of the distribution of liquid wealth at the top is much higher than that of real estate wealth, both in Greece and in all other countries for which micro data are available. This implies that low net worth households are, compared to their high net worth counterparts, much more likely to be liquidity-constrained, thus urgently needing access to their savings in the form of real estate. As a result, also these households are very negatively affected by the real estate market freeze.

The severe negative implications of the WTRE on the economically disadvantaged, even when they own little or no real estate, can be easily understood if one considers its devastating effect on the labour market. As already discussed, the WTRE increases unemployment by at least 70,000–100,000 individuals each year. In Greece, as is the case in most industrialized countries, unemployment hits especially hard those who are less educated,[20] and thus much more likely to be at an economic disadvantage. Hence, we can easily see how short-sighted it is to focus only on who pays the WTRE when considering the overall burden of this tax on the Greek economy.

Interestingly, there is a perception that real estate investment is outdated, especially when compared to the much needed investment in new technologies. According to this view, the essential extinction of housing investment in Greece (as discussed in Section 4) should be of no major concern. It is difficult to agree with this view: all advanced economies devote a substantial part of their private investment to housing, and there is no reason why Greece should be such a large ex-

20 The unemployment rate in Greece in the 3d quarter of 2015 was 13.2 percent for those with postgraduate studies, 20.6 percent for those holding a university degree, 25.5 percent for those with a high school education, and 33.3 percent for those who have not finished primary school (HSA 2015b).

ception, to the extent that its housing investment is currently equal to a startlingly low 1.1 percent of GDP. In addition, if policymakers are keen on convincing households to invest their savings in vehicles other than real estate, they need to work hard towards making Greek banks, government bonds and financial markets trustworthy; this is clearly not true, not now, not over long periods in the past. Hence, it is no wonder that Greek householders, with critical skin in the game—namely the welfare of their families—have historically preferred investing in real estate. Thus it is utterly unfair and unjustifiable to punish them retroactively for being careful with their investments.

Finally, some proponents of the WTRE claim that real estate is taxed everywhere, so Greece should be no exception. The confusion here stems from the fact that, as discussed in Section 2, the WTRE has nothing to do with local real estate taxes, but is rather a pure tax on wealth. Importantly, wealth taxes have been progressively abolished in most countries due to various implementation and fairness considerations, including Germany where the Constitutional Court declared them unconstitutional.

6 Conclusions

The WTRE was dramatically increased during the Greek crisis with the aim of increasing government revenues. It has most likely miserably failed in this aim, while causing a large drop in GDP, and, consequently, a prolongation of the recession. In addition, it has a tremendous human cost, with 70,000 to 100,000 people forced into unemployment each year, while contributing to a freeze in the real estate market that has blocked access to the accumulated savings of many generations. Moreover, the WTRE significantly hinders financial intermediation because the real estate market freeze to which it contributed implies that there is no market for the primary collateral underlying loans.

Reasons for such a dreadful policy failure include the misplaced emphasis on gross tax receipts, the failure to take into account the aggregate implications of a tax on the most important asset that exists in all modern societies, the overestimation of the advantages of the captive tax base that real estate represents, the lack of understanding of the importance of liquidity in households' finances, of the overwhelming importance of real estate in household balance sheets, as well as the complications that the indivisibility of real estate creates when trying to liquidate it and thus access the savings that it embodies. One should also add a misplaced belief in the fairness of a WTRE (due in part to the confusion of concepts as different as income and wealth), and the totally misguided view that most of the problems of heavy real estate taxation can be loaded on the backs of relatively few households through a steeply progressive property tax schedule.

Given the essentially complete failure of the WTRE to increase tax revenues and its considerable cost, both in terms of lost jobs and economic output, this tax should be abolished immediately. This recommendation may sound radical to those targeting only gross tax receipts, but should be much more acceptable to economists worrying about the aggregate implications of a tax on a country's economy, and thus focuses on net instead of gross tax receipts. If policymakers are hesitant to completely abolish the WTRE, then they should at the very least drastically reduce it, and, crucially, also curtail its extreme progressivity that scares away many potential real estate investors.

Greece's greatest need right now is investment, and real estate should be one of its components, especially since it has fallen to astonishingly low levels that are simply not encountered in advanced economies. However, investors need to be treated fairly with respect to taxation. This implies that policymakers—and all major political parties—must commit to reducing wealth taxes and keeping them stable for the medium term at least, as well as to ruling out any radical policy changes similar to the quadrupling of the WTRE as a percentage of GDP. Importantly, investors also need to be reassured that the rule of law will be respected, in contrast to what is currently happening with the policymakers' refusal to adjust cadastral values to reflect the much lower actual ones. If investors are not convinced that the commitment to a fair treatment and reasonable and predictable taxation is genuine, they are not going to invest in Greece, not in real estate, not in anything else.

It is crucial to keep in mind, however, that trust is a very valuable intangible good that is easily and quickly lost but only regained with considerable effort and much time. Regrettably, it is fair to say that the policymakers' actions have violently breached the trust of both actual and potential real estate investors. Consequently, it will take extraordinary commitments from policymakers to restore this trust.

Finally, what has been most striking throughout the whole saga of the WTRE is the fact that policymakers have very little idea about what is going on in the Greek real estate market, as clearly demonstrated by the debacle of the capital gains tax. Most worryingly, there is no indication that they have realized that the real estate market freeze is a pressing emergency, and that increasing taxes four-fold during such an emergency is just about the last thing that one should do. Furthermore, they seem not to have understood the importance of a liquid real estate market, whether as a much-needed boost in aggregate demand in a depressed economy, for the alleviation of liquidity constraints, or for the smooth operation of financial intermediation. To the best of our knowledge, there is no documentation that policymakers have discussed any of issues related to, e. g. the multiplier effect of a discretionary tax like the WTRE, the effect of the WTRE on consumption out of real estate wealth, or of the unpaid household debts and taxes and the impaired financial intermediation that a frozen real estate market induces. Importantly, there is no indication that policymakers consider the state of the market as an indicator of policy effectiveness, fiscal or otherwise. This goes completely against both policymakers' alleged faith in markets as the best vehicle to allocate resources as well as plain common sense. Unless policymakers start to use their common sense and pay attention to what the unprecedented freeze of the Greek real estate market implies for the economy, there is no hope that the latter will recover any time soon. Unfortunately, such a pessimistic outlook is warranted due to the simple fact that it is impossible for a modern economy to function well without a reasonably liquid real estate market, which allows real estate to fulfil its crucially important role as a vehicle for saving, investment, and loan collateral.

References

— Acosta-Ormaechea, S., and J. Yoo (2012): Tax Composition and Growth: A Broad Cross-Country Perspective. IMF Working Paper No. 12/257.
— Arnold, J. (2008): Do Tax Structures Affect Aggregate Economic Growth? Empirical Evidence from a Panel of OECD Countries. OECD Economics Department Working Papers No. 643.

- Arnold, J., B. Brys, C. Heady, A. Johansson, C. Schwellnus, and L. Vartia (2011): Tax policy for economic recovery and growth. The Economic Journal, 121, 59–80.
- Auerbach, A., and Y. Gorodnichenko (2012): Measuring the Output Responses to Fiscal Policy. American Economic Journal: Economic Policy, 4 (2), 1–27.
- Auerbach, A., and Y. Gorodnichenko (2013): Fiscal Multipliers in Recession and Expansion. In: Alesina, A. and F. Giavazzi (eds.): Fiscal Policy after the Financial Crisis. University of Chicago Press.
- Bank of Greece (2015a): Index of Prices of Dwellings (Historical Series). www.bankofgreece.gr/BogDocumentEn/BG_PRICES_INDICES_HISTORICAL_SERIES.xls.
- Bank of Greece (2015b): Office Price Index. www.bankofgreece.gr/BogDocumentEn/OFFICE_PRICE_INDEX.pdf.
- Bank of Greece (2015c): Retail Price Index. www.bankofgreece.gr/BogDocumentEn/RETAIL_PRICE_INDEX.pdf.
- Bank of Greece (2015d): Summary Table of Key Short-term Indicators for the Real Estate Market. www.bankofgreece.gr/BogDocumentEn/TE_SHORT-TERM_INDICES.pdf.
- Bank of Greece (2015e): Monetary Policy Report 2014-2015 (in Greek). www.bankofgreece.gr/BogEkdoseis/NomPol20142015.pdf.
- Blanchard, O., and D. Leigh (2013): Growth Forecast Errors and Fiscal Multipliers. IMF Working Paper No. 13/1.
- Brayton, F., and P. B. Clark (1988): The Macroeconomic and Sectoral Effects of the Economic Recovery Tax Act: Some Simulation Results. In H. Motamen (ed.): Economic Modelling in the OECD Countries. London, Chapman and Hall.
- Campbell, J. Y., and J. F. Cocco (2006): How Do House Prices Affect Consumption? Evidence from Micro Data. Journal of Monetary Economics, 54, 591–621.
- Carroll, C., M. Otsuka, and J. Slacalek (2011): How Large Are Housing and Financial Wealth Effects? A New Approach. Journal of Money, Credit and Banking, 43 (1), 55–79.
- Case, K. E., J. M. Quigley, and R. J. Shiller (2003): Comparing Wealth Effects: The Stock Market Versus the Housing Market. Advances in Macroeconomics 02/2005, 5 (1), 1235–1235.
- European Commission (2011): Communication from the Commission to the European Parliament, the Council, the European Economic and Social Committee and the Committee of Regions. Annual Growth Survey 2012, COM(2011)81 5 final.
- European Commission (2012): Possible Reforms of Real Estate Taxation: Criteria for Successful Policies. European Economy, Occasional Paper No. 119.
- European Commission (2013): Tax Reforms in EU Member States 2013. European Economy, 5.
- Eurostat (2015): National Tax Lists. http://ec.europa.eu/eurostat/statistics-explained/images/c/c4/National_tax_lists_20140528.xls.
- Gilchrist, S., and E. Zakrajsek (2007): Investment and the Cost of Capital: New Evidence from the Corporate Bond Market. NBER Working Paper No. 13174. London.
- Haliassos, M. (2015): Greece: Are we missing the Reform Opportunity of the Crisis? VoxEu. www.voxeu.org/article/greece-seizing-crisis-s-reform-opportunities.
- Hall, R. E., and D. Jorgenson (1967): Tax Policy and Investment Behavior. American Economic Review, 57, 391–414.
- Hellenic Statistical Authority (2014): 2011 Population and Housing Census: Characteristics and amenities of dwellings. www.statistics.gr/en/statistics?p_p_id=documents_WAR_publicationsportlet_INSTANCE_qDQ8fBKKo4lN&p_p_lifecycle=2&p_p_state=normal&p_p_mode=view&p_p_cache-

ability=cacheLevelPage&p_p_col_id=column-2&p_p_col_count=4&p_p_col_pos=1&_documents_WAR_publicationsportlet_INSTANCE_qDQ8fBKKo4lN_javax.faces.resource=document&_documents_WAR_publicationsportlet_INSTANCE_qDQ8fBKKo4lN_ln=downloadResources&_documents_WAR_publicationsportlet_INSTANCE_qDQ8fBKKo4lN_documentID=136273&_documents_WAR_publicationsportlet_INSTANCE_qDQ8fBKKo4lN_locale=en.
— Hellenic Statistical Authority (2015a): Executed notarial acts, by object and value of stamp: 1998–2013. www.statistics.gr/documents/20181/f6b27fab-7937-4171-b848-48f74eab65b7.
— Hellenic Statistical Authority (2015b): Labour Force Survey, 3d Quarter 2015, Press Release. www.statistics.gr/en/statistics?p_p_id=documents_WAR_publicationsportlet_INSTANCE_qDQ8fBKKo4lN&p_p_lifecycle=2&p_p_state=normal&p_p_mode=view&p_p_cacheability=cacheLevelPage&p_p_col_id=column-2&p_p_col_count=4&p_p_col_pos=1&_documents_WAR_publicationsportlet_INSTANCE_qDQ8fBKKo4lN_javax.faces.resource=document&_documents_WAR_publicationsportlet_INSTANCE_qDQ8fBKKo4lN_ln=downloadResources&_documents_WAR_publicationsportlet_INSTANCE_qDQ8fBKKo4lN_documentID=136665&_documents_WAR_publicationsportlet_INSTANCE_qDQ8fBKKo4lN_locale=en.
— Household Finance and Consumption Network (2013a): The Eurosystem Household Finance and Consumption Survey—Methodological Report for the First Wave. ECB Statistics paper series No. 1.
— Household Finance and Consumption Network (2013b): The Eurosystem Household Finance and Consumption Survey—Results from the First Wave. ECB Statistics paper series No. 2.
— International Monetary Fund (2013): Greece: Ex Post Evaluation of Exceptional Access under the 2010 Stand-By Arrangement. IMF Country Report No. 13/156.
— Johansson A., C. Heady, J. Arnold, B. Brys, and L. Vartia (2008): Tax and Economic Growth. OECD Economics Department Working Paper No. 620.
— Mitrakos T., C. Akantziliotou, and V. Vlachostergiou (2014): Current developments and prospects of the Greek property market. www.bankofgreece.gr/BogDocumentEn/PRODEXPO_Oct_2014.pdf.
— Mourre, G., G. M. Isbasoiu, D. Paternoster, and M. Salto (2013): The Cyclically-Adjusted Budget Balance used in the EU Fiscal Framework: an Update. European Economy, Economic Papers No. 478.
— Organization for Economic Cooperation and Development (2015a): Taxation, Details of Tax Revenue—Greece. http://stats.oecd.org.
— Organization for Economic Cooperation and Development (2015b): Taxing Wages 2015. Paris, OECD Publishing.
— Organization for Economic Cooperation and Development (2015c): Annual National Accounts, Main Aggregates, Gross Domestic Product. http://stats.oecd.org.
— Perotti, R. (2012): The Effects of Tax Shocks on Output: Not So Large, but Not Small Either. American Economic Journal: Economic Policy, 4 (2), 214–237.
— Topel, R., and S. Rosen (1988): Housing Investment in the United States. Journal of Political Economy, 96 (4), 718–740.
— Tversky, A., and D. Kahneman (1973): Availability: A Heuristic for judging Frequency and Probability. Cognitive Psychology, 5 (2), 207–232.
— Xing, J. (2012): Tax Structure and Growth: How Robust is the Empirical Evidence? Economics Letters, 117 (1), 379–382.

Taxing Wealth and only Wealth in an Advanced Economy with an Oversized Informal Economy and Vast Tax Evasion: The Case of Greece

GREGORY T. PAPANIKOS

Gregory T. Papanikos, Athens Institute for Education and Research (ATINER) and University of Stirling, Scotland, e-mail:president@atiner.gr

Summary: Greece has the largest underground economy in the eurozone and one of the largest in Europe and the OECD countries. On the other hand, Greece is notoriously known for its sizable and widespread tax evasion primarily because of the large number of self employed and its wide geographical distribution. As documented by many studies, the two depend on a corrupted, inefficient and ineffective public administration. The emphasis is here on the restructuring of the Greek tax system taking into consideration these three structural characteristics of the Greek economy: a large informal sector, a pervasive tax evasion and a corrupt public sector (including the tax authorities). Many attempts to change these structural characteristics have failed primarily because they underestimate the costs and overestimate the benefits of any reform. And this because they assume that people's attitudes (tax morale) and the role institutions can change by a government decree. This paper takes these as given and proposes a tax system that is based exclusively on wealth (property, bank deposits, shares etc) and the abolishment of VAT and all kinds of income taxes. It is argued that this system is more efficient, more effective, more democratic and promotes competitiveness and economic growth.

→ JEL Classification: H21, H26, E62
→ Keywords: Wealth tax, Greece, tax evasion

1 Introduction

This paper proposes a comprehensive lump sum tax on Greek private wealth as the only source of sovereign revenue. The aim is to simplify the Greek tax system, taking into consideration its chronic pathogenesis of tax evasion, corruption and incompetent tax administration. The existing tax system is based on different Value Added Tax (VAT) rates, other sales (excise) taxes, various income taxes (wages, profits, rents, interests, etc), social security contributions, and emergency poll taxes. This system is considered inefficient and ineffective. It is also undemocratic, impedes competitiveness and drives away foreign investment. All these taxes should be abolished and replaced with a flat tax on wealth. Other taxes may exist, but only to correct market failures and externalities, not to be a source of government revenue.

This paper shows that a thorough analysis of the present Greek economic, political, social and technological conditions, supports the argument that a flat tax on wealth is more efficient, more effective, more democratic, and more competitive. As is the case with all taxes, a flat tax on wealth is not a panacea, but under the current Greek state of affairs, it should be considered to be the best of all possible worlds. For example, the economics literature documents (Boadway and Sato 2009) that while VAT promotes production efficiency, it only does so in the formal sector of the economy. The existence of a large informal Greek economy renders this tax inefficient.

The approach followed in this paper is mostly demonstrative. It argues that a flat tax on wealth should be the only source of government revenue and demonstrates it with an example. This is the first time, to my knowledge, that a wealth tax designed to be the only source of government revenue has been proposed. In this study, a wealth tax is proposed for positive and normative reasons. A flat tax on wealth is optimal because it distorts neither producer nor consumer choice. On the other hand, a flat tax on wealth decreases the unfair treatment of rich Greeks. While some of them pay soaring taxes, others, with similar actual high income, pay no tax at all. The latter have accumulated considerable wealth through tax evasion. A wealth tax will correct this unequal treatment of wealthy Greeks. Thus, this paper's proposal has more to do with horizontal equity than with vertical equity. The emphasis is on equality among wealthy Greeks and not between rich and poor households.

The proposal here to introduce a wealth tax is not related to the topical issue of wealth inequality. Piketty (2014, 2015) and many others have discussed this issue, proposing a global wealth tax. They focus on the richest of the rich, i.e. the top 1 percent (Alvaredo et al. 2013). Yunker (2014), using a theoretical framework, concludes that a 3 percent tax on capital wealth is associated with higher output, lower inequality and a considerable improvement in social welfare. Auerbach and Hassett (2015) provide a critical discussion of the idea of a global wealth tax. However, these issues are not related to this paper's proposal for a flat tax on wealth in Greece.

This paper also does not deal with the efficiency of government spending. It proposes neither a smaller nor a larger government. Instead, it assumes that current government spending remains the same. Nevertheless, in the long-term, the proposed tax on wealth will impact governmental size. It will reduce the size of Greek tax authorities and, therefore, the absolute size of public services. It will also reduce the relative size of government spending as a percentage of GDP substantially because implementing a wealth tax while simultaneously eliminating all other taxes will spearhead a process of substantial economic growth. In addition, the reported (official) GDP will increase because the income for tax purposes will not be hidden. The debt to GDP ratio will decrease and the Greek government will be able to borrow at a much lower cost. These important positive side effects of a wealth tax are not further considered in this paper.

This paper is organized in six sections, including this introduction. Section 2 discusses some stylized facts of tax evasion, especially in relation to the self-employed. Section 3 provides a numerical example of how a wealth tax can be designed along with other descriptive examples of unequal treatment of wealthy Greeks. Section 4 presents the four criteria of an optimal tax system: efficiency, effectiveness, democracy (includes transparency, fairness, and equity), and competitiveness; these are discussed in the light of the flat tax on wealth as the only source of government revenue. Section 5 describes some of the difficulties in implementing a wealth tax. The final section, Section 6, concludes.

2 Some stylized facts on the Greek informal economy

The most important reason why a wealth tax would be the best solution has to do with Greece's widespread informal economy, which includes both non-registered companies as well as non-registered employees by otherwise legal, registered, companies. The informal economy is a global phenomenon.[1] There is no country in the world that does not face the challenge of reducing the size of its informal economy. Two reasons can explain the existence of an informal economy.[2] First, people decide to produce in the informal sector because they do not want to pay taxes. The higher the tax rate, the higher the incentive to produce in the informal economy. However, more important than the tax rate, is the tax enforcement, which depends on the administrative cost[3] of tax auditing and tax collection.[4] The latter is critical in countries with slow and corrupt judicial (court) procedures. Second, people produce in the informal sector because some business activities, such as drug and human trafficking, are illegal. Regardless, producing in the informal economy results in the accumulation of personal wealth without paying taxes.

The unreported portion of GDP results in tax evasion. According to Schneider (2015), the shadow economy's share of official GDP in 36 OECD countries ranged from a minimum of 6.5 percent to a maximum of 30.6 percent. The average rate was 18 percent. In Greece, the shadow economy accounted for 22.4 percent of the official GDP. Other studies report higher rates: Berger et al. (2014) claim that the Greek informal economy's contribution to GDP is substantially underestimated. Their evidence shows that the Greek shadow economy exceeds 60 percent of GDP and has been increasing since Greece's 2002 entry to the eurozone.

---

1 See Charmes (2012) for definitions, characteristics and trends of the informal economy.

2 I am aware of the literature that attempts to explain tax evasion as the result of national culture but lacks serious theoretical underpinnings, with weak empirical evidence assuming that one can measure culture and cultural differences. For an example of such a study see Bame-Aldred et al. (2013). I note this aspect here because it is very popular in the international media to portray Greeks as having a culture of tax evasion.

3 All taxes are coercive. The administration cost of implementing a tax system is large and differs between tax systems and tax authorities (countries). Thus, the design of an optimal tax policy is system and country specific. Of course, as Slemrod (1990) points out, the technology of tax collection should be a determinant of an optimal tax policy and this is independent of tax authorities.

4 Tax auditing and tax collection do not coincide. In Greece, a tax audit by tax authorities may result in a tax evasion case, but the tax collection may come later or not at all for many reasons, including the right of the tax evader to appeal the decision in the courts.

Figure 1

Shadow economy and tax rates in 31 OECD countries in 2015

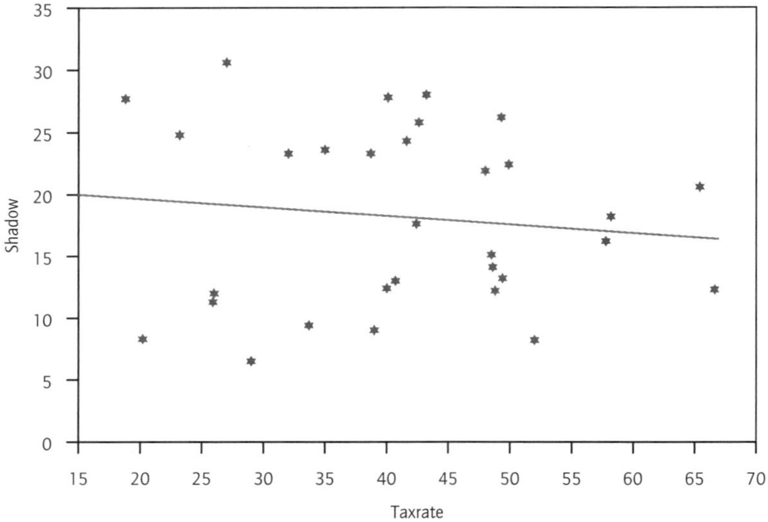

Note: The shadow economy measures are taken from Schneider (2015) and the tax rate variable is a combination of profit tax (percent of profits), labor tax and contribution (percent of profits), and other taxes (percent of profits) retrieved from World Competitiveness Report (http://reports.weforum.org/global-competitiveness-report-2015-2016/competitiveness-rankings/).

The empirical evidence on tax evasion and tax rates is controversial. Levaggi and Menoncin (2012) use a theoretical model where the optimal evasion can be negatively or positively related to the tax rate. Figure 1 is a scatter diagram showing the shadow economy measured by the informal economy's share of official GDP and the tax rate on profits in 31 OECD countries.[5] It appears that the level of the shadow economy is unrelated to the business tax rates. If there is any relationship, it is negative: higher tax rates reduce the shadow economy.

As argued in the literature, the enforcement of the tax law and the deterrence of tax evasion are more important than the level of the tax rate itself.[6] This might explain Figure 1. In an early model developed by Allingham and Sandmo (1972), tax evasion is the result of expected utility maximization taking into consideration the probability of an audit, the size of the fine if caught, the tax rates, and, naturally, income.

5 These include Austria, Belgium, Bulgaria, Croatia, Cyprus, Czech Republic, Denmark, Estonia, Finland, France, Germany, Greece, Hungary, Ireland, Italy, Latvia, Lithuania, Luxembourg, Malta, Netherlands, Norway, Poland, Portugal, Romania, Slovakia, Slovenia, Spain, Sweden, Switzerland, Turkey, and the United Kingdom.

6 For an empirical study on the role of tax enforcement and deterrence, see Pomeranz (2015). A review of field experiments used to increase tax compliance is provided by Hallsworth (2014).

Figure 2

Self-employed and the shadow economy of 31 OECD countries in 2015

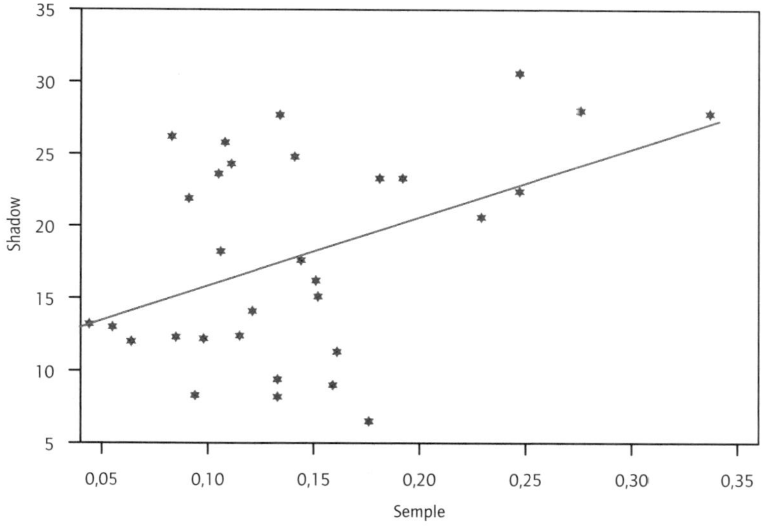

Note: The percentage of self-employed (Semple) is the share of the total number of self-employed in the labor force. Both series are taken from the AMECO database of the Eurostat. The Shadow rates are from Schneider (2015).

In Greece, the large number of self-employed makes the cost of monitoring them by tax authorities extremely high.[7] This is true for countries similar to Greece, such as Spain and Italy; but in Greece it is even higher because of the unique geographical distribution of the self-employed.[8] It is almost impossible for the taxes collected to cover the administrative cost of tax audits, enforcement, and collection.

The number of self-employed as a percentage of the total labor force might explain the extent of the shadow economy better than the level and regular increases in tax rates.[9] Figure 2 shows the relationship between the number of self-employed as a share of the labor force and the shadow economy, measured as a percentage of the official GDP in the OECD countries. Even though there is a high dispersion, the graph shows that there is a strong positive relation between the

7 The self-employed have more opportunities to hide their income and a tax enforcement (deterrence), such as the threat of a tax audit, results in increased compliance by the self-employed relative to the non-self-employed, as documented by Slemrod et al. (2001), Kleven et al. (2011) and Hallsworth et al. (2014).

8 For example, there are more than a hundred small islands, each attracting numerous tourists. Tax enforcement is almost impossible because there are not tax offices on each island. As such tax auditors must travel from Athens and by the time they arrive, everybody is aware of their presence, taking precautions to ensure a favorable outcome of an audit: i.e. they issue the necessary receipts and pay the required VAT.

9 The correlation between the shadow economy and self-employment does not imply causation. Torrini (2005), using data from OECD countries, shows that in countries with tax evasion opportunities, the number of self-employed opportunities increases. But it can be the other way: the existence of self-employment and small businesses may be the cause of tax evasion. This relates to the unique geographical morphology of Greece: On hundreds of small islands, only small business can be profitable.

Figure 3

The Greek shadow economy and the percentage of self-employed, 2003–2015

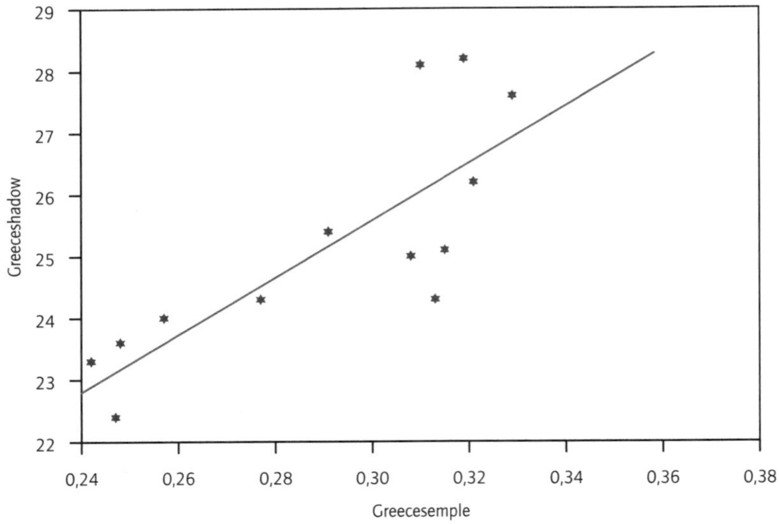

Note: The percentage of Greek self-employed (Greecesemple) is the share of the total number of self-employed in the labor force. Both series are taken from the AMECO database of the Eurostat. The Greek shadow rates (Greeceshadow) are from Schneider (2015).

share of the self-employed and the share of the shadow economy. A one percentage point increase in the self-employment rate increases the shadow economy by 3.1 percent.

Figure 3 shows the same relation using annual Greek data from 2003 to 2015. The impact of the self-employed on the shadow economy is higher than in other OECD countries. The slope of the curve is steeper. Thus, there is a strong positive association between the number of people who are self-employed and the extent of the Greek shadow economy.

According to the European Commission (2013), macroeconomic conditions play an important role in determining how many people decide to work in the shadow economy. The reason is that when the economy is booming more people can find better paid jobs in the formal economy. Thus, the level of the shadow economy is negatively related to GDP growth and positively related to the unemployment rate. This is not the Greek case. Figure 4 shows that GDP growth and the shadow economy are positively related. Figure 5 shows that the unemployment rate is negatively related to the Greek shadow economy.

These observations might be explained by the dynamics of the Greek economy. Tourism is the flagship of Greek economic growth. Tourism is also an area with a very high percentage of shadow economy because of the high cost of tax enforcement. Thus, when tourism flourishes, so does the shadow economy.

Figure 4

The Greek shadow economy and GDP growth, 2003-2015

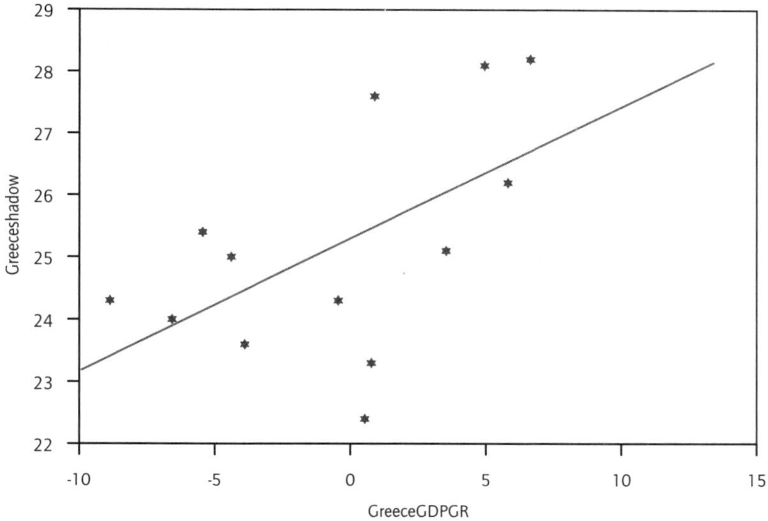

Note: GreeceGDPGR is the real Greek growth of GDP as reported by AMECO database of the Eurostat. The Greek shadow rates (Greeceshadow) are from Schneider (2015).

Figure 5

The Greek shadow economy and the unemployment rate, 2003-2015

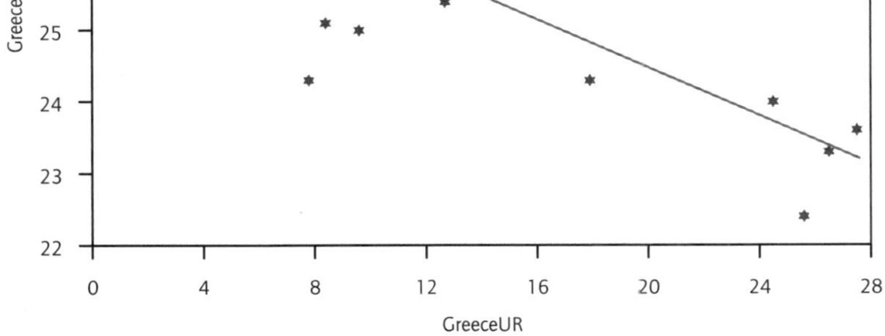

Note: GreeceUR is the Greek unemployment rate as reported by AMECO database of the Eurostat. The Greek shadow rates (Greeceshadow) are from Schneider (2015).

Figure 6

The Greek shadow economy and the inflation rate, 2003–2015

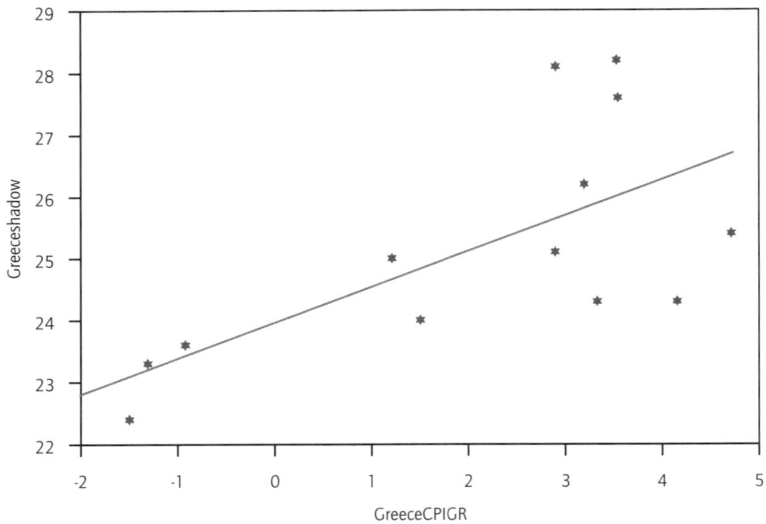

Note: GreeceCPIGR is the Greek inflation rate as reported by AMECO database of the Eurostat. The Greek shadow rates (Greeceshadow) are from Schneider (2015).

Gupta and Ziramba (2010) and Bittencourt et al. (2014) show that a higher level of inflation is associated with a larger shadow economy. Figure 6 shows that there appears to be a strong positive relationship between the inflation rate and the Greek shadow economy.

The above stylized facts show that the Greek shadow economy is positively related to the number of self-employed, GDP growth, and the inflation rate, but negatively related to the unemployment rate. The self-employed evidence is the most important. It is difficult to audit their income, but not difficult to find their wealth and, therefore, tax them. However, this should be accomplished in a very simple and straightforward way as explained in the next section of this paper.

3 Taxing only wealth: A suggestion to simplify the Greek tax system

Wealth is the sum of real estate property, bank deposits, stocks and government bonds held by Greek nationals in Greece and abroad. It may also include other durable consumption goods, such as cars, boats, jewelry and other valuables. It also includes the wealth held by non-Greeks in Greece. As explained in the next section, a tax on such possessions, as the only source of Greece's public revenues, is the most efficient, the most effective, the most democratic, and the most competitive way of coercing citizens to pay their dues. This paper proposes a flat tax on wealth possession. Wealth transfers, including bestowed wealth, should not be taxed. Further, wealth earnings should not be taxed. For example, rents earned from leasing a property should not be taxed. Similarly, dividends from stocks should not be taxed.

The flat tax idea is not new and was proposed by Hall and Rabushka 25 years ago in the USA in an article published in the Wall Street Journal on December 10, 1981, which was then developed into a book; with an updated edition released in 2007. However, their proposal was a flat tax on income and not on wealth. The difference is important in countries with a long history of tax evasion, like Greece. Income taxes are more easily evaded than wealth taxes.

As previously mentioned, a wealth tax is optimal because (a) tax evasion in Greece is not only pervasive but excessively expensive (economically, politically, socially, etc) to reduce; and (b) the Greek tax authorities are corrupt and incompetent. The cost of building a non-corrupt and competent tax administration is too high and would involve a very long term process. Unlike private income, private wealth cannot be hidden. A Greek proverb says: "Cough and wealth cannot be hidden." Technically, someone should be indifferent between taxing his wealth and taxing his income that flows from this wealth. The policy difference is that income can be concealed from tax authorities while wealth is more difficult, if not impossible, to conceal. In addition, those who can hide their income, also have the political power to influence the design of the tax system. This is the reason a wealth tax (property) is met with such fierce political resistance.

As noted earlier, the critical problem in Greece is not so much wealth inequality but the unfair tax treatment of wealthy Greek households. Not all wealthy Greeks pay their due tax. In my book (see Papanikos 2014a), I give an illustrative example of the unfair treatment of two wealthy households headed by physicians. Both medical doctors with similar careers, they started practicing 20 years ago when they were 38 years old. On average, they made an annual income of 500,000 euro in today's money. Doctor A was able to hide all his income. Doctor B was taxed for her total earned income. Assuming a 20 percent income tax rate and annual consumption expenditures of 300,000 euro, today, Doctor A has accumulated wealth (houses, stocks, bank deposits and government bonds) worth 4 million and Doctor B 2 million euro. Doctor B paid 100,000 euro tax per year over the previous 20 years, while Doctor A paid no tax. We assume that both paid the same VAT, excise taxes and any other tax. If income tax was replaced with a wealth tax of 5 percent, Doctor B would pay, as before, 100,000 euro, but Doctor A will pay 200,000 euro per year. This will make up for Doctor B's unfair treatment of the previous years. The total tax revenue increases from 100,000 to 300,000 euro, but it can be designed to give the same revenue as before. Doctor B, the honest doctor, will pay one-third of what she paid annually over the previous 20 years; Doctor A will pay an annual tax of 67,000 euro instead of the zero that he paid in each of the previous 20 years. Both doctors will pay the same total amount of 100,000 per year as they did in all previous 20 years. The tax burden will be different. This example can be extended to any other profession in Greece such as pharmacists, engineers, lawyers, plumbers, electricians, farmers etc.

The proposal for tax wealth here is very similar in design to the one proposed by Bach et al. (2011) for Germany and Lavoie (2014) for the USA. The tax rates are similar to theirs. The only difference is that the wealth tax proposed here is the only tax and is levied on all wealth, not just on the wealthy at the top of the distribution. The proposal here is to tax wealth and not the wealthy. All other taxes are abolished. Many other studies[10] proposed or examine wealth taxes, but these are different from what is proposed here: the wealth tax is the only tax.

10 Eichengreen (1989) provides an argument to tax wealth for lifting the burden of sovereign debt. McDonnell (2013) discusses the implementation of a wealth tax in Ireland designed to improve horizontal and vertical equity; not implemented to be a source of

Table 1 is an example of how a tax on wealth can be designed. Even though the numbers are not based on real data, they should not be very far from today's Greek reality. The starting point is the total amount of revenue required to finance public expenditures. This amount today is around 50 billion euro. The measure of wealth is also critical. As explained in note (5) of the table, wealth is equal to 1,320 billion euro. Thus, a wealth tax rate of 0.3788 is required to generate revenue of 50 billion euro. Mathä et al. (2014) using data from the Eurosystem Household Finance and Consumption Survey estimate the average Greek wealth to be 200,000 euro per household. There are a total of 4,114,150 Greek households reported. Thus, total wealth is equal to 823 billion euro.[11] However, this does not include the non-registered households and the informal economy. Table 1 takes these into consideration.

Table 1 classifies the Greek households into four classes. A more detailed proposal will classify all Greek households according to their wealth. In Papanikos (2014b) I describe in detail the characteristics of the first three classes. Each group belongs to a certain segment of the labor force with various opportunities of tax evasion. Group 1 includes legal and illegal immigrants along with very low skilled native (Greek) workers. Group 2 comprises employees in the government and state controlled enterprises. Group 3 consists of professionals, self-employed, skilled workers, farmers and hetero-employed workers. Members of all groups evade taxes; the opportunities and the levels are different.

A tax on wealth will correct the unfair treatment of the same members in each group and not across groups. For example, two civil engineers who have worked in town planning ("*poleodomia*") for 20 years (belonging to Group 2) have accumulated different wealth because one accepted bribes to issue building permits and the other did not. This extra income, despite how it was "earned," was never taxed. One may argue that the accumulated wealth is due to different saving rates. However, the savings rate required to account for such wealth accumulations is more than 100 percent of the accumulated official earned income.

Table 1 shows that, on average, each group member does not pay a much higher tax than they pay now, with the exception of the poorest households. The latter pay no tax. Contrariwise, the very rich pay 25 percent more tax. Group 2 pays 4 percent more tax (333 euro) and Group 3 pays 3.7 percent more (697 euro). This, however, does not reveal the real difficulty in implementing such a tax. The real resistance will come from all group members that currently pay no tax at all or pay a very small amount because they are able to hide their income. The difference is paid by the other group members who cannot hide their income and, of course, the poorest households, which pay VAT and other expenditure taxes. This explains why voices against a wealth tax come from all segments of society. In each segment, tax evaders exist, exerting a very strong political and social resistance.

A tax on wealth as the only source of Greek government revenue is optimal given the extent of tax evasion, tax compliance and costs of tax auditing. The next section discusses the optimality of this

---

sovereign revenue. The European Commission (2014) also discusses wealth taxes across the European Union along the lines of Piketty's analysis, i.e. to correct for the increasing wealth inequality. This is not the reason a wealth tax is proposed here.

11 According to Eurostat data (AMECO), the net capital stock (OKND) accounted for only 944 billion euro in 2010. If private bank deposits are included, estimated to be more than 250 billion euro in 2010, the total wealth of these two categories exceeds 1,200 billion euro.

Table 1

An example of a flat wealth tax in Greece by household type

Household type[1]	Number of households[2]	Average income[3] (euro)	Total income (bn of euro)	Average tax paid today[4] (euro)	Total tax paid today (bn of euro)	Wealth[5] (bn of euro)	Wealth tax Rate[6]	Total wealth tax (bn of euro)	Wealth tax per household (euro)	Tax difference (euro)
1	2,000,000	10,000	20	1,500	3	0	0.03788	0	0	-1,500
2	1,250,000	40,000	50	8,000	10	275	0.03788	10	8,333	333
3	1,500,000	80,000	120	19,000	29	780	0.03788	30	19,697	697
4	100,000	300,000	30	80,000	8	265	0.03788	10	100,455	20,455
Total	4,850,000		220		50	1,320		50		

Notes:

1 The first three types correspond to Segments C, B and A as explained in more detail in Papanikos (2014b). Type 4 includes business people and other rich households who do not work and earn income from other sources, i. e. by renting their property.

2 Author's estimations based on the hypothesis that the total number of households should be equal to the one found by the national census (about 4 millions) plus the illegal migrants who are not registered as part of the national census process. I assume them about 850,000 households.

3 Author's assessment based on the hypothesis that the total income should equal to 2014 GDP of 179.1 billion as reported by Eurostat plus an estimate of 23.3 percent of the shadow economy as reported by Schneider (2015). Total GDP is equal to 220 billion euro. The essence of the suggestion does not change if different incomes are assumed per household type.

4 It includes all taxes: direct, indirect and social security contributions. The total tax is 50 billion or 22.7 percent of total GDP (official and unofficial). It is assumed that Type 1 pays 15 percent of tax (includes VAT), Type 2, 3 and 4 pays 20 percent, 23.75 percent and 26.7 percent respectively. Different rates do not change the nature of the proposal.

5 According to Piketty & Zucman (2013), the relation of wealth to income is between 6 and 7. Here, it is assumed that wealth is 6 times higher than total income or 1,320 billion euro. However, since wealth is accumulated from past incomes plus inheritances minus consumption, poor households (Type 1 of the table) were not able to accumulate any wealth. They can be considered as the propertyless (wealthless) class. The other household types accumulated wealth proportional to their income. We assume a constant weighted average ratio of wealth to income of 6.6 because total wealth must add up to 1,320 billion euro. Per household type the ratios are 5.5, 6.5 and 8.84 respectively.

6 Lavoie (2014) proposed a wealth tax of 5 percent in the USA which progressively increases to 10 percent for the top 20,000 richest households, without exemptions from other direct and indirect taxes. Bach et al (2011) suggested a similar wealth tax in Germany that ranged from 3.4 percent to 5.3 percent only for the rich. The proposal here for a 3.8 percent wealth tax applies to wealth as a flat rate for all Greek households who possess wealth.

tax using the four criteria mentioned in the introduction of the paper: efficiency, effectiveness, democracy and competitiveness. These four criteria are discussed in many textbooks on public finance. For example, in their classical textbook, Musgrave and Musgrave (1989) discuss these criteria on page 216–217. In this study, these criteria are very similar to the ones suggested in Stiglitz's textbook on the *Economics of Public Sector*, now (2015) in its fourth edition He proposes five criteria: efficiency, administrative simplicity, flexibility, political responsibility and fairness.

4 An optimal tax system for Greece: How the proposal meets the criteria of an optimal tax system

Ramsey (1927) and Mirrlees (1971) laid the foundations of optimal tax policies. Since then, numerous studies have debated the theory and practice of an optimal tax system (Diamond and Saez 2011, Mankiw et al. 2009, Slemrod 1990). There is now an enormous theoretical and empirical literature on optimal tax systems. Most of this work aims at designing a tax system that, one way or another, balances the positive (efficiency) and normative (fairness) aspects of public finance.

Mirrlees himself led a scientific group that reviewed and made recommendations to reform the UK tax system; see Mirrlees et al. (2011) for a summary of his report. As he put it on page 332, "The challenge for the review was to design a tax system that can raise the revenue that the government needs to achieve its spending and distributional ambitions whilst minimising economic and administrative inefficiency, keeping the system as simple and transparent as possible, and avoiding arbitrary tax differentiation across people and forms of economic activity." A critical appraisal of Mirrlees proposals is provided by Feldstein (2012).

For the purposes of this study, an optimal tax system must meet four criteria: efficiency, effectiveness, democracy, and competitiveness. In the remainder of this section, these four criteria are discussed within the context of the current Greek tax system and the paper's proposal of a flat tax on wealth as the only source of sovereign revenue.

The efficiency criterion

The efficiency criterion has two aspects. First, a tax is efficient if it does not distort producers' or consumers' choices. Under this criterion, a lump sum tax on ability is optimal. Mankiew et al. (2009: 149–150) note that, "Actual governments, however, cannot directly observe ability, so the model still fails to deliver useful and realistic prescriptions." But this is not a problem, if ability is directly related to accumulated wealth. Ability *per se* is useless for tax purposes if it does not lead to the production and accumulation of private wealth. Individuals differ in their abilities as long as they differ in their accumulated wealth. Even inherited wealth requires an ability to maintain it. However, ability becomes wealth through effort and the latter might be affected by a wealth tax.

Simons (2015), from the Harvard Business School, develops a descriptive model where individual effort, with entrepreneurship and innovation, produces wealth along with inequality. If entrepreneurship and innovation is a manifestation of wealth generating abilities, then under the appropriate business environment of self interest and freedom, individuals can accumulate personal wealth. A flat tax on wealth should not affect this accumulation process, necessary to promote economic growth. Thus, this paper's proposal to tax only wealth, is efficient and will promote Greek economic growth.

Second, a tax is efficient if it minimizes the administration cost per euro of collected tax. No Greek data exists on the administration cost[12] but it should be very large due to the large number of self employed and independent professionals who are geographically dispersed. A tax on wealth is efficient because it does not require any tax auditing. The tax on real estate property, which was imposed in 2012, was collected through electricity bills. Those who did not pay the tax faced the threat of having their electricity supply cut off. The cost of collecting and enforcing a wealth tax was zero. The electricity bill is also used to collect local taxes and a fixed tax to finance public television and radio broadcasting.

Tax authorities should choose a system that maximizes overall efficiency: production efficiency, consumption efficiency and tax collection efficiency. The current Greek tax system distorts production and consumption efficiency. Efficient producers are driven out of the market because inefficient producers can survive by not paying their taxes: not VAT, not income (profit) tax, and not social security contributions.[13] At the margin, these tax evading cost reductions can be as high as 80 percent of the total production cost.[14] A flat tax on wealth does not create such production inefficiencies.

The effectiveness criterion

The effectiveness of a tax system requires that all citizens pay their due tax. It relates to tax compliance and tax enforcement (deterrence). A tax system can be efficient but not effective. Actually, an ineffective system might be more efficient than an effective tax system. For example, in Greece most of the self-employed and small (family) business people who are geographically dispersed, do not pay any tax or pay very little (the system is ineffective). Large companies and third party tax reporting, pay taxes at a very low administration cost. Tax auditing of the self-employed and small business is too costly and most tax authorities do not bother monitoring them. Therefore, the administration cost is zero. The Greek system is efficient, minimizes the cost per tax collected but not effective, i.e. not all citizens pay their due tax. This is well understood by Greek tax authorities. Whenever there is a demand on tax administration from political authorities to collect more tax revenues, the local tax offices audit their biggest customers. They do not bother to audit the numerous small companies and the self-employed because of the high cost per tax to be collected. They maximize efficiency at the cost of effectiveness.

---

12 European Commission (2014: 107) reports that the average cost of collecting taxes in the European Union was 1.1 euro per 100 euro. Data for Greece is not reported.

13 In the 1980s I asked a civil engineer, who was self-employed building private houses, why he was evading taxes. In Greece they are called "free professionals." He told me that the real choice is not between evading and not evading taxes but between being a civil engineer in Greece or not. If he did not evade taxes, he could not practice his profession. He would be driven out of the market. As with many other civil engineers of his generation, he accumulated considerable wealth without paying the taxes due.

14 This is true in the service sector where the sunk and fixed costs are negligible. A tax evader producer does not pay the 23 percent VAT, the 40 percent social security contributions, or the 25 percent income (profit) tax. For example, a family cleaning company employs illegal migrants and pays them much lower than the minimum wage and without any social security contributions. It pays no VAT and reports no income from profits. Its costs will be reduced by more than 80 percent if it pays half the official minimum wage, i.e. 300 euro per month instead of over 600 euro.

A tax on wealth is an optimal solution to the effectiveness problem. As shown in the previous section, a tax on wealth is effective because all the members of the various social groups pay their due tax, irrespective of whether they are able to hide their income or not. Modern technology allows tax authorities to tax audit all wealth in the form of property, bank deposits and stocks; even the filing of tax returns becomes redundant.

The democracy criterion

In a democratic society, all people should pay taxes according to their ability. The Greek constitution (article 4) states that all Greek citizens contribute according to their ability (power). The thorny issue is how ability is defined and measured. As mentioned above, accumulated private wealth is as close as one can get to a true manifestation of ability.

The democracy criterion relates to vertical and horizontal equity but is more than that. Vertical equity requires that the tax rate should increase with one's ability to pay taxes (i.e. income or wealth). But the most important democratic challenge in Greece is the unfair (horizontal equity) treatment of households with the same wealth (income). Two households may have the same wealth but not pay the same tax because of tax avoidance and tax evasion. This is a true democratic deficit: the unequal treatment of equals. A flat tax on wealth corrects the unfair treatment of two individuals with the same wealth but with different opportunities to hide their income. This aspect of the democracy criterion relates to fairness of the tax system and is one of the five desirable characteristics in Stiglitz's list.

The democracy criterion also relates to the process of tax reforms. Any change of the tax structure is met with strong resistance from political elites. This should be taken into account when an optimal tax policy is designed. Fairfield (2013) examines tax reforms in Latin American countries. The quality of democracy is undermined when economic elites (minorities) are able to impose favorable tax policies either directly (influence politicians and political parties) or indirectly (influence public opinion by controlling or owning the mass media). This is the Greek experience with the 2012 property tax; a tax that favors the poor (propertyless) households has met with fierce resistance from all Greek political parties and the Greek mass media. The allegedly left parties were the fiercest opponents to such a wealth tax implementation and even Greek communists oppose a tax on private property. These are the ones who claim that if they ever come to power, private property will be abolished. The current Greek public opinion is affected by political elites who sturdily oppose any tax on wealth (private property).[15] This aspect of the democracy criterion relates to what Stiglitz calls flexibility, one of the five characteristics of a desirable tax system.

The democratic criterion is very important in reforming the Greek tax system. A tax on wealth (especially a tax on private property) will meet strong opposition because it is the only tax that cannot be evaded. In addition, the corrupted and inept tax authorities are completely sidestepped. They will exert a strong opposition because they will forego income from bribes. The experience

15 In a June 2015 interview with Spiegel Online International (www.spiegel.de/international/europe/eu-commission-president-juncker-on-greece-and-tsipras-a-1039738.html), the President of the European Commission, Jean-Claude Juncker stated, "On the other hand, there are people in Greece who are filthy rich. I have called upon Mr. Tsipras to raise taxes on wealth in his country. Shockingly, his response to my request was not as enthusiastic as I had expected." Most of these rich vote for Mr Tsipras' party, an allegedly left wing party. Mr Tsipras' position is not contradictory. He knows that he gets more votes from social segments that systematically evade taxes and accumulate huge personal wealth. Mr Tsipras, along with many other members of his government, come from these classes. A Greek proverb says "if you blame your 'house,' it will fall on you." In this paper's case, blame equals tax.

with the property tax implemented in 2012 shows that the tax was effective and efficient, even though it met with strong political and social resistance. Democracy is undoubtedly the best of all implemented (practiced) political systems but it does not always lead to optimal policies.[16] This is far from being unique to Greece; Eichengreen (1989) states in the abstract of his paper that, "Property owners are sure to resist its adoption. In a democratic society, their objections are guaranteed to cause delay." I would add, delay until it is scrapped altogether.

Democracy requires transparency. All citizens should know and understand the rules of the tax game. They should feel that they are fairly treated. In Greece, most people feel that the tax system treats them unfairly and for this reason they do not want to pay any tax. If the opportunity arises, they will avoid and evade any tax. In Greece there are mostly two types of tax payers: those who can avoid paying taxes and those who cannot. They will help others to avoid and evade taxes even though there is no direct benefit to them. On the contrary, in many cases they are indirectly harmed because they pay higher taxes than they should. This is an additional reason why a tax system should be as simple as possible. A tax on wealth meets this criterion. Taxing wealth with one tax rate is ideal for Greece's parliamentary democracy. This aspect of the democracy criterion relates to what Stiglitz calls political responsibility.

To overcome the role of political elites, the suggestion to tax wealth and only wealth as the only source of government revenue should be an issue debated and decided through a referendum. This approach will inherently increase tax morale. Togler (2005) finds that tax morale, i.e. citizen's intrinsic motivation to pay taxes, increases with direct democracy. Similarly, Hug and Spörri (2011) find that referendums cement the relationship between trust and tax morale. Persson and Tabellini (1994) develop a theoretical model to compare direct to representative democracy on the issue of capital taxation.

The competitiveness criterion

The optimal tax system should promote national and international competitiveness. This is the only way to promote economic growth. And as mentioned above, Musgrave & Musgrave (1989) consider economic growth to be one of the characteristics of a "good" tax system. The current Greek tax system is not a "good" system. For example, unequal tax evasion among firms inhibits competition. Inefficient firms can survive only because they pay no taxes: VAT, profit taxes and social security contributions. On the other hand, a higher VAT and tax on profits relative to competitive countries reduce exports and the inflow of foreign direct investments. A simple tax on wealth will increase national and international competitiveness, something desperately needed to revitalize the struggling Greek economy.

Summarizing the above discussion, the Greek tax system is inefficient, ineffective, undemocratic, and inhibits competitiveness. A single tax on wealth is optimal in dealing with the Greek informal economy and the resulting vast tax evasion. After all if income is not taxed, there is no incentive not to report it unless it is earned by illegal activities.

---

16 Plato, in 4th century BC, was the first to recognize this deficiency of democracy. He came up with the, elegant, utopian ideal of a benevolent dictator. A philosopher king should rule on eudemonic society. Much later, in the 20th century, Nobel Prize winner Kenneth Arrow persuasively, but not as elegantly, showed that a democracy (a voting system to express social preferences) may not lead to optimal decisions. One of Arrow's assumptions is no dictator.

Apart from the tax evasion issue, taxing wealth has some additional positive implications. For example, Meade (1978) argues in favor of a wealth tax as opposed to an income tax because wealth provides additional utility. In other words, two individuals with the same stream of income should not be taxed the same if one's income comes from wealth and the other's from daily toiling. Income from wealth should be taxed more.

Wealth offers additional utility[17] through the security, the prestige, and the political and social power it provides to its possessor. Wealthy people have the money to bribe (in USA, it is called lobbying) corrupt politicians and media in all developed and less developed countries, to enact laws which provide economic benefits to them. In Greece, wealthy households have the political power to shape public opinion against a wealth tax. Currently, there is not even one Greek mass medium that supports the taxing of real estate. Not a single social group supports it. All oppose the tax, even those who have no real estate property, and regardless of where they lie on the political spectrum, from the far left to the far right.

Wealth possession provides additional economic benefits especially bank financing with favorable terms. In Greece, bank financing of small business and the self-employed is almost impossible unless the borrower possesses wealth, especially real estate property, which is used as collateral. Thus, without wealth it is either impossible to draw a loan from a bank or if it is possible, a higher interest rate must be paid.

The most notable international unsuccessful attempt to implement a tax on wealth was in 1974 when the British Labor party came to power. It was its pre-election promise to implement a wealth tax but it left office without delivering. Glennerster (2012) provides an account of the political bickering using the newly released national archives of that period. He concludes by identifying a number of lessons drawn from this unsuccessful attempt to implement a wealth tax in the UK.

A tax on wealth has been implemented in a number of other countries, including Spain, France, and Italy; but these taxes are in addition to existing taxes, such as VAT, income (profit) tax and social security contributions.[18] They are implemented temporarily to restore fiscal imbalances or to decrease wealth inequality, an argument not made here. A tax on Greek wealth should be levied on a permanent basis because it is efficient, effective, and democratic, while also promoting national and international competitiveness. All other taxes should be abolished.

However, taxing wealth is not an easy ride, especially in Greece. The next section of the paper discusses some of the difficulties in implementing a wealth tax.

17 Chorvat (2006) argues that the only true non-distortionary tax is a tax on utility. Taxing wealth can be a proxy for taxing utility. In other words, it is an indirect utility function based on wealth.

18 See European Commission (2014) for a discussion of various wealth taxes implemented across the European Union.

5 Difficulties in implementing a wealth tax

A careful political, economic, social and technology analysis of the current Greek case will show that a tax on wealth is the only tax that can address corruption and tax evasion. In addition, it will promote economic growth and create more well-paid jobs. However, it is not easy to implement and there is an ongoing debate within the European Union on the merits of a wealth tax (see European Commission 2014: Box 4.2). I summarize below the most important difficulties in implementing a wealth tax.

Political and social resistance

As mentioned above, the economics literature considers a flat tax on wealth (or a tax on ability to pay a tax) as optimal. However, it is recognized that this tax will meet strong political and social resistance. The political aspect of implementing a wealth tax is noted by many studies. Rudnick and Gordon (1996: 10) argue that, "the decision whether to enact a tax or taxes on net wealth or wealth transfer must take into account the country's political, social, and administrative circumstances." Similarly, Boadway et al. (2010: 742) argue that, "to be effective there must be some political consensus on how wealth is taxed."

This is definitely the Greek case: The wealth tax can only become politically and socially acceptable if it is combined with the immediate elimination of all other taxes, particularly VAT and all types of income taxes. By doing so, a wealth tax can get the necessary political support in a parliamentary democracy. This is the only way to battle tax evasion because, as Rudnick and Gordon (1996: 4) state, "A wealth tax base separate from an income tax base can help ensure that taxes not collected on the latter, because of avoidance or evasion, might be collected on the former."

Assessing the true price (value) of wealth

It is claimed that a wealth tax is difficult to implement because the assessment of the real price (value) of wealth, especially real estate property, is cumbersome. In Greece, a small tax on real estate property is based on "objective" (imputed) prices set by the government. Prior to the current economic crisis, the "objective" prices were much lower than the market prices. Since 2010 market prices of real estate property have declined. In some areas (most probably the very rich areas of Athens) the "objective" prices may be higher than the market prices but this might be the result of very low "objective" prices in the first place.

Despite the current criticism in Greece, this is a dilemma only if relative prices of real estate properties have changed, i.e. some properties were hit harder than others. Most probably, house prices have proportionally declined. Reducing "objective" prices to market prices will not affect the amount of tax on each property if the total tax to be collected remains the same. Currently this is close to 3 billion euro. To raise this fixed amount of revenue, if "objective" prices are reduced, the tax rate must accordingly increase.

However, this important problem can be easily sorted out. "Objective" prices can be determined by the sale price of a property and can be adjusted every year. The notary, before preparing the sale contract, publicizes the price and calls everyone who wants to bid for a higher price (say at least 10 percent higher) to do so within 15 days. There is an incentive to reveal the true price of selling. In addition, there will be no incentive to hide the true price since property transfers will not be taxed and all legal fees can be a fixed amount per contract and not proportional to the value of the transferred property.

Wealthy without income

People with wealth may not have the income (liquidity) to pay a wealth tax. A distinction should be made between those who evade taxes by hiding their income and those who pay the full amount of the due tax. Those, who under the current system pay their taxes in full, will, under the new wealth flat tax system, pay less. For them, there will be no liquidity problem any worse than they face under the existing system.

For those who pay no income tax now (presumably they pay part of the current VAT), and who have wealth but no income (assuming that they do not have liquid assets, such as bank deposits), their wealth tax can be paid in installments, which is already common practice in the Greek tax system. Even today, a Greek taxpayer can go to tax authorities and claim liquidity constraints, thus making arrangements to pay in small installments, with up to 100 monthly installments.

Bach et al. (2011) make a similar wealth tax suggestion for Germany. From an economic point of view, taxing the possession of wealth is equivalent to taxing lifetime income and an honest tax payer should be indifferent between the two types of taxes.

A wealth tax will reduce investment and growth

Taxing wealth may reduce savings and investment, and increase consumption. This is only true if a wealth tax is in addition to taxing income and sales. Taxing only wealth with a lump sum tax will have positive economic effects. Investment will increase because profits will not be taxed, although capital stocks as part of wealth will be taxed. Also, the accumulation of wealth will be promoted because wealth inheritance will not be taxed. The proposal here is a revenue-neutral reform of the Greek tax system. Tax revenues will be the same; their source will be different. All revenue will come from a flat tax on private wealth.

A wealth tax affects its distribution

The proposal to tax wealth and only wealth is overall neutral from a distributional point of view, but some people will be affected more than others. This proposal hits hard all those who, throughout their entire economic life, paid no taxes. These segments (particularly the self-employed) of the Greek population possess considerable wealth. Unfortunately for them, they must pay taxes. As Mirrlees et al. (2011: 356) puts it,

> *"Intellectually, the right thing to do is to consider which is the better equilibrium – one in which we are benefiting the self-employed at the expense of everyone else, or one with neutrality between those in different forms of work. Practically, the transition is a challenge."*

This was said for the UK tax system and is even more valid for the Greek tax system with its much higher proportion of self employed.

Despite the above difficulties, the simplification of the Greek tax system is possible and a wealth tax is a way of doing this. The political resistance to a wealth tax will be intense but as the real estate property tax shows, this resistance was not strong enough to abolish it. The tax still exists even though the current coalition government pledged in the pre-election period that they would scrap it. The reason is very simple: this tax is efficient, effective, democratic and, if it becomes the only tax, will promote competitiveness and economic growth.

In 1981, the newly elected socialist government attempted a similar tax but the Minister of National Economy, who suggested the tax, was "decapitated" and the tax was withdrawn because the vested interests of wealthy people in Greece exerted a very strong political resistance.

Today, the technology to implement a wealth tax makes it much easier because all wealth can be electronically audited. This tax will be collected, like the real estate property tax, through electricity bills. This will make the use of Greek tax authorities redundant, which is an additional benefit from a wealth tax implementation.

6 Conclusions

The economic cost of fighting tax evasion is too high in Greece. If the political and social costs are added, then tax compliance is a herculean task. Under these conditions, it is really a puzzle why some Greeks pay taxes. Tax evasion is pervasive among those segments of the population who can hide their income. The self-employed and small businesses systematically conceal their income and employ non-registered workers. They "save" on income tax, VAT and social security contributions.

All these taxes should be abolished not only because they have a high cost of compliance but because they create conditions of unfair competition and production inefficiencies. The lost tax revenue from these sources can be efficiently and effectively replaced by a flat tax on wealth. In Greece, a wealth tax as the only source of government revenue will be democratic. It will also promote the competitiveness necessary to advance economic growth and create well-paid jobs.

References

— Allingham, M. G., and A. Sandmo (1972): Income tax evasion: A theoretical analysis. Journal of Public Economics, 1 (3–4), 323–338.
— Alvaredo, F., A. B. Atkinson, T. Piketty, and E. Saez (2013): The Top 1 Percent in International and Historical Perspective. Journal of Economic Perspectives, 27 (3), 3–20.
— Auerbach, A. J., and K. Hassett (2015): Capital taxation in the twenty-first century. American Economic Review: Papers & Proceedings, 105 (5), 38–42.
— Bach, S., M. Beznoska, and V. Steiner (2011): A wealth tax on the rich to bring down public debt? Revenue and distributional effects of a capital levy. Discussion paper No. 1137. German Institute for Economic Research. Berlin.
— Bame-Aldred, C. W., J. B. Cullen, K. D. Martin, and K. P. Parboteeah (2013): National culture and firm-level tax evasion. Journal of Business Research, 66 (3), 390–396.
— Berger, W., M. Pickhardt, A. Pitsoulis, A. Prinz, and J. Sardà (2014): The hard shadow of the Greek economy: New estimates of the size of the underground economy and its fiscal impact. Applied Economics, 46 (8), 2190–2204.

— Bittencourt, M., R. Gupta, and L. Stander (2014): Tax evasion, financial development and inflation: Theory and empirical evidence. Journal of Banking & Finance, 41 (April), 194–208.
— Boadway, R., E. Chamberlain, and C. Emmerson (2010): Taxation of Wealth and Wealth Transfers in Dimensions of Tax Design. The Mirrlees Review, Institute for Fiscal Studies, Oxford University Press, pp. 737–814. www.ifs.org.uk/uploads/mirrleesreview/dimensions/ch8.pdf
— Boadway, R., and M. Sato (2009): Optimal tax design and enforcement with an informal sector. American Economic Journal: Economic Policy, 1 (1), 1–27.
— Charmes, J. (2012): The informal economy worldwide: Trends and characteristics. The Journal of Applied Economic Research, 6 (2), 103–132.
— Chorvat, T. (2006): Taxing utility. The Journal of Socio-Economics, 35 (1), 1–16.
— Diamond, P., and E. Saez (2011): The case for a progressive tax: From basic research to policy recommendations. Journal of Economic Perspectives, 25 (4), 165–190.
— Eichengreen, B. (1989): The capital levy in theory and practice NBER Working Paper No. 3096.
— European Commission (2013): Europe 2020: Shadow economy and undeclared work. European Commission, Brussels.
— European Commission (2014): Tax Reforms in EU Member States Tax policy challenges for economic growth and fiscal sustainability. European Commission, Brussels.
— Fairfield, T. (2013): Going where the money is: Strategies for taxing economic elites in unequal democracies. World Development, 47 (July), 42–57.
— Feldstein, M. (2012): The Mirrlees Review. Journal of Economic Literature, 50 (3), 781–790.
— Glennerster, H. (2012): Why was a wealth tax for the UK abandoned?: lessons for the policy process and tackling wealth inequality *Journal of Social Policy*, 41 (2), 233–249.
— Gupta, R., and E. Ziramba (2010): Misalignment in the growth-maximizing policies under alternative assumptions of tax evasion. The Journal of Applied Business Research, 26 (3), 69–80.
— Hall, R.E., and A. Rabushka (2007): The Flat Tax. Hoover Institution.
— Hallsworth, M. (2014): The use of field experiments to increase tax compliance. Oxford Review of Economic Policy, 30 (4), 658–679.
— Hallsworth, M., J. List, R. Metcalfe, and I. Vlaev (2014): The behavioralist as tax collector: using natural field experiments to enhance tax compliance. National Bureau of Economic Research Working Paper 20007.
— Hassett, K.A., and A. Mathur (2012): A New Measure of Consumption Inequality. American Enterprise Institute. www.aei.org/wp-content/uploads/2012/06/-a-new-measureof-consumption-inequality_142931647663.pdf.
— Hug, S., and F. Spörri (2011): Referendums, trust, and tax evasion. European Journal of Political Economy, 27 (1), 120–131.
— Kleven, H.J., M.B. Knudsen, C.T. Kreiner, S. Pedersen, and E. Saez (2011): Unwilling or unable to cheat? evidence from a tax audit experiment in Denmark. Econometrica, 79 (3), 651–92.
— Lavoie, R. (2014): Dreaming the impossible dream: is a wealth tax now possible in america? Mimeo. Akron Research Paper No. 14-01.
— Levaggi, R., and F. Menoncin (2012): Tax audits, fines and optimal tax evasion in a dynamic context. Economics Letters, 117 (1), 318–321.

— Mankiw, N. G., M. Weinzierl, and D. Yagan (2009): Optimal taxation in theory and practice Journal of Economic Perspectives, 23 (4), 147–174.
— Mathä, T. Y., A. Porpiglia, and M. Ziegelmeyer (2014): Household wealth in the euro area: The importance of intergenerational transfers, homeownership and house price dynamics. Working Paper Series, No 1690. European Central Bank.
— McDonnell, T. A. (2013): Wealth tax: Options for its implementation in the Republic of Ireland. Nevin Economic Research Institute, NERI WP 2013/No 6. www.nerinstitute.net/download/pdf/neri_wp_no_6_2013_mcdonnell_wealth_tax.pdf
— Meade, J. (1978): The Structure and Reform of Direct Taxation: Report of a Committee chaired by Professor J. E. Meade for the Institute for Fiscal Studies. London, George Allen & Unwin. www.ifs.org.uk/publications/3433.
— Mirrlees, J. A. (1971): An exploration in the theory of optimum income taxation. The Review of Economic Studies, 38 (2), 175–208.
— Mirrlees, J. A., S. Adam, T. Besley, R. Blundell, S. Bond, R. Chote, M. Gammie, P. Johnson, G. Myles, and J. Poterba (2011): The Mirrlees review: Conclusions and recommendations for reform. Fiscal Studies, 32 (3), 331–359.
— Musgrave, R. A., and P. B. Musgrave (1989): Public Finance in Theory and Practice. Fifth Edition. New York, McGraw Hill.
— Papanikos, G. T. (2014a): The Greek economic crisis a class analysis in support of austerity measures. Athens Institute for Education and Research, Athens (in Greek). www.atiner.gr/gtp/2014papbook.pdf
— Papanikos, G. T. (2014b): The Greek labor market, the euro and the current crisis. Singapore Economic Review, 59 (4), S1–S27.
— Persson, T., and G. Tabellini (1994): Representative democracy and capital taxation. Journal of Public Economics, 55 (1), 53–70.
— Piketty, T. (2014): Capital in the twenty-first century. Cambridge, Harvard University Press.
— Piketty, T. (2015): About capital in the twenty-first century. American Economic Review: Papers & Proceedings, 105 (5), 48–53.
— Piketty, T., and G. Zucman (2013): Capital is Back: Wealth-Income Ratios in Rich Countries 1700-010. www.parisschoolofeconomics.com/zucmangabriel/capitalisback/PikettyZucman2013WP.pdf
— Pomeranz, D. (2015): No taxation without information: deterrence and self-enforcement in the value added tax. American Economic Review, 105 (8), 2539–2569.
— Ramsey, F. P. (1927): A contribution to the theory of taxation. Economic Journal, 145 (March), 47–61.
— Rudnick, R. S., and R. K. Gordon (1996): Taxation of wealth. In: Victor Thuronyi (ed.): Tax Law Design and Drafting. Volume 1, Chapter 10. International Monetary Fund. www.imf.org/external/pubs/nft/1998/tlaw/eng/ch10.pdf
— Schneider, F. (2015): Size and development of the shadow economy of 31 European and other OECD countries from 2003 to 2015: Different developments. www.econ.jku.at/members/Schneider/files/publications/2015/ShadEcEurope31.pdf
— Simons, R. (2015): Self-interest: The economist's straightjacket. Harvard Business School, Working Paper 16-045.
— Slemrod, J. (1990): Optimal taxation and optimal tax systems. Journal of Economic Perspectives, 4 (1), 157–178.

— Slemrod, J., M. Blumenthal, and C. Christian (2001): Taxpayer response to an increased probability of audit: Evidence from a controlled experiment in Minnesota. Journal of Public Economic, 79 (3): 455–83.
— Stiglitz, J. E. (2000): Economics of the Public Sector. Third Edition. New York, W. W. Norton & Company, Inc.
— Torgler, B. (2005): Tax Morale and Direct Democracy. European Journal of Political Economy, 21 (2), 525–531.
— Torrini, R. (2005): Cross-country differences in self-employment rates: the role of institutions. Labour Economics, 12 (5), 661–683.
— Yunker, J. (2014): Capital wealth taxation: theory and application. Review of Political Economy, 26 (1), 85–110.

Product Market Reforms in Greece—Unblocking Investments and Exports

KASPAR RICHTER, GABRIELE GIUDICE AND ANGELO COZZI*

Kaspar Richter, European Commission, Brussels, e-mail: Kaspar.Richter@ec.europa.eu
Gabriele Giudice, European Commission, Brussels, e-mail: Gabriele.Giudice@ec.europa.eu
Angelo Cozzi, European Commission, Brussels, e-mail: Angelo.Cozzi@ec.europa.eu

Summary: While Greece's poor record on investment and exports predates the crisis, the deep economic recession has made addressing long-standing weaknesses a priority. This paper takes a closer look at selected structural reforms that are critical for bolstering investments and exports in Greece. We investigate the areas of licensing, competition, professions, land use, and trade facilitation. In all areas significant progress has been made since 2010. However, many reforms are only partially implemented and with delays. Based on the challenges at, and progress since, the outset of the crisis, we chart the way forward in each of the five areas, discussing what needs to be done to improve the patchy reform record, thus unblocking investment and exports for Greece.

→ JEL Classification: J44, K23, L43, O24; O52, R52
→ Keywords: Barriers to competition, business licensing, Greece, land use, structural reforms, trade facilitation

* We are grateful to Declan Costello, Dimitris Loukas and Dimitris Rokos for useful suggestions as well as the anonymous reviewer for insightful comments. The views expressed in this paper are those of the authors and should not be attributed to the European Commission.

1 Introduction

The way out of the crisis in Greece depends critically on a wide range of institutional, economic and social reforms, including making product markets friendlier for investment and exports, as well as making goods and services better and cheaper for consumers. During the economic crisis, companies, lacking financing and customers, downsized or went out of business. This severely curtailed investment and exports in Greece. However, even before the crisis, business investment, both domestic and foreign, and exports were low in Greece. Weak product markets and feeble innovation have held back Greek GDP and productivity growth since the early 1980s (Figure 1 and Figure 2). Greece's predominately small and inward-looking enterprises (Figure 3) were not just poorly equipped to reap the benefits of the European single market and globalisation, but also, in the absence of established export channels, fully exposed to the collapse in domestic demand (Figure 4). Businesses struggled, especially as competitiveness deteriorated in the run-up to the crisis, which contributed to the loss of 30 positions between 2003 and 2007 in the World Economic Forum global competitiveness ranking (Schwab et al. 2007, Sala-i-Martin and Schwab 2004).

Improving competitiveness requires not only lowering wage costs through labour market reforms but also improvements in non-wage competitiveness through product market reforms. The poor record on investment and exports relates to a host of long-term constraints confronting Greek businesses: fragmented and complicated regulations; unpredictable, time-consuming and costly procedures; restrictions to entry and on fees or prices; lack of clear property rights; and a complicated spatial planning system. Such weaknesses explain a significant part of Greece's export gap compared to similar countries in terms of GDP and geographical position. Böwer et al. (2014) estimate that Greece exports about one-third less than what regular international trade patterns suggest. For example, exports of goods and services as percent of GDP were only 33 percent in 2014, compared to 43 percent for the EU.

Figure 1

Growth in Greece lagged behind the EU15 since EU membership in 1981

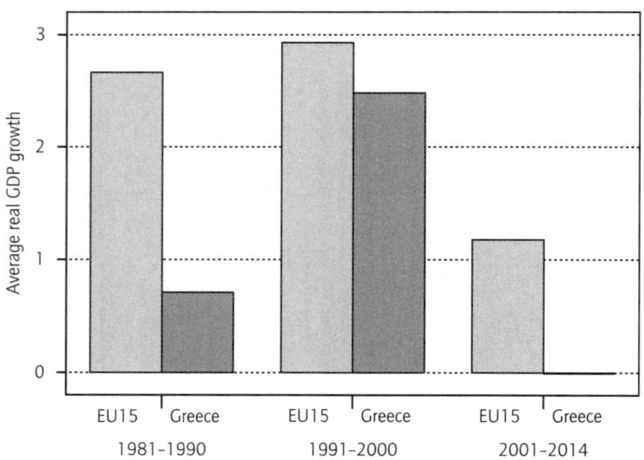

Source: Ameco.

Figure 2

A reason for the weaker growth performance is low total factor productivity growth

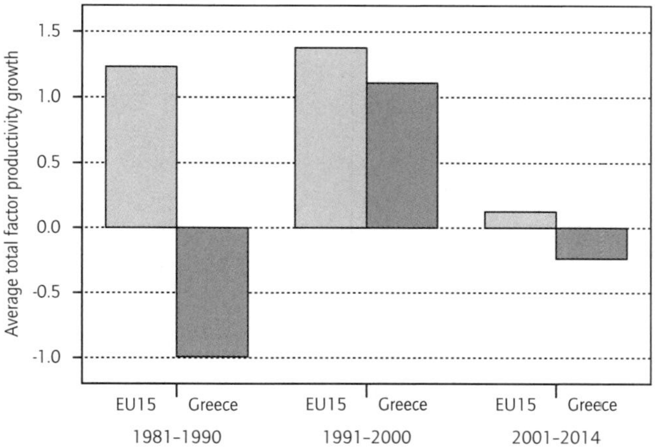

Source: Ameco.

Figure 3

Micro-enterprises in Greece matter more for jobs and value added than in other EU countries

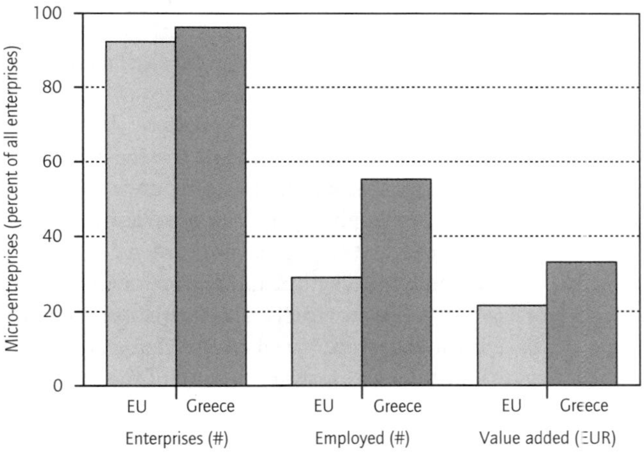

Source: Eurostat.

Since the beginning of the economic adjustment programmes in Greece in May 2010, Greece has been working towards, among others, removing barriers to competition, reducing the administrative burden on businesses, opening regulated professions and improving land management. Contrary to perceptions that the programme was centred only on fiscal adjustment and financial

Figure 4

During the crisis, exports held up much better than domestic demand in Greece

2014

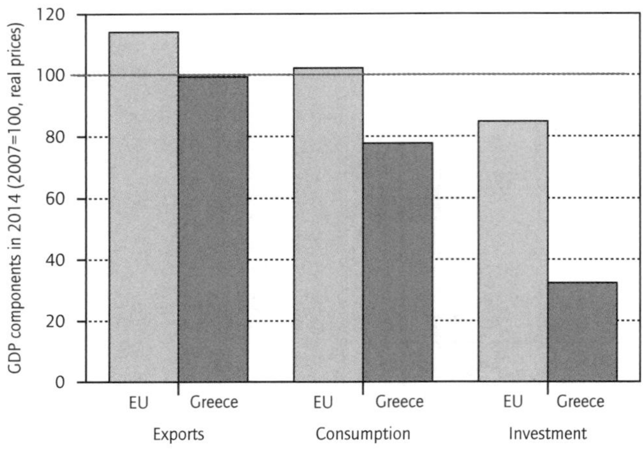

Source: Eurostat.

stabilisation, it included from the outset a strong focus on product market and other structural reforms. Over time, the structural reform pillar of the programmes became more detailed to address delays in implementation in the face of strong vested interests, low social capital and weak administrative capacity.

In this paper, we take a closer look at selected product market reforms in Greece critical for bolstering economic activity. We will focus on five areas affecting the business environment in which investments and exports take place: licensing, competition, professions, land use, and trade facilitation. Since data tracking structural reforms in these areas are rare, we draw on a broad range of quantitative and qualitative evidence both from within and outside of Greece. For key reform measures in each area, the paper assesses whether structural reforms were partially or fully implemented and whether results have been delivered. Based on the challenges at the outset of the crisis and the evident progress, we chart the way forward in each of the five areas, discussing what needs to be done to improve the patchy reform record, thus unblocking investment and exports for Greece.

2 Licensing

At the onset of the crisis, licensing regulations in Greece were a principle bottleneck for investment. Numerous and fragmented regulations as well as complicated and time-consuming procedures made the licensing process both costly and highly uncertain for businesses. This red tape led to significant administrative burdens, facilitated corruption, and, most importantly, discouraged investors. It contributed to the low pre-crisis levels of business investment and FDI inflows into Greece as compared to other European countries (Figure 5 and Figure 6).

In response to the crisis, improving business licensing to encourage investment was a priority of the Greek government. To facilitate the creation of new businesses, one of the first actions was to establish a one-stop shop approach in 2010, following the example of countries such as Austria and the Netherlands. In April 2011, the General Electronic Commercial Registry (GEMI) was launched, which is a unified company registration that allows for the electronic processing of business registration documents (European Commission, 2014). GEMI is connected to 3,200 notary offices and about 60 chambers of commerce that provide consultation and serve as one-stop shop for businesses. Furthermore, in 2012 a new capital company type (IKE) without minimum capital requirement was created in order to facilitate the establishment of new businesses.

In an effort to attract large scale public and private investments, the fast track licensing was introduced in 2010 and enhanced in 2013 for investments exceeding certain value or job creation thresholds. It provides an expedited licensing procedure for strategic investments facilitated by Enterprise Greece, the investment and trade promotion agency, under the guidance of the Ministry of Economy. Projects are approved by a specialised inter-ministerial committee for strategic investments. According to Enterprise Greece, 10 projects have been approved under the fast track mechanism, including five related to solar parks and three to tourism. These projects are estimated to have created more than 3,000 jobs.

For the bulk of Greek companies, the simplification of standard licensing procedures is a priority, as they are too small to benefit from fast-track procedures. In 2011, an initial simplification of licensing procedures in the manufacturing sector and for business parks was adopted, although it took up to 2014 before these changes were implemented. In 2014, a fundamental overhaul of

Figure 5

Business investment in Greece was low already before the crisis

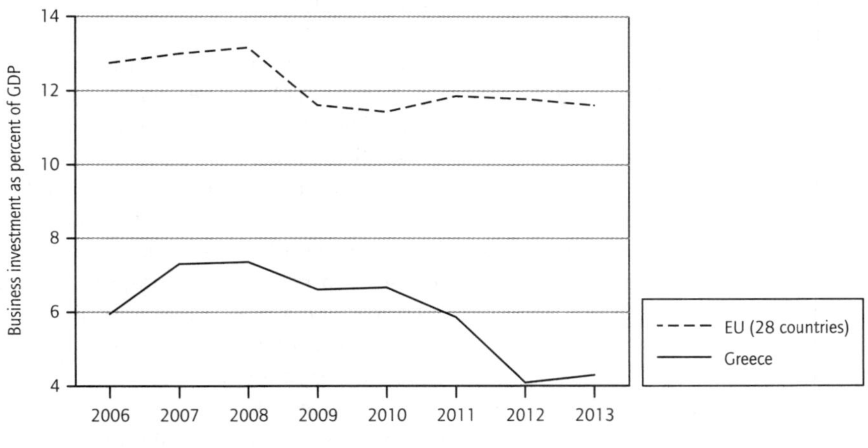

Source: Eurostat.

Figure 6

FDI inflows to Greece were low already before the crisis

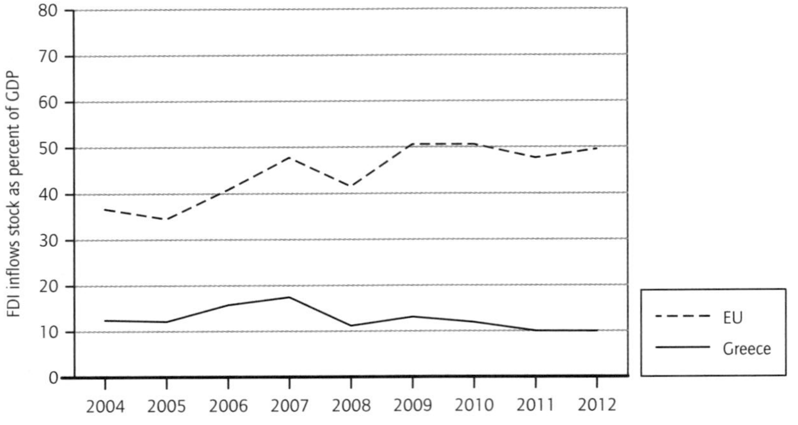

Source: Eurostat.

the system was launched with support of the World Bank. It aims to create an integrated licensing framework where the licensing procedure differs according to the risks involved in an economic activity. While high risk categories continue to rely on an the established *ex ante* permit system, low and medium risk categories are moved to a system of self-declaration where *ex post* assessments of compliance are outsourced to accredited third parties. On this basis, in late 2014, the authorities simplified 103 licenses for the operation of low-risk economic activities in the industrial sector and eliminated horizontal licensing requirements linked to fire safety.

Another important concern for investors were strict requirements on environmental licensing. Before the crisis, environmental licensing was the most time consuming of all licensing procedures and did not actually result in environmental protection (Ministry for the Environment, Energy and Climate Change 2013). The major problem was the disproportionate amount of project and activity types that required the submission and evaluation of environmental licensing files. It exceeded by far the standards prescribed by the relevant 2011 EU Directive, creating an unnecessary administrative burden for private businesses and public administration. Table 1 shows the annual average numbers of environmental licensing case-files in 11 EU countries from 2005 to 2009. As can be seen, the number of environmental licensing cases per million inhabitants in Greece was over 30 times than the number in France, the country with the second most environmental licensing cases, and was more than 600 times than the number in Austria. Furthermore, particularly for larger projects with a potentially significant impact on the environment, the time needed for approval often exceeded 20 months, sometimes taking up to 42 months. For an investment project of 1 million euro in the mining sector, a six-month delay in the environmental permitting process is estimated to lead to opportunity costs of 65,000 euro (SEV 2014). A large part of these delays was due to compulsory preliminary impact assessments, as well as the final approval through a Joint Ministerial Decision, often by up to 4 Ministers. Finally, the strong focus of administrative capacities on *ex ante* environmental assessment studies, given the limited

Table 1

Before the reform, the number of environmental licensing cases-files in Greece exceeded by far the numbers of other EU countries

Member State	Average number of Environmental Licensing Cases-Files/year	Population	Annual number of Environmental Licensing Cases-Files/million residents	GNP in billion euro	Annual number of Environmental Licensing Cases-Files/billion euro
Austria	23	8,375,290	3	284.4	0,09
UK	334	62,008,048	5	1,696.6	0,20
Finland	38	5,351,427	7	180.3	0,21
Germany	1,000	81,802,257	12	2,498.8	0,40
Hungary	152	10,014,324	15	98.4	1,54
Belgium	183	10,839,905	17	352.9	0,52
Denmark	125	5,529,449	23	234.0	0,53
Spain	1,054	45,989,016	23	1,062.6	0,99
Poland	2,200	38,167,329	58	354.3	6,21
France	3,867	64,716,310	60	1,932.8	2,00
Greece	21,534	11,305,118	1,902	230.2	93,4

Source: Ministry for the Environment, Energy and Climate Change (2013).

public budget, led to a lack of compliance control during the operation phase of the projects, the stage when actual environmental harm is most likely to occur.

In 2011, the Greek legislators radically simplified the environmental licensing procedures for a wide range of projects and activities, addressing most of the problems outlined above. Most importantly, following common EU practice, it introduced a new category of projects, abolishing the requirement to present an environmental report for a many projects with an usually small environmental impact. Furthermore, while preliminary assessment reports used to be compulsory, with the reform they became optional and the validity of previous environmental conditions approvals was prolonged to 10 years. Therefore, as seen in Table 2, the number of assessment reports decreased almost 90 percent in 2012. Additional reform measures included a reduction of time delays, a standardization of the required contents of assessment reports, a plan to set up a digital environmental registry, as well as increasing the efficiency of compliance controls and increasing the number of inspections. As far as economic benefits are concerned, the Greek Ministry of Environment, Energy and Climate Change estimates that the reduction of administrative burden leads to total savings of around 85 million euro per year, more than half of it benefitting the private sector.

Thanks to such licensing and business registration reforms, the ranking of Greece in the World Bank Doing Business report has improved significantly (Figure 7). For starting a business, Greece reduced the gap to the best performance from 29 percent in 2010 to 9 percent in 2015 (World Bank 2015). In 2013, Greece recorded the largest improvement in this category of any country since the Doing Business ranking was started (World Bank 2013). Relatedly, the time needed to set up a business was reduced significantly for the new capital company type IKE between 2012

Table 2

The number of environmental licensing case-files decreased significantly after the implementation of Law 4014/2011

Assessment type	Number of assessment reports		
	2005-2009 average	2012	Reduction in percent
Cases-Files of DAEC renewal/ amendment	1,589	769	51.6
Environmental Impact Assessment reports (EIA)	3,807	1,540	59.5
Preliminary Assessment reports	2,816	66	97.7
Environmental reports with less significant environmental impact	13,322	0	100.0
Total	21,534	2,375	89.0

Source: Ministry for the Environment, Energy and Climate Change (2013).

and 2015, as seen in Figure 8. Furthermore, IKE has become increasingly popular, representing close to three in four of newly capital companies in 2014 (Figure 9).

However, even though there has been significant progress, much remains to be done to make these reforms fully operational and lift Greece from the bottom to top ranks of business friendliness among EU countries. For the investment and environmental licensing reforms, key outstanding measures include the following:

- Existing provisions for investment licensing must be streamlined based on a careful screening in line with the 2014 law. These legislative reforms require parallel multi-year efforts in other areas, such as the development of certified business-to-business service providers that can act as consultants to investors and as auditors for compliance; the reorganization of the public administration involved in training, accreditation procedures and evaluations; and the development of the IT infrastructure.

- Important parts of the 2011 environmental licensing legislation still require implementation (OECD 2014). This includes the introduction of private reviewers for environmental impact assessments and the drafting of environmental permits. This reform will speed up the process and allow civil servants to focus on the most important projects. In addition, the online environmental-licensing platform based on a digital environmental registry needs to be made operational.

Figure 7

The doing business distance-to-frontier score (frontier = 100) increased significantly in most areas over the last 5 years

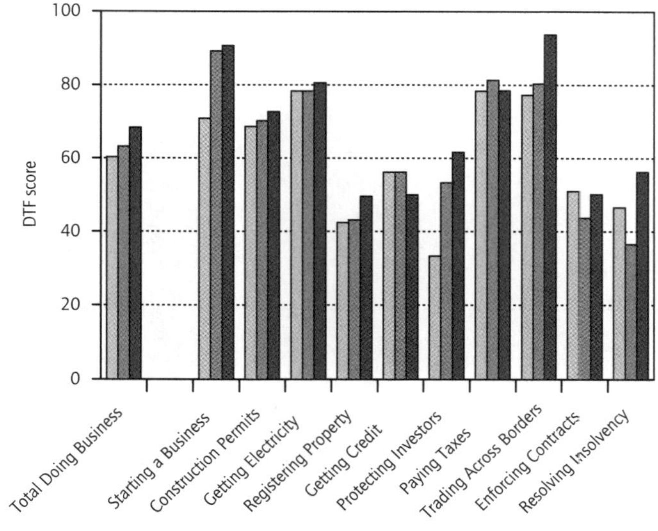

Source: World Bank.

Figure 8

The average duration of business registration of the new capital company type "IKE" decreased substantially since its introduction in 2012

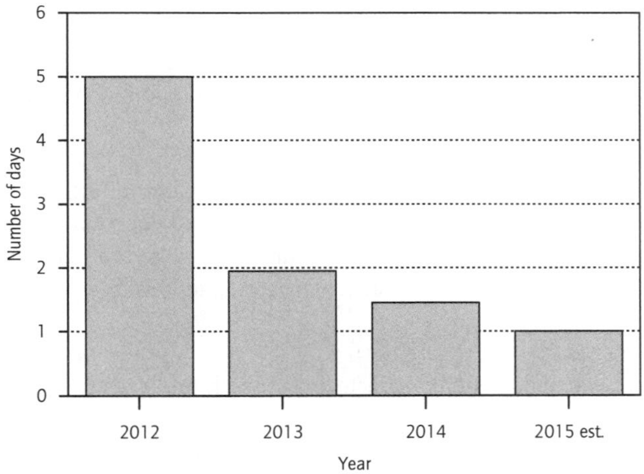

Source: GEMI, Ministry of Development (2015).

Figure 9

Distribution of new capital companies in 2014

Private Companies (IKE) seem to be an attractive alternative to the regular Limited Liability Company (LTD) and the Societe Anonyme (SA)

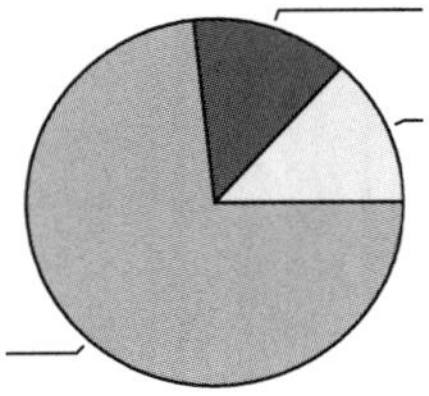

Source: GEMI, Ministry of Development (2015).

3 Competition

Legislative barriers to competition, often adopted under the influence of rent-seeking firms (Mitsopoulos and Pelagidis 2009), have contributed in Greece to inefficient production and high consumer prices. Fostering competition and lowering prices are a key part of the economic adjustment in Greece. For consumers, this makes the pay check last longer and widens their choice. As prices fall, more people can afford the products, overall demand increases and well-run businesses take a bigger slice of the market, allowing them to grow and expand, including to foreign markets.

Various regulatory restrictions for competition have been abolished in Greece with the support of the OECD and the Hellenic Competition Commission. Some of the reforms, such as the deregulation of Sunday trade and sales of over-the-counter medicines, are following general liberalization trends across European and OECD countries, while other reforms, such as lifting the 5 day shelf life restriction for fresh milk removed restrictions specific to Greece. In the following, we discuss the deregulation efforts for Sunday trade, fresh milk and baby milk to illustrate the economic reasoning and implementation difficulties of such reforms.

Regulations on Sunday trade vary significantly across European countries. For example, Sunday trading is completely liberalized in Sweden, generally forbidden in Norway, and depends on the city or region in France and Germany, respectively. In Greece, Sunday trade was forbidden for all retailers except for specific authorised shops such as restaurants, cafes, and kiosks, as well as shops located in certain touristic areas.

The restriction of Sunday trading has several detrimental effects on competition. It restricts consumer choice, puts students and others willing to work on Sundays at a disadvantage, and adds to congestion. The economic literature on liberalization of Sunday trade in other countries points toward a positive effect on employment (Pilat 1997, Goos 2004), mainly due to an increase in the number of workers employed instead of hours worked (Gradus 1996, Skuterud 2005). The effect on sales volumes is also positive (Goos 2004, Prodromidis, Petralias and Petros 2012) or neutral (Reddy 2012), while it is ambiguous for market concentration and prices (Reddy 2012, Inderst and Irmen 2005), perhaps as it depends on a range of other factors. For Greece, the OECD estimated that deregulating Sunday trading hours would lead to around 30,000 new jobs and 2.5 billion euro of additional annual expenditures (OECD 2014b). Among the reforms considered and quantified by the OECD, this would have, by far, the largest effect.

Despite the expectation of positive economic effects, including on job creation, the efforts to liberalise Sunday trading in Greece were met with resistance (Eurofound 2015): employees feared uncontrolled flexibility and employers a detrimental effect on small retailers.

Notwithstanding such resistance, in 2013 the authorities allowed shops of all sizes to open on 7 Sundays each year. In addition, for small shops, regional administrations can decide whether to allow trading on additional Sundays. In July 2014, Sunday trade was expanded to all commercial shops in three touristic areas for a one year pilot exercise that could possibly followed by a general liberalisation throughout the country. However, in autumn 2014, the Council of State, Greece's supreme administrative court, suspended temporarily this pilot, and the final verdict, as of December 2015, is still pending.

While many EU countries have rules for Sunday trading, Greece had special regulations for the milk sector that reduced competition, restricted consumer choice, and increased consumer prices. In Greece, there was a unique distinction of milk based on pasteurization temperatures that had implications on whether it was marketable as "fresh" or not. Such fresh milk had a fixed shelf-life of five days, in contrast to an average shelf life of around 10 days of comparable milk across Europe (OECD 2014b). For all other types of milk or dairy products, shelf life was at the discretion of manufacturers, as is common throughout Europe, including for fresh milk. This specific restriction in Greece therefore harmed competition in several ways. In particular, Greek milk producers were protected from foreign milk imports; consumer choice in some areas was restricted; small, remote producers were put at a competitive disadvantage as they did not have enough time to supply urban centres; and the short shelf-life led to excessive logistic costs of collection and return of expired products. As a result of these restrictions, producer prices and retail prices of fresh milk were around 35 percent higher in Greece than the EU average between 2008 and 2012. The OECD estimated a consumer benefit of 33 million euro with the abolition of the five day restriction (OECD 2014b).

Perhaps due to the resistance of the local milk producers supplying urban centres, in April 2014, the Greek government introduced a marginal reform: it increased the shelf-life of fresh pasteurized milk from 5 to 7 days, while at the same time introducing an additional definition for milk packaged within 24 hours of milking and a shelf-life of two days. Data from the price observatory of the Ministry of Economy suggests that this measure failed to bring down prices as of spring 2015. In August 2015, the government abolished the differentiation of milk based on pasteurisation procedures and the associated shelf life restriction in line with other EU countries. While it is too early to assess the impact of this measure, this example illustrates how sometimes the interests of the few can significantly delay reforms for the potential benefit of the many.

A related product group—milk formulas for infants (0 to 6 months)—was subject to a different type of restriction, namely the prohibition of sales through all retail channels except pharmacies. In 2011, however, the Hellenic Competition Commission (HCC) argued that this prohibition was unjustified as it limited price and distribution competition. The HCC pointed out that baby milk prices in Greece were higher than in other EU countries and such differences did not exist for the freely sold milk formulas for older infants. Since the composition, marketing, and advertising

Figure 10

Product market regulations eased in the last 15 years but remain below EU average

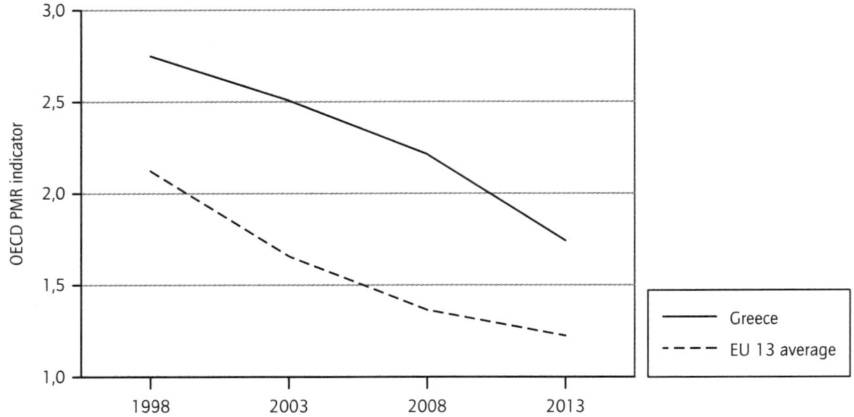

Source: OECD, EU 13 refers to countries with available data in 1998.

of baby milk formulas is already covered by EU legislation, the potential additional benefits of restricting the retail distribution channel on infant health and the promotion of breastfeeding did not outweigh its anticompetitive effects. Following the HCC opinion, the prohibition was lifted in January 2012. Prices were 12 percent lower in supermarkets in May 2012 than in pharmacies in March 2011.

In order to build on the improvements since the onset of the crisis (Figure 10), additional reforms are needed to strengthen competition in Greece.

- There still are several regulatory barriers in many sectors that need to be lifted. This includes, among others, the sectors of beverages and petroleum manufacturing (OECD 2015) and of wholesale trade, construction, e-commerce and manufacturing where assessments will be forthcoming.

- Steps are under way to strengthen the capacity of the Hellenic Competition Commission to advocate reforms in favour of a level-playing field for markets participants. This would also ensure that advocacy efforts do not come at the expense of the enforcement of competition rules.

4 Professions

In the late 2000s, closed professions were another source of large rents and economic inefficiencies. While some regulations on professional services are needed for consumer protection, the restrictions in Greece were among the most stringent among EU and OECD countries. This curbed competition, kept firm sizes small and held back innovation. Strict regulations also translated into large mark-ups and high prices for professional services, including accountants, architects, customs brokers, dockworkers, engineers, lawyers, notaries, and others. While professional services represented only around 2½ percent of output and 7 percent of employment, they have important spill-over effects across the whole economy, notably, by increasing the transaction costs of firms and lowering the purchasing power of consumers. The Greek research institute IOBE calculated that the deregulation of a number of services in Greece could yield GDP gains of over 10 percent in the long-term (IOBE 2010). Such reforms could also help in burden sharing of the costs of adjustment by reducing rents of well-off vested interests and lowering prices.

The reform of regulated professions proceeded in stages and remains incomplete. The initial step was the adoption of framework legislation in early 2011 to establish the principle of professional freedom. The legislative changes abolished in principle, among others, fixed prices or compulsory minimum fees and the requirement for an administrative license to practice a profession, substituting instead a simple notification accompanied by the necessary supporting credentials.

Despite of these sweeping changes, the impact of the reform was delayed for a number of reasons. Initially, the scope of the law was not specified, so it was unclear to which professions the provisions of the law would apply. The scope of the law was provided subsequently in spring 2013, with the government publishing the list of the 150 professions falling under the provisions of the law in July 2013.

In addition, while the law established a general principle of professional freedom, it did not directly abolish each of the unnecessary restrictions in force. As a result, the legal situation was uncertain until such restrictions were explicitly revoked on the basis of a thorough screening of the existing legislation.

The 2011 law also provided for a 4-month period during which restrictions that are justified on public policy grounds, either by addressing market failures, or pursuing non-economic objectives, could be reinstated by decree. Professional associations responded with requests for derogations, although often with delays. The government submitted these requests to the Hellenic Competition Commission for opinion in order to ensure that the reinstatement of restrictions was limited to public interest cases only, as envisaged by the legislation. Based on the opinion of the Hellenic Competition Commission, the government then revised the relevant regulations. While this process ran its course as foreseen, the timeline proved to be too ambitious. The Hellenic Competition Commission provided opinions on requests of derogation throughout 2012, and by end 2013, some regulations still needed to be adjusted in line with these opinions.

In addition to the general part, the law also had a specific part. This part focused on high economic impact professions, namely notaries, lawyers and law firms, engineers and auditors. In addition, separate laws dealt with pharmacists, technical professions, and trucks and transportation companies. The liberalisation of these professions in the 2011 laws was partial. Additional reforms were needed to open up these professions further, such as through the adoption of the code of lawyers in September 2013.

More reforms followed in 2014, when steps were taken to liberalise other professions and services, including actuaries, chartered valuers, electricians, geo-technicians, one-day clinics, and the sales of plant-protecting material, fertilisers and pesticides. Furthermore, following the opinion of the Hellenic Competition Commission, the government took steps to remove unjustified or disproportionate activities reserved to qualified professionals of engineers, architects, geologists and land surveyors. In summer 2015, the authorities broadened the geographic area in which court bailiffs can be active and clarified the criteria for the determination of court bailiffs' fees. In addition, in order to support the recovery in the housing market, the authorities reduced the fee of notary acts for property transactions up to 120,000 euro from 1 percent to 0.8 percent.

International comparisons confirm the reform progress in recent years. The professional services regulation index of the OECD assesses legal restrictions for four professions. According to this index, the regulations of professional services were significantly loosened between 2008 and 2013, although legal professions remain highly regulated.

Building on work in 2012, the Centre of Planning and Economic Research (KEPE), a research institute of the Ministry of Development, assessed in July 2013 the liberalisation of 20 professions under the 2011 law (KEPE 2013). A key contribution of this report was to apply the OECD methodology in order to measure regulations for these 20 professions. The main finding was that the reforms liberalised professions substantially. The regulation index, which ranges from zero (no restriction) to 12 (maximum restrictions) declined on average from 5.8 before the reform to 2.3 after the reforms. As a result, 74 percent of the restrictions of the 20 professions were abolished. For non-scientific professions, the share went up to 83 percent. However, this assessment focused on changes in primary legislation only and did not assess whether the legal changes were effectively applied in practice and whether the remaining restrictions are justified or proportional for safeguarding public interest.

Figure 11

The producer prices for key business services decreased significantly between 2010 and 2014

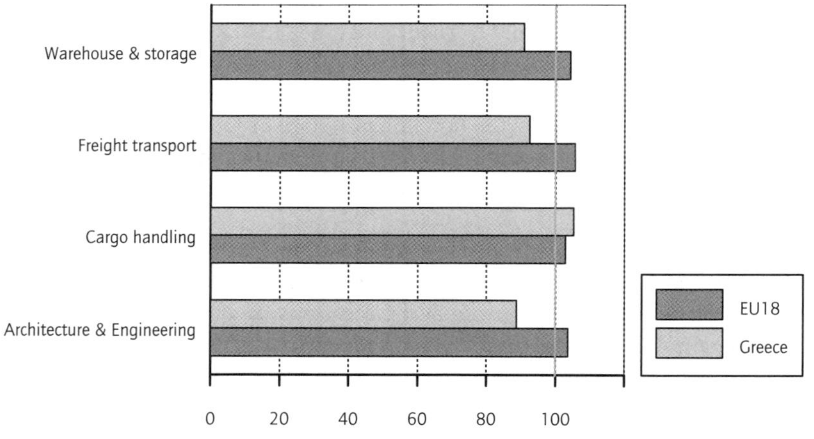

Source: Eurostat.

The KEPE report also looked at prices for professional services. The evidence was inconclusive: there was no clear indication that more open professions performed better on price changes; or that the 20 professions performed better than other professions. This could be because the regulation index might not capture well changes in *de facto* liberalisation, and the liberalisation efforts to date remain work in progress. However, comparisons of certain professional services with the euro area suggest price reductions (Figure 11). For example, prices of business services for architecture and engineering, freight transport, as well as warehouse and storage declined noticeably between 2010 and the last quarter of 2014, while prices for cargo handling increased moderately. By contrast, prices in the euro area increased across all four categories over the same period. Clearly, this is only indicative evidence as it is difficult to disentangle the price effects of the opening of professions from changes in the level and composition of demand.

Finally, the Ministry of Finance has compiled monitoring indicators for the liberalisation of some 20 professions, including changes in the number of professionals since 2011 (Table 3). The number increased for most professions, despite the economic crisis, indicating that reforms helped to open access for new professionals, although other factors also could have played a role, such as for energy inspectors (changes in energy regulations for buildings) and tax accountants (move toward electronic transactions).

Table 3

The number of professionals increased in many areas despite the economic downturn

	2011	2012	2013	2014
Lawyers	42,025	41,861	42,022	42,052
Law Firms	81	86	528	558
Pharmacies	10,223	10,412	10,516	10,547
Auditors	983	1,050	1,037	1,040
Audit firms	28	39	42	45
Accountants and tax consultants	66,072	68,212	71,094	74,644
Energy inspectors of buildings	5364,	8,327	9,608	12,625
Energy inspectors of heating systems	3,506	5,740	1,673	2,347
Energy inspectors of air conditioning systems	3,376	5,555	1,286	1,785
Stevedores			1,511	3,610
Travel agents	4,105	4,079	4,328	4,650
Tourist guides	1,904	1,915	1,997	2,119
Private labour consultancy offices	95	91	91	93
Custom brokers	2,256	2,115	2,629	2,686
Real estate agents	5,050	4,986	5,053	4,924
Actuaries	74	77	82	82
Chartered valuers		11	217	335
Geo-technicians (agronomists)	19,597	19,952	20,241	20,768

Note: 2012, 2013 and 2014 refer to the fourth quarter.
Source: Ministry of Finance (2015).

Greece has advanced in the liberalisation of profession as confirmed by the improvement of professional services indicators and the increase in the number of professionals for some key professions. However, the liberalisation was uneven across professions. Further progress will depend on tackling remaining rigidities and monitoring the effectiveness of reforms to identify needs for further adjustments. One example in this regard is the engineering profession. For electricians and mechanical engineers, 2014 legislation in principle opened market access but there are concerns that the law is not leading to changes in actual practice. For civil engineers, architects, geologists and land surveyors, the 2014 law provided for a presidential decree for activities in complex technical projects, which still needs to be issued.

5 Land use

Good governance of land is crucial for property rights, economic activity and social cohesion. This requires a clear record of the current land use and land rights. As the only EU country without a computerised nationwide land registry, an important priority for Greece is the completion of such a land registry by 2020.

While Greece set up a system of land registries in 1853 (Tzinieri 2015), this person-based deeds system does not allow for tracking down property by location. In 1995, the national cadastral project was launched with the objective of creating a digitalised and property-based deeds system that links each property title with detailed legal and technical information, including ownership and location, in order to guarantee property rights and facilitate property transfers. Among the 37 countries that computerized their land registries between 2011 and 2015, the time required to register property fell by almost two-fifths (World Bank 2015).

In 2013, in order to accelerate the completion of the cadastre, the authorities adopted a law clarifying the political and administrative responsibilities for the cadastral project, allowing for the setting up of new operational cadastral offices, reducing the period of appeals, and making available the cadastral data to the Ministry of Finance for taxation purposes.

However, progress in tendering and completing the project remains limited. After four generations of cadastral surveys, the registration of titles and cadastral maps are complete and operational for around one-fourth of the total number of titles, covering about 7 percent of the country.

The mapping of the forest land is completed for over one-fifth of the territory, although only less than 1 percent of the forestry maps are legally certified. The production of forestry maps is crucial in view of Constitutional provisions that lead to a presumption of public ownership of forest land, even in urban fringes where forests have given way to urban settlements with direct or implicit approval of public authorities. By contrast, across the European Union, about three-fifths of forests are in private ownership (European Environmental Agency 2015).

Improvements in three areas are crucial for the success of the cadastral and forestry mapping:

- The Greek agency in charge of the creation and management of the cadastre needs adequate administrative and financial independence to manage efficiently large mapping projects. The company should continue to move toward a project management culture, with a focus on efficient tender design and procedures in order to save time and money in awarding cadastre projects.

- As the new cadastral and forestry maps are being completed, the current system of close to 400 land registry offices must be transformed into a system of 16 cadastral offices under the Ministry of Environment. The first two modern cadastral offices in Attica and Thessaloniki opened in 2014 and are fully operational.

- In order to support land management and make better use of available information, government agencies have to integrate electronically information on property titles and property transactions with geocoded data on archaeological sites, industrial development, spatial plans, forestry land, coastal zones, protected areas and public property.

The absence of a fully operational cadastre is only one factor in the weaknesses of Greek land administration. Another are ineffective spatial policies, which have given rise to problems such as construction without prior planning in urban fringes, along the coast and on islands; a lack of communal and green space in urban areas; the need for reforestation of degraded forestlands; as well as a fragmented, costly and time-consuming planning system (OECD 2009).

In 2014, the land use framework was improved in three aspects. Spatial planning was rationalized by halving the number of planning levels, more equalized between national, regional and local levels, thus facilitating strategic investment and privatisation, and devolving powers to local levels to modify existing plans in line with economic needs. In addition, forestry legislation streamlined the procedure for characterising a piece of land as forest and simplified investments while aligning safeguards with the environmental licensing law. Finally, legislation defining coastal zones was adopted.

More steps are needed to make these reforms effective. First, implementing legislation on the spatial and forestry laws remains to be adopted. This includes, among others, the guidelines and the procedures of the new spatial plans and the scientific criteria for the definition of forests and forest land in line with Constitutional provisions. Second, legislation to clarify the uses of coastal zones and to tackle the issue of illegally occupied properties remains pending. Finally, administrative capacity has to be strengthened in order to implement land use legislation coherently.

6 Trade facilitation

While trade openness is a hallmark of many countries in the European Union, Greece is a fairly closed economy. EU member states have integrated with their neighbours and other regions in the world through trade in goods and services, thereby supporting economic growth and convergence. However, despite strong reliance on tourism and maritime services, Greece has lagged behind other EU countries in trade integration, which has reduced the benefits of the single market and globalisation. Facilitating exports is important for avoiding the emergence of external imbalances once growth returns and imports start picking up.

Recognising the need to simplify administrative procedures and lower the time and costs for exporters, in October 2012 Greece adopted a national trade facilitation strategy. It foresees a roadmap with 25 actions to streamline pre-customs procedures, set up a national single window for exports and overhaul customs procedures. Three years after the adoption of the strategy, progress is uneven.

There has been some limited improvement of pre-customs procedures and the national single window. Using business process analysis (UNESCAP/UNECE 2012), the authorities have analysed export procedures, including procedural, regulatory and documentary requirements, for seven products (kiwi, feta cheese, olive oil, cosmetics, canned peaches, aluminium frames, and metallic pipes). The results are the basis for simplifications of these requirements. In addition, the authorities have screened national legislation of key export product for the main countries of destination with a view to simplify requirements. For fresh fruits and vegetables, the authorities have enrolled more than 20 exporters in the authorised trader scheme and automated risk-based controls. Regarding the national single window, the authorities have set up an electronic platform for customs and taken initial steps to link this system with the corresponding platform of the Ministry of Agriculture for fresh fruits and vegetables.

Reforms have advanced more with regard to customs. Following the advice of the World Customs Organization, export procedures have been substantially revamped. Key measures include the streamlining of the export clearance process (such as allowing the presentation of goods at other appointed locations than the Customs office and requesting supporting documents only when declarations are selected for controls), the automatic clearance of low risk declarations with a timer functionality, the implementation of an e-payment system and the standardisation of customs fees.

The World Bank's Doing Business ranking confirms the improvement in trade facilitation. Greece reduced the gap to the best performance from 23 percent in 2011 to only 6 percent in 2015 in trading across borders. Out of 189 countries, Greece ranks 27th in 2015 on trading across borders, the best performance for Greece among the 10 topics measured by the Doing Business ranking. Indicators of the Greek customs validate the progress. Export clearance steps were cut from about 9 to 11 to 2 to 3. And while almost all export declarations were controlled before the reforms, during the first half of 2015, only one in twenty declarations were controlled using a risk based approach.

Despite these achievements, more progress is needed in key areas:

- The business process analysis and the screening of national legislation for key commodities and destination countries must be translated into actual simplifications in line with good EU practices. These advances would also help toward setting-up a national single window through the creation of an integrated electronic platform of customs and relevant government agencies that would enable traders to interact paperless through a single window with authorities, and thereby avoid unnecessary delays and costs in cross-border movement of goods and services.

- Much of the reform effort in Greece focused on exports. Similar improvements are ongoing for imports, including an electronic clearance process and risk-based controls. For example, while virtually all import declarations were controlled in early 2014, by mid-2015 only one in three declarations were controlled on an at risk-basis.

- The full implementation of an electronic platform, the streamlining of customs procedures, a renewed emphasis on anti-smuggling, and a commitment to reinforce independence requires a reorganisation of the customs administration. Based on a strategy adopted in late 2014, the customs administration is, among others, in the process of strengthening the role of regional offices in supervising and controlling frontline customs offices, redesigning the workflow for customs procedures, aligning skills and job profiles, and building up *ex post* audit capacities.

- The facilitation of trade needs to go hand in hand with the promotion of exports and attraction of foreign direct investment. A first step was the 2014 creation of Enterprise Greece with the dual mandate of both export and investment promotion.

7 Conclusion

Faced with a deep structural economic crisis, Greece has launched a wide set of reforms to attract investment and generate exports, often facing stark resistance from vested interests. Some reforms are yielding results: selected investment and environmental licensing procedures have been streamlined, barriers to competition have been removed, for example in the retail sector, access to and exercise of various professions has become easier, the cadastral agency has strengthened its capacity, land use legislation has been modernised, and customs procedures have been rationalised. These are only some of the achievements. Their full economic benefit will only become visible once the economic recovery is solidly under way.

However, the accomplishments are matched by the remaining challenges. While international comparisons suggest that Greece has improved its business environment markedly since the crisis, it remains behind EU averages. Many reforms are only partially implemented and with delays. Much remains to be done in all five areas discussed in the paper. This includes, among others, the reform of investment licensing, the removal of barriers to competition in the wholesale and construction sectors, the opening of the engineering profession, the completion of the cadastral and forestry mapping, and the setting-up of a national single windows for exports. This is likely to require a sustained effort for years to come.

Progress is needed across these domains to eliminate bottlenecks. For example, investment is held back not just by complicated licensing procedures but also by a fragmented spatial planning system. Exports rely not only on efficient customs procedures but also on a friendly business environment for traders to expand production. And in view of the predominance of micro enterprises in Greece, a fast track approach for large companies is not enough. Restrictions must also be lifted for small businesses.

Furthermore, beyond the five areas presented in the paper, other factors are critical for a sustainable economic recovery. This includes a stable financial sector, a broad-based and equitable tax system, an efficient judicial system, a well-run public administration and an adequately regulated energy sector.

Five ingredients are critical for these reforms to succeed. As the remaining challenges remain large, the approach has to be comprehensive. This also helps to limit concessions to vested interest groups (Mitsopoulos and Pelagidis 2009). After more than five years of difficult adjustments, persistence in the reform effort tailored to country circumstances is needed to see through the required changes. Central coordination of the reform agenda is crucial as most reforms require multiple ministries or agencies to act. Implementation support is essential. Legislative changes need to translate into the administrative and operational changes on the ground that will help investors and exporters, whether small or large, to prosper. Finally, monitoring and evaluation is important to continuously improve the design and implementation of such reforms.

References

- Böwer, U., V. Michou, and U. Christoph (2014): The Puzzle of the Missing Greek Exports. European Economy – Economic Papers 518. European Commission, Brussels.
- Eurofound (2015): Greece: Changes to shop opening hours and working time. www.eurofound.europa.eu/printpdf/observatories/eurwork/articles/working-conditions-industrial-relations/greece-changes-to-shop-opening-hours-and-working-time (retrieved on 22.10.2015).
- European Commission (2014): The Second Economic Adjustment Programme for Greece: Fourth Review. DG ECFIN Occasional Papers 192.
- European Environmental Agency (2015): State and Outlook—Forests.
- Goos, M. (2004): Sinking the Blues: The Impact of Shop Closing Hours on Labour and Product Markets. Centre for Economic Performance Discussion Paper Series, No. 664.
- Gradus, R. (1996): The Economic Effects of Extending Shop Opening Hours. Journal of Economics, 64 (3), 247–263.
- Inderst, I., and A. Irmen (2005): Shopping Hours and Price Competition. European Economic Review, 49 (5), 1105–1124.
- IOBE (2010): The Greek Economy, Vol. 1/10. IOBE, Athens.
- KEPE (2013): Impact Evaluation of Deregulation of Professions with Significant Contribution to the Greek Economy. Centre of Planning and Economic Research, Athens.
- Ministry for the Environment, Energy and Climate Change (2013): Review of the implementation of law 4014/2011 examining the degree to which licensing procedures have been simplified and shortened. Athens.
- Mitsoppoulos, M., and T. Pelagidis (2009): Vikings in Greece: kleptocratic interest groups in a closed, rent-seeking economy. Cato Journal, 29 (3).
- OECD (2009): OECD Environmental Performance Reviews: Greece 2009.
- OECD (2014a): Measurement and Reduction of Administrative Burden in 13 sectors in Greece. Environment. OECD Publishing.
- OECD (2014b): OECD Competition Assessment Reviews: Greece. OECD Publishing.
- OECD (2015): Competition assessment of laws and regulations in four sub-sectors of the manufacturing industry in Greece. OECD Publishing.
- Pilat, D. (1997): Regulation and Performance in the Distribution Sector. OECD Economics Department Working Papers 180. OECD Publishing.
- Prodromidis, P., A. Petralias, and S. Petros (2012): The economic impact of deregulating Sunday. KEPE working paper.
- Reddy, K. (2012): Price Effects of shopping Hours Regulation: Evidence from Germany. Economic Affairs, 32 (1), 48–54.
- Sala-i-Martin, X., and K. Schwab (2004): The Global Competitiveness Report 2003–2004. World Economic Forum.

— Schwab, K., M. Porter, and X. Sala-i-Martin (2008): The Global Competitiveness Report 2007–2008. World Economic Forum.
— SEV Hellenic Federation of Enterprises (2014): Ex-post impact assessment of environmental licensing law. Athens.
— Skuterud, M. (2005): The Impact of Sunday Shopping on Employment and Hours of Work in the Retail Sector. European Economic Review, 49 (8), 1953–1978.
— Tzineri, I. (2015): The present landscape of land registration in Greece. European Land Registry Association.
— UNESCAP/UNECE (2012): Business Process Analysis Guide to Simplify Trade Procedures. UNESCAP Publishing.
— World Bank (2013): Doing Business 2014: Understanding Regulations for Small and Medium-Size Enterprises. Washington, D.C.
— World Bank (2015): Doing Business 2016: Measuring Regulatory Quality and Efficiency. Washington, D.C.

The Greek Economic Crisis, Labor Markets and Policies

VASILIKI BOZANI AND NICK DRYDAKIS

Vasiliki Bozani, Economics Research Centre, University of Cyprus, Nicosia, Cyprus, e-mail: bozani.vasiliki@ucy.ac.cy
Nick Drydakis, Lord Ashcroft International Business School, Anglia Ruskin University, Cambridge, and IZA, Bonn, e-mail: nick.drydakis@anglia.ac.uk

Summary: The historic decision at the Euro Summit on July 12. 2015, to continue supporting Greece as a member of the EU and the euro family, provided Greece the chance to return to growth and sustainability, provided it takes the necessary steps to continue with its reforms. Jointly the Greek government with its partners (European Commission, European Central Bank and the International Monetary Fund), agreed that the success of economic policy decisions would be determined by the concentration on social policies. Policy initiatives should view reforms not as a debate between more versus less regulation, but rather as a matter of good versus bad regulation. Encouraging productive investment represents one of the main engines to sustain not just recovery but also promote productive transformations. Moreover one of the most pressing priorities for the Greek government should be to provide immediate support to vulnerable groups, to help alleviate the impact of the economic crisis, and set the stage for stable future economic growth.

→ JEL Classification: E24, E50, E60, J01, O52
→ Keywords: Economic crisis, labor markets, policies

1 Introduction: The structural patterns of the crisis

The outbreak in 2008 of the ongoing economic crisis and its consequences for EMU economies, in particular Greece, raised a number of questions about the sustainability of the economic model. Despite the differences among European economies—namely inflation, unemployment, and competitiveness levels—the adherence of EMU principles on inflation targeting as well as on the convergence criteria set by the Stability and Growth Pact (SGP), led to the establishment of a dual growth model within the euro area (Arestis and Sawyer 2011a and 2011b, Hein 2014, Stockhammer 2012). On the one hand, the North-core countries (Austria, Belgium, Finland, Germany and the Netherlands) achieved growth under an export-led model, while on the other hand, the South-periphery countries (Greece, Spain, Ireland) followed a debt-led growth model[1] (Stockhammer 2012 and 2013, Hein 2014). In the name of a cohesively single financial and capital market, the periphery economies were covering their deficit problems by borrowing money from the core economies. The implied inequalities and the negativities stemming from them came up after the outbreak of the current crisis and resulted in destabilizing the *addictive borrowing dependence* of peripheral countries on the core EMU countries (Arestis and Sawyer 2011a and 2011b Hein 2014). On these grounds, the euro crisis can be considered as a balance-of-payment crisis or, alternatively, as an external-debt sustainability crisis (Mastromatteo and Rossi 2015).

Regarding the Greek case, the general economic crisis further expanded its high-level deficits, pushing the economy toward the experience of a sovereign debt crisis without its government being able to raise funds on the financial markets in order to resolve it. The Greek attempts to reduce the possibility of a government default by reversing any future upward-trend in the magnitude of public debt ratio, were finally assisted by rescue packages known as *Memorandums I and II* (2010, 2012); these were provided jointly by the European Commission, European Central Bank and the International Monetary Fund (the well-known *Troika* that has been renamed by the new government as *Institutions*). The main intention of the Memorandums was to help the Greek government to comply with the benchmark deficit and debt levels set by the SGP. In practice, the Memorandums were simply borrowing agreements that pushed the Greek economy into vicious circles of continuous borrowing, stemming mainly from the obligation to implement fiscal consolidation, labor market reforms and structural changes, in order for competitiveness to be regained; otherwise Greece could either exit the euro or default[2] (Frangakis 2015, Stockhammer 2013, Calcango 2012, Arestis and Sawyer 2011b).

---

1 The main characteristics of debt-led growth models are the expansion of economic activity parallel to extended inflows of foreign capital and the expansion of income inequalities, against (low) income labor profits, thereby causing the stagnation of real investment, since such decisions are profit driven. On the other hand, economies of export-led model base their ability to run surpluses on exports, since their domestic demand is relatively low (Barku et al. 2012, Stockhammer 2012, Hein 2014).

2 All these reforms could have been avoided if Greece could devaluate its own currency directly and faced imbalances (Mastrommateo and Rossi 2012, Arestis and Sawyer 2011b).

2 Labor market reforms during 2010–2014[3]

Concentrating our attention on the case of Greece, we examine the labor market reforms that were undertaken in order to improve Greek labor market regulations, thereby reducing unemployment rates (ILO 2014). In addition, the implementation of a range of labor market policies[4] seeks to increase the degree of labor market flexibility, as well as to improve the matching between labor demand and supply, thereby increasing the possibility of potential workers finding employment (Immervoll and Scarpetta 2012, Cazes et al. 2009).

The adopted policy packages were determined by the assumption that the combination of fiscal austerity with internal devaluation (wage and price deflation) and appropriate structural reforms would expand the economy by improving investment, competitiveness, and exports. On these grounds, the reduction of unit cost would work to improve competitiveness and exports, so as to balance the negative consequences on domestic demand (Blanchard et al. 2014). Thus, any attempt to improve the labor market environment was rooted in the need to increase its flexibility. This target could be achieved by adopting the suggested reforms, which concerned the following two aspects: first, the downward squeeze of the minimum wage, in order to re-set the base for wage determination; and, second, the reduction in public wages, in order to improve fiscal conditions and potentially affect private sector wages. In addition, the following measures were suggested: the replacement of collective agreements with firm-level wage agreements, so that wages reflect the actual level of firms' productivity; changes in the social fund contributions; the overcoming of obstacles against dismissals; the abolishment of life-tenure contracts, in addition to the enhancement of temporary employment, so as to meet the fixed and constant needs of the enterprise; the introduction of a more flexible or fewer working hours scheme, in order to reallocate workforce toward more productively. Obviously, the direction of these reforms suggests as a solution for the Greek problem: the creation of a more flexible labor market environment. However a number of studies find these suggestions responsible for unemployment (Blanchard et al. 2014, ILO 2014).

The question remains as to what extent these reforms have been undertaken. By examining the *LABREF database*, we conclude that since *Memorandum I* (2010), many and continuous reforms were undertaken (until 2013, the last available data). In terms of labor market institutions, the majority of these reforms concern changes in labor taxation, in an attempt to reduce tax evasion and contemporaneously increase revenues in social funds. Significant reforms have been adopted relating to the introduction of flexible contracts (i. e. temporary contracts) and working-hours programs, while steps have been taken in reducing the notice and severance payments as well as the expansion of collective dismissals. Among the most important reforms are those referring to the freezing and progressive reduction of the public-sector wages and pensions, as well as changes to the minimum wage; all these decisions for reducing the public expenditures however instead of improving affect negative economic activity since they do only reduce aggregate demand. As

3 In our attempt to examine the changes implied by borrowing agreements, as the starting point of our analysis we us 2010, the year that Memorandum I was introduced.

4 Following the methodology of European Commission (2006) labor market policies are distinguished into (a) *services* (counseling, mediation); (b) *measures* (training, job sharing, subsidies, support to employment, public works), both of which consist Active Labor Market Policies; and (c) *support* (financial support to the unemployed and early retirement) representing the Passive Labor Market Policies measures. In practice the appropriate combination of these policies is required for expanding economic activity and appropriately addressing unemployment problems.

for reforms related to labor market policies, these have been concentrated on discouraging early retirement as well as on establishing strict eligibility criteria for receiving unemployment or other social-welfare benefits; although in order to balance this, social assistance benefits for specifically vulnerable groups have been provided. On the other hand, in an attempt to motivate the unemployed, young people, and women, as well as those close to retirement, numerous reforms introducing programs related to subsidized employment, the direct creation of jobs, and training have been made.

Despite these useful institutional and legislation changes, an open issue is the ability of all these reforms to reduce unemployment, not because of their inappropriateness but because of the continuously changing Greek macroeconomic conditions. Additional doubts are also triggered by the relatively unstable political environment that characterizes Greece the last couple of years as well as the unwillingness of the political system to take up the cost of restructuring the social and economic relations.

3 The effect of austerity on the Greek economy

Any second thought about blindly implementing the social partners' policy suggestions (i.e. reduction of the size of the public sector, privatization and deregulation programs for the transport sector and energy, regulated professions, the judicial system and the pension system) (Frangakis 2015, OEC 2010), gradually faded away. It was believed that the crisis should be considered as an opportunity to get rid of pre-crisis economic and social structures that were consistent with negativities (Barkbu et al. 2012). However, imposing strict austerity and labor reform measures in a country suffering from recession would have only had catastrophic results, with unexpectedly adverse effects on income distribution, unemployment and output growth (Frangakis 2015, Calgano 2012, Stockhammer 2012)

Hence the extreme and inconsistent interventions for reducing pensions and wages, as well as the generosity (in terms of both eligibility levels and duration) and the relatively high coverage rate of both unemployment and social benefits in a society where unemployment had continuously expanded, were all factors that not only devastated income distribution, but also expanded further the pre-crisis income inequalities and poverty for specific groups (mainly pensioner unemployed, disabled people) in society. In turn, this resulted in a sharp reduction in living standards[5] (Giannitsis and Zografakis 2015, Matsagannis 2013); with these conditions having severe social consequences due to the asymmetry of the taxation system across income groups. This situation also had negative effects on health and social security, the existence of which became a luxury for most individuals, although during crises the opposite is expected (Drydakis 2015, Gianitsis and Zografakis 2015, Matsaganis 2013). As a result, it is not unusual nowadays for households to have at least one unemployed or partly employed member who has faced a sharp reduction in income and is unable to afford basic necessities or to pay their taxes.

---

5 The lower living standards that resulted from the crisis are not necessarily combined with expansions in income inequality and poverty, as long as the poverty line is determined as a proportion of average income (Matsaganis 2013). Besides even in the pre-crisis period, Greece was a country with high poverty rates (OECD 2013) while persistence on austerity measures seemingly appear to expand it.

But the social crisis was not the only "side effect" of the policy packages; it also had adverse effects on the real economy. Thus, despite its problems, Greece remained focused on the suggested policies and the European focus on inflation, in order to increase its competitiveness without risking its liquidity. It succeeded in reducing its prices, with the *HCPI* (Harmonised Index of Consumer Prices) squeezed downward by 6.1 percentage points, relative to the 1.2 percentage point reduction achieved across eurozone (19 countries) countries during the 2010–2014 period.[6] It is important to note that the relatively high levels of HICP in 2010 and 2011 are attributed to increases in the Value Added Tax from 19 percent to 23 percent, as a part of the fiscal devaluation program (Frangakis 2015). Moreover, in line with policy suggestions, the real unit labor cost appeared to have fallen by 11.8 percentage points over 2010 to 2013 period (data availability until 2013), while the eurozone reduction was just 0.1 percentage points over the same period. Comparing real (or even nominal) unit labor costs in Greece with those in the eurozone, allows us to consider the achievement of internal devaluation. However the fact that the devaluation was not followed by the expected results in terms of competitiveness, investment and exports indicates that aggregate demand has negatively been affected. The implementation of this policy suggestion across members in the eurozone, without considering the specific national characteristics, does partly explain the reasons about which the expected effects are not exported.

Any other fear about characterizing this policy package as misguided is reflected in the negatively signed output growth rates, which though have been improved over time they inform us about the actual abilities of Greek economy. The eurozone's output growth was negative only in 2012 and 2013; while the Greek output growth was negative from 2010 to 2013 and positive only in 2014. The aggregate output growth (for the same period) shrunk by 24.51 percentage points in Greece, versus 3.41 percentage points increase in eurozone. Additionally, the expansion in total revenues during 2010–2014 by only 5.1 percentage points and its combination with an expenditure shrunk by 2.6 percentage points, give the illusion about macroeconomic improvement. However, the fact that such changes are achieved mainly through increases in taxation, downward pressures on public expenditures, pensions and wages suggest the possibility for future problems.

In particular, the increases in public debt of 32.4 percentage points from 2010 to 2014 do not indicate that Greece is out of the crisis period. On the contrary, while eurozone unemployment rise by just 1.5 percentage points between 2010 and 2014, in Greece it skyrocketed by 13.8 percentage points. Specific subgroups have fared more poorly: Greece's youth unemployment rate, up by 19.4 percentage points since 2010, appears to be the driving force for the expansion of total unemployment; something policy should address. Further, it is heartbreaking the expansion of long-term unemployment by 28.9 percentage points over the period under consideration; a fact that requires the reconstruction of policies, since the higher the long-term unemployment rate, the harder it is to solve the problem.

Undoubtedly, Troika's policy package had not the expected effects, as it pushed the Greek economy into a prolonged recession. So, given that the program failed to achieve its targets of restoring price competiveness, expanding growth expansion and maintaining public debt sustainability (OECD 2013), the question arising is what should be done in order to bring an end to the depression.

6 For the analysis that follows we have use data from the Eurostat Database. See Appendix.

4 Strategic actions for Greece

Regardless of adhering to the programmes' suggestions, fiscal austerity should be addressed as a consequence and not as the cause of the crisis, since the two different growth models characterizing the eurozone indicate that the crisis had flourished due to private over-indebtedness and financial deregulation; it was not a crisis caused by fiscal profligacy (Mastromatteo and Rossi 2015, Calcagno 2012). In other words, the Greek fiscal austerity experiment failed; such failure was driven by the concentration on labor market reforms and their treatment as the main and not as the substitute instrument for pushing the economy out of recession (Cazes et al. 2012), while the absence of any attention to the demand side of the labor market made this result inevitable (Stockhammer and Klar 2010, Stockhammer et al. 2014). Moreover the fact that reforms were concentrated on the labor market, while little attention was paid to reforming the product market (i. e. lowering start-up costs or the high mark-up levels), inhibits improving economic activity and employment expansion (Blanchard and Giavazzi 2003, Gersbach 2000). In addition, product market reforms would facilitate employment expansion not by replacing labor market reforms, but rather by treating them as complementarities (Annett 2007, Blanchard and Giavazzi 2003, Gersbach 2000). According to evidence provided by Papageorgiou and Vourvachaki (2015), structural reforms to Greek product and labor markets can positively impact the macroeconomic environment and growth levels (both in the short- and long-run); the degree of this impact essentially determined by the adopted fiscal policy instrument.

In other words, in order for the labor market reforms to flourish, they should be combined with reforms in the product market as well as with policies concentrating on aggregate demand stimulation and income re-distribution, and, in turn, the policies should be restructured, recognizing the failures of the current policies, thus moderating the effects of the current recession (Hein 2014, Sawyer 2013, Stockhammer 2012, 2013, Barkbu et al. 2012). These suggestions should have been evident from the disappointing results, in terms of employment and growth, which were reached by the German attempt to face its structural problems by focusing on the supply side of labor while paid no attention to the demand side in order to reverse the situation and stabilize the domestic demand (Herzog-Stein et al. 2013). However, the question is to what extent Greece and its partners are willing to face the core of the Greek crisis.

Given these thoughts, the historic decision at the Euro Summit on July 12, 2015, to continue supporting Greece as members of the EU and the euro family provides a chance for Greece to return to growth and sustainability (European Commission 2015). The Greek government should implement best practices across the range of labor market legislations through constructive dialogue with its social partners (ILO 2014); in addition, jointly agreed policy approaches are important in order for social policies to be sustainable and successful (European Commission 2015, ILO 2014). This can be achieved by modernizing legislation through a process of consultation with the social partners, thus benefiting from the expertise of think tanks and international organizations (ILO 2014). The participation of all key actors and social partners increases the likelihood of bringing about sustainable solutions, especially in times of crisis (ILO 2014). Tripartite social dialogue and collective bargaining would benefit from more profound labor market monitoring, including monitoring of wages, working conditions, and price developments (ILO 2014).

Currently, the Greek government is reviewing, through a consultation process, the existing frameworks for collective dismissals, industrial action, and collective bargaining, taking into account best practices elsewhere in Europe (European Commission 2015). The Greek government is also working to adopt legislation for a unified wage grid reform, in line with the agreed wage bill targets, including decompressing the wage distribution across the wage spectrum in accordance with staff skills and responsibilities (European Commission 2015). Policy initiatives should approach employment protection legislation reforms not as a debate over more or less regulation, but rather as a matter of good versus bad regulation (ILO 2014). Balanced labor market reforms must seek to achieve both high-quality employment creation and adequate income security, while reconciling firms' need to adjust over the business cycle (ILO 2014).

An improved interaction between social protection measures and labor market programs would improve the effectiveness of government efforts to ensure that workers remain attached to the labor market and retain and improve their skills (ILO 2014). The suggestion that employees should keep full access to social security contributions, sick leave and maternity leave, eventually entitling them to unemployment benefits, along with the need to maintain the financial stability of the fund, shows the government's intention to secure these measures (World Bank 2015, ILO 2014). Providing comprehensive social protection that allows life to be lived with dignity (European Commission 2015) is the starting point, with the government ensuring the autonomy and effective representation of workers and employees (ILO 2014). In addition, Greece should employ social dialogue to connect companies with trade unions in order to provide worker representation through designated bodies at the enterprise level (ILO 2014).

In addition, as the Greek government acknowledges that the approach not only needs to balance flexibility and fairness for employees and employers, it also needs to consider the very high unemployment rate (European Commission 2015). The most pressing priority for the government should be to provide immediate support to the most vulnerable in order to help alleviate the impact of the economic crisis (European Commission 2015, Bank of Greece 2014). The collective mission should be to get people back to work and prevent the entrenchment of long-term unemployment (ILO 2014). The long-term unemployed are at particular risk of poverty and social exclusion, and their support from social security is meager. Income support should be linked to the duration of unemployment, so that resources directed to participants increase in line with the risk of long-term unemployment (International Labor Office 2014). The minimum allocation for emergency social measures should be increased; thus they would need to be designed in a way that optimizes their impact on poverty reduction and labor market inclusion through improved targeting (ILO 2014, Bank of Greece 2014). Better targeting would allow improved poverty-reduction efforts and help to improve the financial efficiency of social protection (ILO 2014, Bank of Greece, 2014).

Currently, Greece is trapped in a vicious cycle where low tax revenues induce higher corporate and labor taxation, which in turn pushes firms to exit the formal economy, hire uninsured workers, and/or downsize their business activity (World Bank, 2015, ILO 2014, 2015). The Greek government must take action to fight undeclared work, thus strengthening the competitiveness of legal companies and protecting workers, in addition to ensuring tax and social security revenues (IMF 2015, ILO 2014). Therefore, the government should strengthen the tax collection system through mandatory declarations and penalties, in an effort to enlarge the tax base and reduce informality (World Bank 2015, International Labor Office 2014). Improving the tax system is crucial to increasing financial resources for social security purposes, while meeting fiscal adjustment targets (World Bank 2015).

To strengthen the capacities of the labor inspectorate, action should be directed toward designing inclusive labor inspection (ILO 2014). In addition, Greece should further enhance the legislation for temporary employment, so as to meet the needs of business (ILO 2014). In addition, the government should implement training programs aimed at providing youth with entrepreneurial skills and the guidance needed to start a business (European Commission 2015, OECD 2015b, ILO 2014).

Eventually, more flexible legislation could apply to specific sectors, where the seasonal nature of the activities requires a fixed information system (ILO 2014). Greece is also advised to continue its efforts to increase the effectiveness of reduced working-hour schemes, through the implementation of training measures in companies that have reduced working hours; in addition, shifting the workforce from declining economic sectors to more productive ones should be considered (ILO 2014). The government should be committed to compensating employees who are temporarily employed in work-sharing schemes up to a certain percentage of their foregone income (ILO 2014).

But none of the suggested reforms will work unless attention is also turned to the demand side of the economy. Thus, among its priorities should be the encouragement of productive investment, which represents one of the main starting points to both sustain the recovery and promote productive transformations (ILO 2014). Given the productivity structure of the Greek economy and its opportunities, Greece is required to create a public financial institution with the mandate of providing credit to SMEs, while promoting the participation of private institutions in their credit products (European Commission 2015, OECD 2015b, ILO 2014). Hence, direct public loans and European Investment Bank/EU funds could be combined with government credit guarantees, in order to spur private investor involvement (OECD 2015b). In addition, policy initiatives could attempt to enhance the quality of entrepreneurial activities for specific target groups that are perceived as facing the highest barriers to entrepreneurship (OECD 2015b). Moreover, in order to re-enforce investment, it is suggested that SMEs should benefit from a reduction in their tax and social security contributions for creating high skilled research jobs (ILO 2014). The government should provide firms, especially in their early stages, with dedicated support programs, such as mentoring, nurturing and coaching programs (OECD 2015b), while policies to foster firms' investment in innovation should be complemented by efforts to strengthen the collaboration between academic research and businesses (ILO 2014, Herrmann and Kritikos 2013). The government should strengthen the mechanism of co-funding among various entities, in order to foster risk sharing.

Finally, it is critically important for Greece to promote the acquisition of sector-specific skills among the workforce, while re-connecting the market strategy toward value added services (ILO 2014). For instance, Greece should enhance the profitability of the tourism industry by enhancing the quality of services provided (European Commission 2015, ILO 2014). Meanwhile, for agrifood businesses, policies should be implemented to strengthen the integration of their products into the tourism industry value-chain (ILO 2014). It is highly recommended that providing further incentives for investment in renewable energy could provide a series of positive externalities in terms of investments and job creation (European Commission 2015, ILO 2014).

5 Funding opportunities for the Greek economy

Although the above suggested reforms aim at improving the labor market, while simultaneously mediating, if not resolving, some of the chronic pathogeneses of the Greek society, we also must consider whether these can be undertaken by an economy with virtually no liquidity.

Given this possibility, and recognizing the need to boost domestic demand, one of the significant decisions taken by the European Commission in June 2015 created a Structural Reform Support Service that is designed to offer support in such areas as labor market policies and improving the business environment, including assistance for the efficient and effective use of EU structural funds (European Commission 2015). In July 2015, the Commission committed itself to make a number of proposals (such as the early release of remaining EU payments and increasing the rate of pre-financing for 2014–2020 programs) in order to immediately improve liquidity, so that investments can be made now, with their beneficial impact on growth and jobs (European Commission 2015, OECD 2015a). According to the European Commission (2015), 35 billion euro from the European Structural and Investment Funds will become available to Greece between 2015–2017; these funds could be mobilized to create jobs and sustainable growth through (i) investment in innovative SMEs, in order to improve the business environment; (ii) youth employment initiatives, in order to enable young people to have a first job experience; and (iii) social funding that supports an active labor market and social inclusion (European Commission 2015; Bank of Greece 2014, Herrmann and Kritikos 2013). In addition, Greek farmers should continue to benefit from payments, both in terms of direct payment and income support, as well as measures that support key agricultural markets in order to help make the agricultural sector competitive (European Commission 2015, ILO 2014). Funding should support also coastal communities in creating a basis for sustainable fishing (European Commission 2015).

This funding will contribute to a spirit of entrepreneurship and job creation, improve education and vocational training systems, while also modernizing public administration (European Commission 2015, OECD 2015a). This fund will help thousands of SMEs benefit from investments in research and innovation, to cooperate with research institutes, and to boost their future competitiveness (European Commission 2015, Herrmann and Kritikos 2013). Based on the figures given, at least 250,000 unemployed people should receive support, along with 180,000 who are already employed but could benefit from additional training, as well as around 30,000 migrants and Roma people, 33,000 living in jobless homes, 10,000 disabled people, and 80,000 other disadvantaged people (European Commission 2015).

In 2016, the Commission will review the allocation of cohesion policy funding, and it is also likely to increase further the amount of EU funding available for investment in Greece (European Commission 2015). One immediate task would be for the Commission to support Greece in maximizing its absorption of EU funds, ensuring the fastest possible take-off of investment, as well as ensuring that sound financial management requirements and relevant deadlines are met (European Commission 2015). It is essential for Greece to fully respect the basic EU legal requirements, in terms of EU rules, in order to build trust and credibility with its partners and internationally. It is essential that Greece quickly returns to financial stability, so that it can make use of the substantial EU support available in the form of grants, loans and technical assistance to build a secure future (European Commission 2015, OECD 2015a). Reducing unemployment and increasing growth while simultaneously managing tightening financial conditions, tackling structural challenges, as well as reducing the uncertainty of the economic and political environment (European Commission 2015, ILO 2014) is the challenge facing Greece. These problems could disrupt the efforts of many investment plans, and challenge the attempts of the Greek authorities to make good use of the EU's and international partners' financial support.

6 Conclusions

It is highly recommended that, in order to return to the path of job creation and economic growth, Greece must continue with reforms affecting both labor demand and supply, while also starting product market reforms. The country should develop a comprehensive social protection strategy effectively linked to the labor market and optimizes poverty-reducing effects through better targeting. The country should review its central social dialogue mechanisms and consultative processes, with the goal of improving its effectiveness, especially in terms of monitoring labor market and wage developments, in order to support evidence-based policy-making and effective collective bargaining. Effective collective bargaining at appropriate levels and organizing the decentralization process are necessary for improving confidence and creating a stable environment for growth and investment. But nothing can be achieved if aggregate demand is not boosted; this is why consideration should be given to reforming the product market, promoting investments in the real economy, improving access to credit for SMEs, and leveraging the human capital present in the country. Moreover, support should be given to large companies to maintain their focus on innovation, while public institutions should promote the growth in SMEs that can link into large companies' supply chains and collaborate in their research. In addition, there is a need for a tax regime that balances issues of competitiveness and revenues with a comprehensive strategy to implement sustained productivity and innovation, in order to promote the shift from the informal sector to the formal sector. In addition, the country needs to take steps to improve the regulations concerning economically dependent self-employment and temporary employment. Changes could aim to link the associations of self-employment and temporary work to some specific characteristics that define the status of economically dependent self-employment. Therefore, it is crucial for the government to create a public financial institution with the mandate of providing credit to SMEs, while promoting the participation of private institutions with their credit products. All the above, make it clear that the only route for Greece to escape from continuous borrowing and to achieve healthy growth rates is to enact reforms that will resolve any structural problems, while creating a friendly and financially stable environment for investment.

In general, the case of Greece should teach us that attention should be focused on diagnosing the problem correctly, so that the medicine does not have side effects. Also, there is no "one size policy" that fits everyone and contemporaneously, since policies should be determined with respect to the specific macroeconomic characteristics and needs of each economy; otherwise, only additional problems will be caused. Further, the fact that these reforms are undertaken with time delay and only as a part of the Memorandums in order to ensure future funding and not that robust growth is established explains the reason for their failure. Moreover, the refusal to accept the essence of some of these reforms for improving the well-known pathogeneses in the economic system reflects the inability to understand what is really required to fuel economic activity. In addition, policy suggestions should not only seek to help Greece escape from the current economic crisis, but they should also ensure the long-run survival of the Greek economy after the end of this "adventure".

One it is for sure, it is time for Greece to understand that this is no time to postpone decisions; now is the time to take advantage of the opportunities provided to it, and to prioritize them in the best possible way. Equally, its social partners should understand that there is no room for additional experiments, recognize the possible mistakes in their policy suggestions, and to look at every alternative; otherwise Greece will only be driven into a deeper recession.

Appendix

Table 1

Variable/Time	GEO	2010	2011	2012	2013	2014	2014-2010
HCPI (all items)	Greece	4,7	3,1	1,0	-0,9	-1,4	-6.1
	eurozone	1,6	2,7	2,5	1,4	0,4	-1.2
GDP growth rate	Greece	-5.47	-9.14	-7.27	-3.25	0.62	6.09
	eurozone	2.05	1.63	-0.85	-0.28	0.86	-1.19
Unemployment rate (total)	Greece	12.7	17.9	24.5	27.5	26.5	13.8
	eurozone	10.1	10.2	11.4	12.0	11.6	1.5
Youth Unemployment Rate (age group under 24)	Greece	33.0	44.7	55.3	58.3	52.4	19.4
	eurozone	21.3	21.3	23.5	24.4	23.7	2.4
Unemployment rate (age group: 25-74)	Greece	8.9	9.0	10.1	10.8	10.4	1.5
	eurozone	11.2	15.9	22.3	25.4	24.8	13.6
Long-term Unemployment*	Greece	44.6	49.3	59.1	67.1	73.5	28.9
	eurozone	42.5	45.3	46.5	49.7	52.5	10.0
Nominal ULC** (growth rate of nominal unit cost)	Greece	113.1 (-0.1)	111.0 (-1.8)	105.4 (-5.1)	98.1 (-6.8)		-15.0 (-6.7)
	eurozone	109.7 (-0.6)	110.7 (0.8)	112.7 (1.9)	114.1 (1.2)		4.4 (1.8)
Real ULC** (growth rate of real unit cost)	Greece	98.6 (-1.3)	95.8 (-2.9)	91.2 (-4.8)	86.8 (-4.9)		-11.8 (-3.6)
	eurozone	101.4 (-1.4)	101.0 (-0.4)	101.6 (0.6)	101.3 (-0.3)		-0.1 (1.1)
Governmental expenditures	Greece	52.5	54.2	55.2	60.8	49.9	-2.6
	eurozone	50.5	49.1	49.7	49.6	49.4	-1.1
Governmental revenues	Greece	41.3	44.0	46.3	48.3	46.4	5.1
	eurozone	44.3	44.9	46.1	46.6	46.8	2.5
Net lending/Net Borrowing	Greece	-11.2	-10.2	-8.8	-12.4	-3.6	7.6
	eurozone	-6.2	-4.2	-3.7	-3.0	-2.6	3.6
Public Debt	Greece	146.2	172.0	159.4	177.0	178.6	32.4
	eurozone	83.8	86.0	89.3	91.1	92.1	8.3
Interest Payable	Greece	5.9	7.3	5.1	4.0	3.9	-2.0
	eurozone	2.7	3.0	3.0	2.8	2.7	0.0

* Long term-unemployment as a percentage of total unemployment.
** 2010-2013.

Database

Countries: Greece, Eurozone: (EA11-2000, EA12-2006, EA13-2007, EA15-2008, EA16-2010, EA17-2013, EA18-2014, EA19).
HICP (all items): Harmonized Index of Consumer Prices, (2005=100)-annual data (average index and rate of change). Source: Eurostat Database (2015).
GDP: Gross Domestic Product and main components (output, expenditures and income) in

constant prices 2005. Source: Eurostat Database (2015).
UNR: Unemployment Rate by sex and age groups-annual average percent. Source: Eurostat Database (2015).
Long-term UNR: Long-term unemployment in percent of unemployment. Source: Eurostat Database (2015).
Nominal ULC: Nominal Unit Labour Cost in constant prices 2005 (2005=100). Source: Eurostat Database (2015).
Real ULC: Real Unit Labour Cost in constant prices 2005 (2005=100). Source: Eurostat Database (2015).
Governmental Expenditures: Total general government expenditures as a percentage of GDP. Source: Eurostat Database (2015).
Governmental Revenues: Total general government revenues as a percentage of GDP. Source: Eurostat Database (2015).
Net lending/Net Borrowing: Net lending (+)/Net Borrowing (–) of the general government as a percentage of GDP. Source: Eurostat Database (2015).
Public Debt: Government (general government) consolidated gross debt as a percentage of GDP. Source: Eurostat Database (2015).
Interest Payable: Interest Payable (general government) as a percentage of GDP. Source: Eurostat Database (2015).

References

- Annett, A. (2007): Lessons from Successful Labor Market Reformers in Europe. IMF Policy Discussion Paper. No. 07/1. International Monetary Fund, Washington, D.C.
- Arestis, P., and M. Sawyer (2011a): The Design Faults of the Economic and Monetary Union. Journal of Contemporary European Studies, 19 (1), 21–32.
- Arestis P., and M. Sawyer (2011b): The Ongoing Euro Crisis. Challenge, 54 (11), 6–13.
- Bank of Greece (2014): Inequality, Poverty and Social Welfare in Greece. Distributional Effects of Austerity. Bank of Greece, Athens.
- Barkbu, B., J. Rahman, and R. Valdes. a staff team. (2012): Fostering Growth in Europe Now. IMF Staff Discussion Note. No.12/07. International Monetary Fund, Washington, D.C.
- Blanchard, O.J., and F. Giavazzi (2003): Macroeconomic Effects of Regulation and Deregulation in Goods and Labor Markets. Quarterly Journal of Economics, 118 (3), 879–907.
- Blanchard, O.J., F. Jaumotte, and P. Loungani (2014): Labor Market Policies and IMF Advice in Advanced Economies During the Great Recession. IZA Journal of Labor Policy, 3 (2), 1–23.
- Calcagno, A. (2012): Can Austerity Work? Review of Keynesian Economics, 1 (1), 24–36.
- Cazes, S., S. Verick, and C. Heuer (2009): Labour Market Policies in Times of Crisis. Employment Working Paper. No.35. International Labor Organization, Geneva.
- Drydakis, N. (2015): The Effect of Unemployment on Self-reported Health and Mental Health in Greece from 2008 to 2013: A Longitudinal Study Before and During the Financial Crisis. Social Science and Medicine, 128, 43–51.
- European Commission (2006): Employment in Europe 2006 Corrigendum. European Commission, Brussels.
- European Commission (2015): Communication From the Commission to the European Parliament, The Council, The European Economic and Social Committee and the Com-

mittee of the Regions. A New Start for Jobs and Growth in Greece. European Commission, Brussels.
- Frangakis, M. (2015): Public Debt Crisis, Austerity and Deflation: The Case of Greece. Review of Keynesian Economics, 3 (3), 295–331.
- Gersbach, H. (2000): Promoting Product Market Competition to Reduce Unemployment in Europe: An Alternative Approach. Kyklos, 53 (2), 117–134.
- Giannitsis, T., and S. Zografakis (2015): Greece: Solidarity and Adjustment in Times of Crisis, Study No. 38. Dusseldorf, German: IMK, Macroeconomic Policy Institute of the Hands-Boeckler-Fooundations.
- Hein, E. (2014): The Crisis of Finance-Dominated Capitalism in the Euro Area, Deficiencies in the Economic Policy Architecture and Deflationary Stagnation Policies. Journal of Post Keynesian Economics, 36 (2), 325–354.
- Herrmann, B., and S. A. Kritikos (2013): Growing out of the Crisis: Hidden Assets to Greece's Transition to an Innovation Economy. IZA Journal of European Labor Studies, 2, 14.
- Herzog-Stein, A., F. Lindner, and R. Zwiener (2013): Is the Supply Side All That Counts? How Germany's One-Sided Economic Policy Has Squandered Opportunities And Is Damaging Europe. Report No. 87e. IMK, Macroeconomic Policy Institute of the Hands-Boeckler- Fooundations, Dusseldorf.
- Immervoll, H., and S. Scarpetta (2012): Activation and Employment Support Policies in OECD Countries. An Overview of Current Approaches. IZA Journal of Labor Policy, 1 (9), 1–20.
- International Labor Office (2014): Productive Jobs for Greece. International Labor Office, Geneva.
- International Monetary Fund (2015): Greece: A Preliminary Draft Debt Sustainability Analysis. International Monetary Fund, Washington, D. C.
- Mastromatteo, G., and S. Rossi (2015): The Economics of Deflation in the Euro Area: A Critique of Fiscal Austerity. Review of Keynesian Economics, 3 (2), 326–350.
- Matsaganis. M. (2013): The Greek Crisis: Social Impact and Policy Responses. Friedrich Ebert Stiftung, Berlin.
- Organisation for Economic Co-operation and Development (2010): Greece at a Glance: Policies for a Sustainable Recovery. Organisation for Economic Co-operation and Development, Paris.
- Organisation for Economic Co-operation and Development (2013): Economic Surveys: Greece. Organisation for Economic Co-operation and Development, Paris.
- Organisation for Economic Co-operation and Development (2015a): Employment Outlook. Organisation for Economic Co-operation and Development, Paris.
- Organisation for Economic Co-operation and Development (2015b): Financing SMEs and Entrepreneurs 2015: An OECD Scoreboard. Organisation for Economic Co-operation and Development, Paris.
- Papageorgiou, D., and E. Vourvachaki (2015): The macroeconomic Impact of Structural Reforms in Product and Labour Markets: Trade-offs and Complementarities. Working Paper. No. 197. Bank of Greece, Athens.
- Sawyer, M. (2013): Alternative Economic Policies For The Economic and Monetary Union. Contributions to Political Economy, 32 (1), 11–27.
- Stockhammer, E. (2013): Rising Inequality as a Cause of the Present Crisis, Rising Inequality As A Cause of the Present Crisis. Cambridge Journal of Economics, 39 (3), 935–958.

— Stockhammer, E. (2012): Euro-Keynesianism? The Financial Crisis in Europe. Radical Philosophy, 175, September/October, 2–10.
— Stockhammer, E., A. L. Guschanski, and K. Kohler (2014): Unemployment, Capital Accumulation and Labour Market Institutions in the Great Recession. European Journal of Economics and Economic Policies Intervention, 11 (2), 182–194.
— Stockhammer, E., and E. Klar (2011): Capital Accumulation, Labour Market Institutions and Unemployment in the Medium Run. Cambridge Journal of Economics, 35 (2), 437–457.
— World Bank (2015): Global Economic Perspectives. World Bank, Washington, D. C.

Database

EUROSTAT Database, National Accounts, Population and Social Conditions, Labour Market. Brussels, European Commission.
Labour Market Reforms (LABREF) Database. Brussels, European Commission.

Greece in Economic Crisis: The Case of Health and Education

XENI DASSIOU

Xeni Dassiou, Department of Economics, City University London, Northampton Square, London, e-mail: x.dassiou@city.ac.uk

Summary: In 2010 the Greek economy entered a deep economic crisis. This was the result of an accumulation of structural problems in the economy, including overspending and loss of competitiveness during the previous decades, translating into persistently large budget and trade deficits. In 2015, under its third EU and IMF bailout, Greece has entered a spiral of depression that has led to its economy shrinking by one-third and unemployment skyrocketing to more than 25 percent, both a result of the austerity measures introduced as required to receive bailout funding. As a consequence, the health and education sectors have each experienced a reduction in public spending of more than one-third. We look at these two sectors before the crisis in the early 2000s, finding that a combination of delays, lack of enforcement, and reversals of urgently needed reforms resulted in obvious weaknesses not being corrected. This has prevented these two systems from delivering the social principles of equity in provision, equal opportunities for all, universal coverage, accessibility, and affordability. Healthcare and education both lack oversight and evaluation mechanisms to ensure quality of service for its users. Additionally, there are no cost containment/efficiency mechanisms on the procurement side to avoid wasting taxpayers' money and valuable resources. This means that Greece has high cost/low outcome education and health systems. When the economic crisis struck, the ability of these two systems to deliver the above mentioned social objectives further deteriorated, as lower per capita spending on education, health and social protection lowered entitlements, benefits, and outcomes while increasing the burden of out of pocket expenses, user charges etc. We conclude by arguing that there is a need for a radical change in the institutional framework and governance of these two systems, by establishing truly independent regulators or agencies, answerable only to parliament) that can effectively exercise oversight over both the quality and the cost in the provision of health and education.

→ JEL Classification: I11, I18, I21, I28
→ Keywords: Reforms, evaluation, regulation, equity, austerity

1 Introduction

Starting from 2010, Greece is in the midst of a severe economic crisis that has led to a drastic reduction in the funding of essential public services to an extent that the country's social coherence is starting to unravel. Debt has reached a staggering 178.6 percent of the GDP (the latest available figure from the Hellenic Statistical Authority for 2014), the result of a downward spiral in competitiveness, exports, and output, combined with years of excessive public spending and continued budget deficits until a budget primary surplus was achieved in 2013 and 2014. The three bailout austerity programmes between 2010 and 2015 underlie the 26.6 percent unemployment rate in 2014 and a fall in mean income of more than 25 percent. Household disposable income decreased by 11 percent, 9.9 percent, 7.9 percent and 8 percent in 2010, 2011, 2012 and 2013 respectively. Real GDP contracted at the rate of 5.4 percent, 8.9 percent, 6.6 percent and 3.9 percent over the same 4 years, returning to a paltry growth of 0.8 in 2014 while further reductions are predicted for 2015 and 2016 following a recent third bailout.

Since 2010, the vast majority of Greek people can no longer afford private health care, instead relying on public hospitals,[1] while a large number of pupils has transferred from private to public schools.[2] As a result, there has been a 28 percent increase in the demand for public hospitals between 2009 and 2013 as well as a 15 percent increase in the demand for places in public schools for the school year 2010/11.

An increase in co-payments for medicines and other user charges, together with the loss of social insurance health coverage by the unemployed and self-employed (Kentikelenis et al. 2014) has compounded problems, while on the funding side there has been a sharp contraction in public spending. Total public funding on health expenditures decreased by 31.39 percent over the 2009–2013 period.[3] At the same time educational spending was reduced by 33 percent over the same period, with, according to Stratis (2014), a further 8.1 percent planned reduction for 2015.

In this paper we first discuss, in Section 2, the principles that should characterise a health and an education system in their provision of services to the citizens of a country. We then explain, in Sections 3 and 4, that even before the crisis both the education and health sectors were unreformed, lacking independent oversight and evaluation mechanisms that should provide incentives to promote value for money and ensure efficient resource usage. Once the economic crisis struck, the spending cuts hit these two sectors hard; sectors that were cost inefficient, bloated, and characterised by unequal access, leading to a sharp increase in unmet medical needs in health and under provision (e. g. in the form of teacher and teaching materials shortages) in education. As Greece's bailout monitors emphasized spending cuts over ensuring the implementation of reforms, the symptoms were treated, but not their underlying causes. New health and

1 Data for 2009-2011 show increases in admissions to public hospitals as patients can no longer afford private payments or access to private health insurance. Several authors report on a marked deterioration in accessibility, especially for vulnerable people (uninsured, unemployed, migrants, older people, children etc.), increases in suicide rates combined with a decrease in the spending for mental health, 40 percent cuts in hospital budgets, shortages in staff and medical supplies, and corruption in procurement and bribes (for example, see Economou et al. 2014a, Kentikelenis et al. 2011, 2014, Karanikolos et al. 2013, Karamitri et al. 2013, Kentikelenis and Papanicolas 2012, Karamanoli 2011 etc.).

2 What happens now? The fallout of Greece's education cuts at: http://learnnow.org/departments/global-learning/the-state-of-public-education-in-greece-2

3 Calculated using data in Table 3, Hellenic Statistical Authority 2015.

education reforms were few and piecemeal, presented to the people as a result of austerity rather than sensible changes. Many of the reforms voted in by parliament were never implemented or, with trade union pressure, the reforms were reversed or seriously watered down. An exception in education, highlighted in Section 3, saw the introduction of a higher education evaluation system in order to secure EU research funding long before the crisis. For health care, an exception is the 2014 introduction of a standard health package for all citizens following decades of unequal access (promoting some equity in the system), the introduction of e-prescriptions, and the implementation of the OECD based accounting system in hospitals increasing transparency in the payment and procurement systems. As we argue in the conclusions presented in Section 5, Greece still needs to promote radical reform by introducing an institutional framework of independent regulation, oversight and evaluation that is answerable to, but not controlled by, the state. Such a system needs to be understood, supported and owned by the people of Greece as a way to ensure that the services that they are entitled to as taxpayers and citizens of the country are provided in a sustainable, cost efficient and equitable way, thus ensuring universal access and quality.

2 Models of education and health provision

2.1 Supply and demand criteria in health and education

Every country has an obligation to provide healthcare and education as these two services are essential to enable the people of the country to effectively participate as citizens in society. The provision of these services must satisfy, on the supply side, the main social criteria of equity, equal opportunities for all, universal coverage, accessibility, and, where appropriate, affordability. On the demand side, as both services are experience, or even credence, goods, their quality cannot be easily ascertained by direct users, either before its use or, in many cases, even after.[4] Moreover, as there is an informational asymmetry on the users' side, the state must ensure not only the continuity and sustainability in the provision of such services, but also their quality, irrespective of whether these are publically or privately provided. Hence there is a need for an institutional framework ensuring the independent regulation of such systems using a transparent system of evaluation, assessment, oversight, and accountability in their provision.

Since the late 1990s, there has been an attempt in some developed countries, such as the UK, to transform the provision of such services into "user choice" public service markets, where the focus is on the promotion of competition and, through it, increased user choice, without sacrificing any of the above social principles, a theme discussed in more detail below.

OECD countries offer a variety of models in health and education provision. The acceptance of services provided by private-for-profit companies, social companies (mutuals, charities etc.) and state providers varies across populations. For example; US families are used to the idea of paying for their children's university education as private universities were established earlier than public universities (Musselin 2010). Similar arrangements apply to countries like Cyprus. In Greece, education is viewed as being an exclusive concern of the state (Education Act 1985), and its con-

4 See Dassiou et al. (2015, 2016), on credence goods in terms of time lags (time required to establish quality through criteria such as survival rates, employment outcomes etc.), difficulty of establishing a counterfactual, or problems of attrition (e.g. health and education being two factors among many that define educational or health outcomes).

stitution prohibits the establishment of private universities. Total private spending on health was consistently about 1/3 of total health spending in the years immediately before the recession and was even higher in the early 2000s.[5]

2.2 Health and education as merit goods

Health and education are categorised as merit goods in economic theory i.e. they are characterised by large positive externalities in their consumption.[6] While such services are not public goods, as they are both rival (e.g. prone to congestion and hence there is rivalry in their consumption) and excludable (e.g. in principle it is possible to exclude people from being served), the social benefit to society of "consuming" health and education services significantly exceeds the private benefit to the direct beneficiary. If the provision of these goods was left solely to the private sector, these services would be massively under consumed and society would miss the large positive externalities. In other words, the market mechanism cannot meet the wider policy objectives as the users do not internalise the full social benefits of their actions. Hence state funding is required to correct a market failure (under consumption) for these two merit goods, whose significant spill overs are not wholly captured by their immediate users.

While state funding is therefore justified, in principle there is no reason why the state could not just hand out vouchers or direct payments to users, letting them choose a supplier. This approach creates a user choice based quasi- market approach where the providers chase the funding by the state, now in the hands of the consumers of such services. Providers have an incentive to compete with each other for consumers' custom. This should lead to improvements in quality and innovation. For example, Sweden gives parents vouchers that they are able to redeem not only in state schools, but also in private schools, where they have the choice to top up if required.[7] The UK started offering personal budgets to older and disabled people wishing to buy their own care, while UK universities compete with each other for students, while the state (through the Student Loans Company) provides the latter with loans to "purchase" tertiary education. The reason why this does not happen more widely is that even if we assume hypothetically that all the users had the ability to effectively choose in this manner (plurality of providers, free entry and exit in the market, ability of users to access, assess and act on information regarding all aspects of the service etc.), the state may wish to pursue different objectives like fairness, equity, social justice, and, most importantly, implement budget constraints in their provision.

Ultimately, even where the user may exercise choice by directly purchasing the service, the user's choice is restricted by the funding for the service from the state or the relevant regional/local authority. For example, in the case of school choice in the UK, it would be more accurate to say that the user (the parent) can state a preference rather than being able to exercise the right to choose which school their child attends. Hence the choice of available school places is restricted by how many schools there are in the area, as well as the capacity of these schools.

---

5 See OECD data on Government expenditure by function (COFOG). https://stats.oecd.org/Index.aspx?DataSetCode=SNA_TABLE11#

6 For a closer analysis on merit goods, externalities and market failures, the reader can refer to any microeconomics or industrial organisation textbook (e.g. Griffiths and Wall 2000).

7 This is far more radical that it may seem at a first glance. It means that taxpayers' money in the provision of education ends up with private firms and also that the taxpayers using private education no longer cross-subsidize (by paying for a service they do not use) the ones using state provision.

3 The Greek education system

3.1 Primary and secondary education

The education system in Greece has the following structure: primary education (PE), lower secondary education (gymnasium—LSE) followed by upper secondary education (USE) in lyceums or technical vocational schools (EPALs). Education is mandatory until the completion of gymnasium at 15. Students aged 15–18 complete either lyceum or go to a technical school; both lasting 3 years.

Higher education consists of universities and vocationally oriented technological education institutes (TEIs), both offering 4 year study programmes. Graduates of lyceums are eligible to take national exams that determine eligibility for entry into universities and TEIs, while graduates of EPALs are eligible for admission to TEIs and, as of 2009,[8] also universities. Further education also exists, in the form of vocational education institutes (IEKs) (Xochellis and Kesidou 2007). There is plethora of such institutes across the country, both public and private (the duration of study at these is two years, with a further 6 months of work experience).

According to Eurostat data, Greece's spending on education as a percentage of the GDP is one of the lowest in Europe, at 4.1 percent in 2005, compared to 6.8 percent in Germany, 5.4 percent for the UK, 6 percent in Sweden and 8 percent in Denmark (2006 figures). About 6–7 percent of all pupils attend private schools. However there is another form of private education spending, in the form of a parallel system created since the mid-1990s. Private cramming groups (phrontistiria) or home tutors are used by the majority of pupils who wish to be admitted to university during the last year (or last two years) of upper secondary education (Papapolydorou 2010: p. 123). In 2008 spending on phrontistiria was, on average, 20 percent of a household's expenditure. Prices for daily 3-hour lessons are around 500 euros per month. Obviously pupils from more affluent families can afford to spend more time taking such lessons; the BBC reports that children from affluent families spend 4 times more time in these classes than those from less affluent families.[9] Given the one-third reduction in median income and an unemployment rate at around 25 percent, this gap in affordability has increased further, violating the principles of equal opportunity and accessibility to higher education.[10] Many public school teachers also work in such tuition centres in order to supplement their low salaries. Obviously if the students are taught by the same teacher both at school and at the tuition centre, there is a conflict of interest leading to perverse incentives.

Although, maximum class size is defined by law to be 25 pupils in primary education and 30 in secondary education, in practice many schools in Greece have significantly fewer pupils.

---

8 With the aim of promoting equality of access in tertiary education, as working class students were over represented in EPALs and, hence, effectively excluded from access to the more academic type of higher education offered by universities.

9 www.bbc.co.uk/news/business-34384671

10 Hanushek and Wößmann (2006) find that Greece is the second most inequitable country after Germany, as measured by the increase in inequality between primary and secondary education. Also the parents' occupational status is largely related to the student performance and this correlation is stronger in Greece that in other non-selective countries such as Scandinavian ones.

The 2011 OECD report stressed that pupils to teacher rates (as highlighted in tables 1–3) were very low in Greece compared to the OECD averages: the figures for 2007 were 10.1, 7.7 and 7.3 in PE, LSE and USE, respectively, versus OECD averages of 16.0, 13.2 and 12.5. To correct for the existence of schools with very few pupils, in 2011 the government consolidated 1,933 schools into 877 schools. This decrease in the number of schools is reflected in Tables 1 and 2, showing primary and lower secondary education, as well as, to a lesser extent, in Table 3, showing upper secondary education.

The need to improve efficiency and rationalisation in the coverage of the school networks is limited by the geographic diversity of Greece. Approximately 54 percent of primary school students are clustered in two regions: Attica and Central Macedonia, with pupils concentrated in the city of Athens and Thessaloniki respectively. The remainder of pupils are dispersed across thousands of communities in mountainous, isolated, regions across Greece and on its 227 populated islands, of which only 78 have more than 100 residents.

Net teaching time in Greece is strikingly lower than both OECD and EU averages. This, combined with persistently low pupils to teacher ratios, leads to high salary costs in education, despite low teacher salaries. In addition, teaching time is inversely related to qualifications and experience, meaning that the less prepared and less experienced teachers have to teach more. Some modest increases in teaching hours were introduced in 2013 with the aim of bringing these to OECD averages by 2015, albeit once more by increasing the teaching hours of junior staff more than those of senior staff. Unfortunately many of the policy recommendations either were never implemented or were reversed, and it is only at the time of writing this paper, in late 2015, that there is talk of evaluating and approving the OECD 2011 recommendations for implementation in the 2016/17 teaching year, if not later. This is unfortunate as it misleadingly links sensible reforms, which should have been implemented years ago when the Greek economy was experiencing fast growth, to austerity measures in the minds of parents and pupils.

Schools in Greece have no autonomy and virtually no say in the hiring of teachers, their dismissal, establishing starting salaries or increases, or formulating the school budget. All of these decisions rest with the regional or national education authority. This is in stark contrast with what is common practice in other OECD countries. As the selection and remuneration of teachers is isolated from the school itself, the teachers have no incentives to build a commitment to the school that they are appointed to. Teachers are hired using a waiting list where ranking is determined using various socio-economic criteria. Progression rules are based on seniority rather than criteria relating to their effectiveness or training related experience as teachers.

The OECD 2011 policy recommendations suggest a simple conceptual framework of evaluation and analysis with assessment at different levels: at the pupil level (in the classroom), teacher appraisal (by the school leadership), school assessment (by the local authority), and system evaluation (by the regulator or education department).

However, what is required in the long term is that the budget allocations to schools should follow a carefully set up algorithm using a per-pupil funding formula with weights for age, education level, family income, and other background characteristics, including special needs and learning difficulties. The formula would allow funds according to school location, teacher positions, operational costs and investments. For this to be implemented a reliable database is needed, with live data reporting on pupils, teachers, and schools, including information on buildings

Table 1

Primary education (primary schools): School units, teaching staff and pupils, end of the school years 2000/01–2012/13

Type of school	2000/01	2001/02	2002/03	2003/04	2004/05	2005/06	2006/07	2007/08	2008/09	2009/10	2010/11	2011/12	2012/13
Public													
School units	5,708	5,600	5,541	5,471	5,398	5,297	5,220	5,174	5,127	5.075	4.991	4.392	4.350
Teaching staff	48,872	50,986	52,775	57,305	59,387	60,814	63,513	64,058	64,977	66.409	66.018	63.396	61.726
Pupils	593,094	597,847	600,254	605,961	599,843	596,652	593,583	590,491	590,640	589.578	590.203	590.070	588.832
Pupils per teacher	12.1	11.7	11.4	10.6	10.1	9.8	9.3	9.2	9.0	8,9	8,9	9,3	9,5
Private													
School units	386	389	384	383	380	378	374	372	369	365	365	354	348
Teaching staff	3,218	3,334	3,360	3,465	3,495	3,602	3,829	3,985	4,041	4.066	3.967	3.918	3.831
Pupils	46,838	48,484	48,233	48,819	47,700	46,548	46,378	46,818	46,836	46.357	43.845	43.221	41.211
Pupils per teacher	14.6	14.5	14.4	14.1	13.6	12.9	12.1	11.7	11.6	11,4	11,1	11,0	10,8

1 Also including –"absent" teachers, but only for public schools. Absent teachers are the teachers with a fixed post in the school unit who are absent for more than 20 working days(due to illness, training, maternity leave, etc.) and their replacement is pending, as well as the teachers who are seconded to other administrative posts of the Ministry of Education and Religious Affairs, Culture and Sports or elsewhere.

Source: Hellenic Statistical Authority at: www.statistics.gr/portal/page/portal/ESYE/PAGE-themes?p_param=A1401&r_param=SED12&y_param=2012_00&mytabs=0

Table 2

Secondary education (lower secondary schools): School units, teaching staff and pupils, end of the school years 2000/01–2012/13

Type of school	2000/01	2001/02	2002/03	2003/04	2004/05	2005/06	2006/07	2007/08	2008/09	2009/10	2010/11	2011/12	2012/13
Public													
School units	1,760	1,762	1,723	1,811	1,797	1,834	1,847	1,851	1,859	1,860	1,826	1,729	1,729
Teaching staff(1)	37,340	38,757	38,892	41,627	43,137	44,477	46,606	47,727	49,335	50,208	46,762	43,071	40,585
Pupils	329,842	318,897	305,448	307,218	308,861	317,091	325,514	322,391	322,242	318,875	315,606	308,185	304,863
Pupils per teacher	8.8	8.2	7.9	7.4	7.2	7.1	7.0	6.8	6.5	6.4	6.7	7.2	7.5
Private													
School units	110	105	96	107	107	112	111	106	109	105	102	100	98
Teaching staff	2,327	2,135	2,095	2,297	2,309	2,446	2,495	2,473	2,523	2,397	2,277	2,202	2,080
Pupils	18,916	17,253	16,233	16,115	16,290	17,144	18,251	18,716	19,073	18,063	16,399	16,217	15,087

1 Also including –"absent" teachers, but only for public schools, Absent teachers are the teachers with a fixed post in the school unit who are absent for more than 20 working days(due to illness, training, maternity leave, etc,) and their replacement is pending, as well as the teachers who are seconded to other administrative posts of the Ministry of Education and Religious Affairs, Culture and Sports or elsewhere,

Source: Hellenic Statistical Authority at: www,statistics,gr/portal/page/portal/ESYE/PAGE-themes?p_param=A1401&r_param=SED12&y_param=2012_00&mytabs=0

Table 3

Secondary general education (upper secondary schools): School units, teaching staff and pupils, end of the school years 2000/01–2012/13

Type of school	2000/01	2001/02	2002/03	2003/04	2004/05	2005/06	2006/07	2007/08	2008/09	2009/10	2010/11	2011/12	2012/13
Public													
School units	1,199	1,146	1,171	1,191	1,212	1,246	1,252	1,264	1,264	1,265	1,244	1,228	1,225
Teaching staff(1)	23,484	23,420	23,605	24,428	26,014	28,099	27,028	28,122	28,756	29,197	28,015	25,817	25,567
Pupils	225,057	214,361	212,628	217,530	219,134	222,519	217,061	223,527	225,507	231,766	231,593	232,145	230,998
Pupils per teacher	9.6	9.2	9.0	8.9	8.4	7.9	8.0	7.9	7.8	7.9	8.3	9.0	9.0
Private													
School units	90	92	97	99	100	106	109	105	103	96	94	92	93
Teaching staff	1,897	1,989	1,993	2,075	2,020	2,172	2,103	2,036	1,927	1,821	1,768	1,855	1,760
Pupils	16,157	15,804	16,119	16,193	15,963	16,456	15,825	16,125	16,219	15,675	15,627	15,572	14,894
Pupils per teacher	8.5	7.9	8.1	7.8	7.9	7.6	7.5	7.9	8.4	8.6	8.8	8.4	8.5

1 Also including –"absent" teachers, but only for public schools. Absent teachers are the teachers with a fixed post in the school unit who are absent for more than 20 working days(due to illness, training, maternity leave, etc.) and their replacement is pending, as well as the teachers who are seconded to other administrative posts of the Ministry of Education and Religious Affairs, Culture and Sports or elsewhere.
Source: Hellenic Statistical Authority at: www.statistics.gr/portal/page/portal/ESYE/PAGE-themes?p_param=A1401&r_param=SED12&y_param=2012_00&mytabs=0

and infrastructure. The system should encourage the formation of clusters where small schools team up with larger ones by sharing resources, teachers, management, and best practice teaching methods, while allowing for an alternative approach for small primary schools in isolated regions.

Incentives should be built into the system, not only in the form of sticks but also carrots recognizing and rewarding on the basis of output/outcomes (e.g. pupils' performance and learning achievement, as well as teaching, assessment, and leadership quality). Success should not just be recognised in the remuneration of the school's management and teaching staff, but also advertised to parents and pupils in order to secure their support of the reforms.

3.2 Tertiary education

Greece has 22 universities, while there are 16 TEIs operating a total of 212 departments in 46 municipalities. The establishment of a plethora of TEI locations since the mid-1990s means that Greece has the highest number of tertiary education enrolments per 100,000 people, at 5,478, in the world.[11] Although Greek universities have low graduation rates—around 17 percent in 2007, as opposed to an OECD average exceeding 35 percent—data from the same year suggests that graduation rates in TEIs at 12 percent in 2007, are above both OECD and EU averages at 10 percent and 8 percent respectively.

As Figure 2 illustrates, enrolment in Universities significantly increased until 2005, then decreased slightly before stabilising. The diagram reflects the caps in student numbers set by the state rather than actual demand as reflected by the number of pupils taking the higher education entrance examination. As an indication, in 2014 there were around 105,000 students taking the national entrance exams, but only 70,305 open positions at higher education institutions around the country. While it is relatively easy to gain entry in to a higher education institution, it is very difficult to gain entry at a university, especially the pupil's first preference, with many ending up at a TEI instead. Figure 1 shows the numbers of teaching staff and graduates in Greek universities. The relative static number of graduates, around 10,000–14,000 each year, despite the increasing number of students, reflects the aforementioned low graduation rates from Greek universities.

In the 1990s the EU emerged as a major funding source for academic research in higher education. The Bologna Process (1999) established the principles of an evaluation and quality assurance framework, and paved the way for the creation of a national system of quality assurance to be implemented by all EU countries (Mattheou 2004). The establishment of such a framework, was a pre-requisite for Greece to implement as part of the process of European unification, and also necessary to secure access to European funds for academic research. Universities wishing to participate in European projects had to familiarise themselves with evaluation mechanisms and discourse. As a result, they adopted criteria from the EU toolkit including internal and external evaluation, accountability, quality and efficiency. As part of the Europeanization process, universities had to offer new degrees with a more pragmatic orientation (vocation-wise) in finance, business and technology. Moreover, the EU's Operational Programme of Education and Initial Vocational Training (OPEIVT) led to the establishment of new university departments and TEIs across the country, as well as an increase in teaching staff numbers as shown in Figure 1. How-

11 OECD (2011: p. 65).

Figure 1

Tertiary education in Greece over 2000–2012

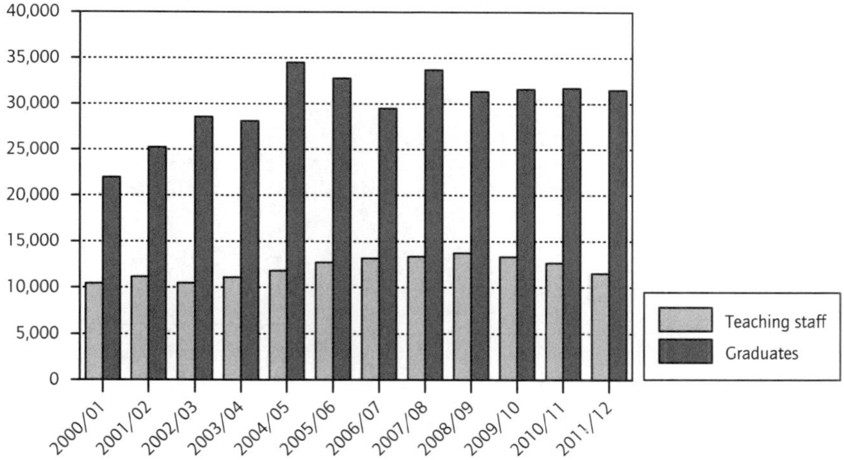

Source: Constructed by the author using ELSTAT (Hellenic Statistical Authority) data on tertiary education.

ever the creation of these more served mayoral and local community ambitions, resulting in the creation of "flying professors,"[12] rather than the intended objective of fostering innovation and entrepreneurship in underdeveloped regions of Greece or responding to genuine demand from potential students in the region. In addition, a complex system of transfers of students between universities and TEIs in different regions using ad hoc and ever changing socioeconomic criteria, means that many departments in the regions end up with far fewer students that they planned for and vice versa for metropolitan areas such as Athens and Thessaloniki.

Despite the backlash (Prokou 2010), evaluation mechanisms in Greek universities were formally implemented in 2005; these included both internal and external evaluation, the use of evaluation indicators, the implementation of the European Credits Transfer Scheme (ECTS), and 4-year Development Academic Planning as a requirement for universities seeking to secure public funding (Zmas 2015).

Regardless of the significant reductions in research, investment, infrastructure and operational costs funding since 2011, the improvements made since the mid-1990s are becoming visible: Greek universities now have quality assurance mechanisms and the majority also have established mechanisms for internal and external evaluation, while an increasing number of institutions are finally adopting Development Academic Planning.

However when it comes to the student unions there is still a "beyond reasonable involvement in the political process in university campuses" (OECD 2011: p. 77) that started in the 1980s and persists to this day, endangering not just academic freedom but also the quality of teaching and

12 Academic staff that taught for 1–2 days per week at a regional university or TEI, who then flew back home on subsidised tickets.

Figure 2

The number of students in Greek tertiary education over 2000–2012

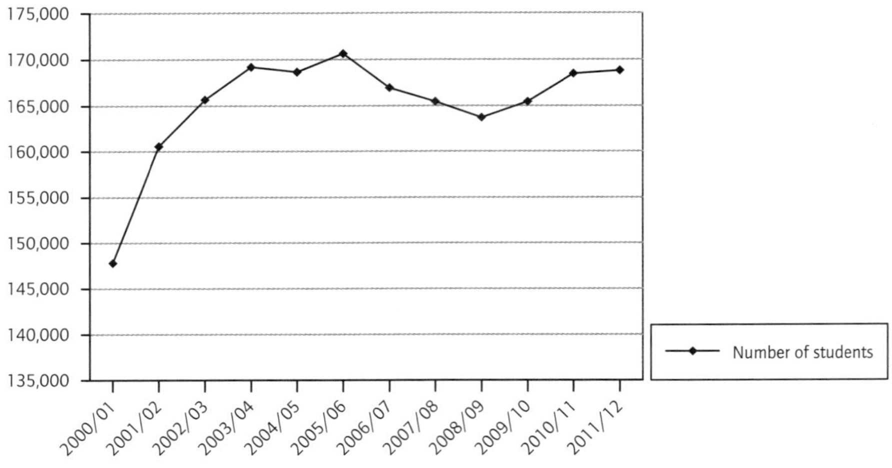

Source: Constructed by the author using ELSTAT (Hellenic Statistical Authority) data on tertiary education.

learning in higher education institutions. In terms of attainment, Greek universities are still low in research league tables, while the employment prospects of Greek graduates are the bleakest in the EU with an almost 20 percent unemployment rate. The introduction of a law in 2011 based on the bailout requirements led to the merging of university departments and a change in university management with the aspiration of sharpening the strategic focus of universities to conducting innovative research that will lead to an improvement of their position in the research league rankings, attaining international recognition, as well as ensuring financial and administrative autonomy from the state.

4 The Greek health system

The Greek public health system is a hybrid that includes a compulsory social insurance aspect, together with a National Health System (ESY), as well as co-payments by patients.[13] In addition the private sector includes profit making hospitals, diagnostic centres and independent practices. Table 4[14] gives a brief description of the three types of health systems typically found in most countries; we see that Greece is a combination of all three types.

13 For drugs there is typically a 25 percent co-payment fee. There are also fees for private afternoon outpatient clinic consultations. In the last 2–3 years fees for morning outpatient clinics and hospital admissions were introduced, but both were withdrawn following public outcry. (See Zaracostas 2011, and Doctors of the World 2013a, 2013b, on increases in user fees and access to health care.)

14 This is a much reduced and modified version of a table constructed by Professor Mireia Jofre-Bonet as part of her lecture notes at City University London for the MSc in Economic Evaluation in Health Care.

The post war era saw the creation of a plethora of Social Security Funds (SSFs) in Greece (over 300 in 2001) providing health coverage to their members. According to Economou (2010) these have been merged into 4 funds covering 95 percent of the population in 2010, and the plan is to integrate all schemes into one by January 2018.[15] There is no regulator or other institutional body governing the relationship between ESY and the SSFs; nor is there a jurisdictional map. ESY is taxpayer funded while SSFs depend on employer contributions, employee contributions, as well as state subsidies funded by the taxpayers. This hybrid system has led to two sources of entitlement: the first is based on citizenship for access to outpatient services provided by ESY only, and the second is based on employment status, provided by insurance fund membership for access to doctors, diagnostic tests, etc. (see footnote 15), as well as access to inpatient services (e.g. hospitals) provided by the ESY. This has meant that health coverage was largely dependent on being employed or self-employed (with wives and children also enjoying coverage as the dependants of the insured). As a consequence, the fall in employment as a result of the economic crisis, combined with the fact that a large number of people are self-employed (40.6 percent of male and 31.2 percent of females according to 2012 figures provided by the OECD) meant that many people found themselves without coverage after one year in unemployment (recently this has been increased to two years) or with no coverage at all after ceasing their self-employment activity and/or stopping self-insurance payments.

Table 5 (constructed using Eurostat online data) shows the split between different financing agents in 2012 for different OECD countries. Private expenditure on health (including private payments and private insurance) in Greece is 31.8 percent, one of the highest by European standards, only surpassed by Cyprus, Bulgaria and Latvia, while being broadly similar to that for Portugal, Hungary, Lithuania and Switzerland.

Figure 3[16] shows the split among the three sources of health spending in Greece between 2009 and 2013, where we see the private funding share increase from 30.3 percent to 35.6 percent of total spending, while the role of social security funds shrank from 43.1 percent to 34.3 percent over the same period (because, as discussed above, there was an increase in unemployment, a reduction in the number of self-employed as many small businesses failed, while many self-employed could no longer afford to pay their own social security contributions or contributions for their employees). Figure 4,[17] shows the split of total funding to public funding (government spending plus social security funds) and private funding, with the former decreasing by almost 38 percent over 2009–2103 and the latter by 20 percent, amounting to a fall in total health spending of 32 percent. The fact that public funding fell faster than private funding explains the increase in the share of private funding as seen in Figure 3. Both are the result of the economic crisis and the imposition of austerity in Greece, which has led to a reduction in both availability and affordability of healthcare in Greece.

15 These plethora of funds linked to different occupational groups gave different levels of health benefits coverage and access to health to their members (not directly linked to the level of contributions), violating equity, universality and social fairness objectives. The government provided subsidies to these funds also varied. Fortunately, as we report below, reforms since 2010 led to a standardization of health benefits package for all citizens (Economou et al. 2014).

16 Chart 3, p. 7, Press Release, System of Health Accounts of year 2013 & revision of SHA data of years 2009–2011, Hellenic Statistical Authority, 2015. www.statistics.gr/portal/page/portal/ESYE/BUCKET/A2103/PressReleases/A2103_SHE35_DT_AN_00_2013_01_F_EN.pdf

17 Chart 2, ibid.

Table 4

Comparision of different health systems

	Private health insurance	Social health insurance	Taxation
Key features	1. Insurance is voluntary 2. Premiums are paid by the individuals and /or their employer 3. Premiums are based on individual risk status 4. Insurance providers may be profit maximisers or have goals other than profit maximization 5. Insurance provision may be via indemnity plans or managed care organisations (MCOs)	1. Insurance is compulsory for all or part of the population 2. Premiums are usually paid in the form of a hypotheca-ted payroll tax 3. Payments are related to ability to pay usually as a pro-portion of income; they are not related to individual risk 4. Payments are made into a social insurance fund	1. Insurance is compulsory for the whole population 2. Premiums are paid in the form of tax payments made to the government 3. Payments are related to ability to pay; they are not related to individual risk 4. Taxes can be: indirect or direct; general or hypotheca-ted; set locally, regionally or nationally
Countries with predominantly this type of system	USA, Switzerland	France, Germany, Luxemburg, Netherlands	Denmark, Finland, Ireland, Italy, Norway, Portugal, Spain, Sweden, UK
Dealing with affordability	1. Retrospective reimbur-sement 2. Selective contracting and vertical integration between the third party payers and health care providers	Compulsory insurance in which payments are related to ability to pay	Compulsory insurance in which payments are related to ability to pay

Source: See footnote 14.

Given that health is free at the point of use, overconsumption may lead to waste. To prevent overspending, choice may be exercised on behalf of the user by the family doctor. In many health systems, general practitioners and family physicians form what is commonly called the primary care level, while the secondary health care sector includes specialised care and hospitals. In several northern European countries including the UK, as well as in Italy, Portugal, and Spain, the primary care level plays the role of the "gatekeeper" to the health system. The patient is not authorised to consult a specialist if she has not first consulted a general practitioner with whom she has a record.

Given that the family doctor should also promote the interests of the patient, a gatekeeping arrangement may lead to an obvious conflict. For example, in the UK a family doctor acts an agent for the patient (advising him on treatment options, choice of specialists, hospitals etc.), as well as an agent for the state in his roles of gatekeeper and budget-holder. This means that she may face conflicting incentives in her dual role.[18] Interestingly, referral by a general practitioner to a specialist or a hospital is necessary even in the case where the patient elects to go private. This

18 See Van Stolk et al. (2010) on the double agency issue: providers are expected to act as agents of both patients and payers. The shifting of the responsibility for commissioning care to GPs has given rise to questions concerning the commissioning skills, capacity, and incentives of GPs to ensure value for money for both their patients and the taxpayers (see Crowe et. al. 2014).

Table 5

Healthcare expenditure by financing agent, 2012

In percent of current healthcare expenditure

	General government excluding social security funds	Social security funds	Private insurance enterprises (including private social insurance)	Private household out-of-pocket expenditure	Non-profit institutions serving households	Corporations (other than health insurance)
Belgium	10.9	64.3	4.2	20.4	0.2	0.0
Bulgaria[1]	15.5	38.8	0.4	44.5	0.5	0.4
Czech Republic	4.5	79.2	0.2	15.3	0.4	0.3
Denmark	85.2	0.0	1.8	12.9	0.1	0.0
Germany	6.8	70.4	9.6	12.2	0.5	0.5
Estonia	10.5	69.1	0.3	18.4	0.0	1.4
Greece	28.7	39.3	3.0	28.8	0.1	0.0
Spain	67.0	4.7	5.8	22.1	0.4	:
France	3.9	73.8	13.8	7.8	0.0	0.6
Croatia	2.6	76.9	7.7	12.8	:	:
Cyprus	45.7	0.7	4.5	47.2	0.2	1.7
Latvia[2]	59.6	0.0	2.5	37.8	0.2	0.0
Lithuania	9.0	58.1	0.8	31.8	0.0	0.1
Luxembourg	8.6	74.0	4.6	11.6	1.2	0.0
Hungary	8.1	53.8	2.7	29.1	2.0	4.2
Netherlands	7.5	78.3	5.5	6.0	1.3	1.5
Austria	32.6	44.6	4.8	16.7	1.2	0.1
Poland	6.4	63.6	0.8	24.3	1.4	3.6
Portugal[1]	64.2	1.3	4.9	28.9	0.1	0.5
Romania	12.1	67.8	0.2	19.5	0.1	0.3
Slovenia[1]	1.8	71.3	13.7	12.2	0.1	1.0
Slovakia[1]	7.2	66.5	0.0	23.6	1.0	1.7
Finland	59.7	15.1	2.2	19.6	1.0	2.5
Sweden	81.2	:	0.3	17.5	0.2	0.8
Norway	73.6	11.4	:	:	:	:
Switzerland	20.3	45.5	7.2	26.0	1.0	:
Australia[1]	68.3	:	8.8	19.4	0.6	2.9
Canada[1]	68.5	1.4	12.9	15.5	:	1.6
Japan[1]	9.6	72.8	2.5	14.1	:	1.0
New Zealand[1]	74.9	7.8	4.8	10.9	1.6	0.0
South Korea	11.4	44.4	5.8	37.6	0.6	0.1
United States	5.3	43.3	34.8	12.5	3.9	0.2

1 2011.
2 2010.
Source: Eurostat (online data code: hlth_sha_hf).

Figure 3

Funding on health expenditures
In percent

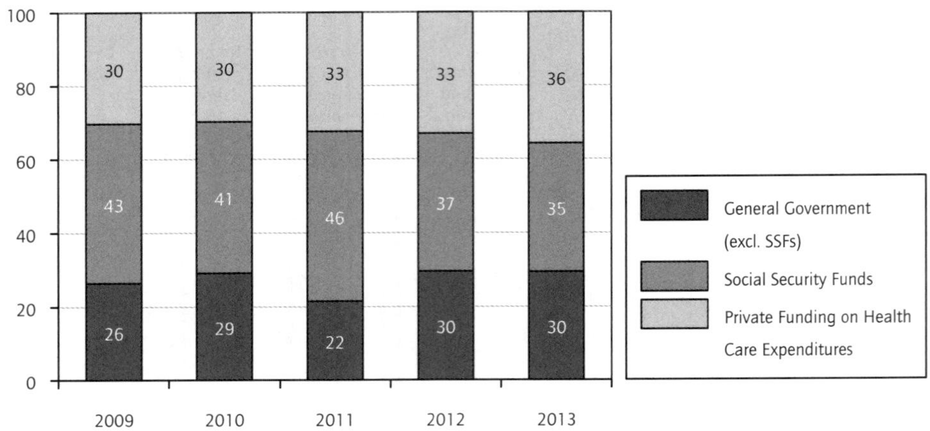

Source: See footnote 16.

is because private healthcare is not only provided by the 200 or so private hospitals, but also by private patient units in National Health Service hospitals.[19]

This 'gate' system is not present in Greece (nor in Belgium, France, Germany, and Luxemburg). In terms of user choice, Greek patients enjoy a more market oriented approach than the UK. They can choose any public hospital to receive treatment and have access, as part of primary care, to any specialised doctor, provided that the doctor is contracted with the patient's insurance fund. The pay of primary care doctors is on a "fee per service" basis, which leads to "supplier-induced demand" (Van Stolk et al. 2010, p. 18), where doctors use the information asymmetry to alter patient preferences and provide more services than necessary, thus leading to a waste of taxpayers' money.

Economou (2010) reports on sensible reforms introduced between 2001 and 2004, which, following the 2004 election, were either abolished or never implemented. Fortunately reforms since 2010 have led to the standardization of health benefits package for all citizens (Economou et al. 2014b), thus restoring equity, along with the introduction of a prospective payments system for hospital care, the implementation of the system of health accounting used by the OECD, the introduction of more transparency in the system of procurement, the introduction of e-prescriptions, and the increased use of generic drugs in prescriptions. However the improvements that such reforms would have brought would have been more pronounced and better received by people if they had been implemented when the economy was growing fast in the early 2000s,

19 The German system differs substantially, as the funding is patient–based, so data on patients are not centralised, but are sent to the sickness benefit fund of each patient with the aim of financing the care for each patient and subsequently covering the costs of the hospitals.

Figure 4

Total funding on health expenditures by financing agency

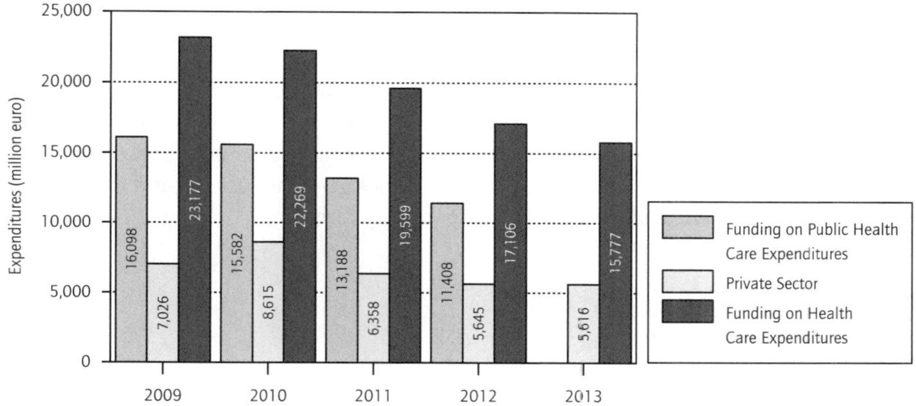

Source: See footnote 17.

rather than during the economic crisis and presented to its citizens as a necessary by-product of the economic austerity.

Regarding universality and accessibility, the economic crisis led to medical needs increasing among both unemployed and employed people (Dubois and Anderson, 2013). In the European Quality of Life survey respondents indicated distance (45 percent of respondents), delay of appointment (67 percent) waiting time to see a doctor (66 percent) and cost (64 percent) as a barriers to access in to healthcare in 2011; in addition there was a 50 percent increase in the reporting of unmet medical need in 2011 relative to 2007. A study by Karamitri et al. (2013) looks at the perceptions of health professionals on the accessibility to health services by vulnerable people. Physicians report bureaucratic procedures, the lack of translation of access procedures and medical interpreters, as well as the lack of a link between primary and secondary healthcare, leading to a clustering of vulnerable people in emergency departments, as the main impediments to access. The Thales European project in Greece is one example of attempting to remove barriers to informed access by establishing a website as well as information kiosks in large cities in Greece with information translated into different languages, on access to publicly funded services, on the rights of migrants with regard to access to healthcare services, on co-payments, and on the identification of symptoms of infectious diseases.

The lack of a health regulator in Greece leaves the problem of asymmetric information on the demand side unaddressed, as there is no one to oversee the quality of health care provided to the users of the health system. It is also problematic on the procurement side, given the lack of institutional oversight over the purchasing activities of insurance funds, thus leaving room for corruption and nepotism. Reimbursement levels and the prices paid to providers are regulated by the central government. A large part of the private sector enters into contracts with the social insurance funds, mainly providing primary care. In 2011 the government briefly investigated the option of transforming PODY (former EOPYY), the provider of primary care, to a purchaser only body that commissions health care services from providers. However this step is not realistic unless the system is first subjected to independent oversight and regulation to ensure transparency in procurement through the establishment of an independent agency.

The other missing piece of the puzzle is the incentives for doctors. As we already noted, the fee for service pay that contracted doctors receive creates perverse incentives to overspend rather than economize. Doctors in hospitals receive a modest salary and there is no clear system for promotion given the lack of an evaluation system. As a consequence, some of these doctors also retain a private practice, while others solicit or accept bribes given by patients and their relatives who hope to jump the queue and/or receive prompt quality care.

5 Conclusions

The severe problems in funding for health and education induced by austerity measures (imposed as part of three successive bailouts) are magnified by a lack of coherence and continuity: even before the economic crisis (in fact, ever since the restoration of democracy in 1974) Greece has had a large number of education and health ministers with terms of service that, on average, amount to a few months, not years. This means that no minister has ever had the time to design a coherent policy, own it, and then implement it. The constant change of ministers has accelerated since 2008 as the negotiation of three bailout programmes has led to a political crisis in the country, with each party in government toppled after a maximum of 2 years, rather than serving a full 4 year term. Consequently, a completely new ministerial team is introduced by each successive new government as it takes office, in addition to the frequent reshuffling of ministerial positions in education and health by any given government. This has led to a further deterioration in policy design and implementation, just when it was most sorely needed: many laws were passed without proper design or stakeholder consultation only to be reversed by later governments or never implemented, unless said laws were pre-requisites for accessing bailout funding. In other words, there is a persistent and significant divergence between the enactment and the enforcement of legislation in the health and education sector. The state controls all economic activity related to the provision of health and education. Any attempts for reform, for rationalizing, evaluating or improving are either resisted or stalled.

Under these circumstances, it is clear that only a paradigm shift can provide a legitimate response capable of winning back the trust of the citizens, both as taxpayers and as the users of these services. The country urgently needs the establishment of an institutional framework for independent regulation (with a regulator/agency answerable only to the parliament rather than the government) in health and education so that a competent small group of health technologists, economists, healthcare managers and education specialists become responsible for monitoring these sectors, overseeing the implementation of policy, ensuring continuity, performing oversight and evaluating the system in order to protect the interests of the users, both present and future (i. e. ensure the system is sustainable). This is similar to the current regulatory arrangements in the European Union surrounding utility services (e. g. national watchdogs in energy markets, telecoms, etc.).

Reforms need to be coherent and fully owned with a strategy plan that clearly sets out the benefits and the risks. The system should include an evaluation system with clear rules and with incentives in the form of a carrot (reward) and stick (punishment) approach. The anxieties and concerns of citizens should be addressed, with the reforms explained in a way that simplifies the stakes, making the necessity for specific reforms understandable. Finally the regulator should be granted independence, with a clear de-coupling from the state that allows it to overcome embedded resistance to the implementation of reforms from interest groups.

References

— BMJ (2011): 342:d200. www.bmj.com/content/342/bmj.d200 (accessed on 19 October 2015).
— Bologna Declaration (1999): The European higher education area, Bologna, June 19.
— Crowe, D., T. Gash, and H. Kippin (2014): Beyond big contracts. London, Institute for Government.
— Dassiou, X., P. Langham, C. Nancarrow, A. Scharaschkin, and D. Ward (2015): Public service markets; their economics, institutional oversight and regulation. Palgrave Communications (forthcoming).
— Dassiou, X., P. Langham, C. Nancarrow, A. Scharaschkin, and D. Ward (2016): New development: exploring public service markets. Public Money & Management, CIPFA (forthcoming).
— Doctors of the World (2013a): Access to healthcare in Europe in times of crisis and rising xenophobia: An overview of the situation of people excluded from healthcare systems.
— Doctors of the World (2013b): Access to health care for vulnerable groups in the European Union in 2012. www.europarl.europa.eu/document/activities/cont/201302/20130208ATT60776/20130208ATT60776EN.pdf
— Dubois, H., and H. Anderson (2013): Impacts of the crisis on access to healthcare services in the EU. Dublin, European Foundation for the Improvement of Living and Working Conditions.
— Economou C. (2010): Greece: Health system review. Health Systems in Transition, 12 (7), 1–180.
— Economou, C., D. Kaitelidou, D. Katsikas, O. Siskou, and M. Zafiropoulou (2014a): Impacts of the economic crisis on access to healthcare services in Greece with a focus on the vulnerable groups of the population. Social Cohesion and Development, 9 (2), 99–115.
— Economou, C., D. Kaitelidou, A. Kentikelenis, A. Sissouras, and A. Maresso (2014b): The impact of the financial crisis on the health system and health in Greece. World Health Organization for the European Observatory on Health Systems and Policies.
— Griffiths, A., and S. Wall (2000): Intermediate microeconomics: theory and applications, 2nd ed. Essex, Pearson Education Limited.
— Hanushek, E.A., and L. Wößmann (2006): Does educational tracking affect performance and inequality? Differences-in-differences evidence across countries. The Economic Journal, 116, C63–C76.
— Hellenic Statistical Authority (2015): System of health accounts (SHA) of year 2013 & revision of SHA data of years 2009-2012. Press Release 17 July 2015 at: www.statistics.gr/portal/page/portal/ESYE/BUCKET/A2103/PressReleases/A2103_SHE35_DT_AN_00_2013_01_F_EN.pdf
— Karamanoli, E. (2011): Debt crisis strains Greece's ailing health system. Lancet, 378, 303–304.

— Karamitri, I., T. Bellali, P. Galanis, and D. Kaitelidou (2013): The Accessibility of vulnerable groups to health services in Greece: a Delphi study on the perceptions of health professionals. The International Journal of Health Planning and Management, 28, 35–47.
— Karanikolos, M., P. Mladovsky, J. Cylus, S. Thomson, S. Basu, D. Stuckler, J. P. Mackenbach, and M. McKee (2013): Financial crisis, austerity, and health in Europe. The Lancet, 381 (9784), 1323–1331.
— Kentikelenis, A., M. Karanikolos, I. Papanicolas, S. Basu, M. McKee and D. Stuckler (2011): Health effects of financial crisis: omens of a Greek tragedy. Lancet, 378, 1457–1458.
— Kentikelenis, A., M. Karanikolos, A. Reeves, M. McKee, and D. Stuckler (2014): Greece's health crisis: from austerity to denialism. The Lancet, 383 (9918), 748–753.
— Kentikelenis, A., and I. Papanicolas (2012): Economic crisis, austerity and the Greek public health system. European Journal of Public Health, 22, 4–5.
— Mattheou, D., (2004): Marketing a new institutional identity for the University in Europe. The Bologna Process and the national context. In: E. Bulk-Berge, S. Holm-Larsen, and S. Wiborg (eds.): Education across borders- comparative studies. Oslo, Didakta, 57–72.
— Musselin, C. (2010): Universities and pricing on higher education markets. In: D. Mattheou (ed.): Changing Educational Landscapes. Chapter 4, 75–90.
— OECD (2011): Education policy advice for Greece; strong reformers and successful reformers in education. OECD publishing.
— Papapolydorou, M. (2010): Educational Inequalities in Greece, Sweden and the United Kingdom: A Comparative Analysis of the Origins. In: D. Mattheou (ed.): Changing Educational Landscapes, Chapter 7, 119–133.
— Pickles, M. (2015): Greek tragedy for education opportunities. BBC News, September 30. www.bbc.com/news/business-34384671 (accessed 2 December 2015).
— Prokou, E. (2010): University reform in Greece: a shift from intrinsic to extrinsic values. In: D. Mattheou (ed.): Changing Educational Landscapes, Chapter 3, 59–74.
— Stratis, A. (2014): Impact of the financial crisis on Greek Higher Education. www.iu.qs.com/2014/02/impact-of-the-financial-crisis-on-greek-higher-education/ (accessed on 7 October 2015).
— Van Stolk, C., G. Bjornsson, and S. Goshev (2010): Provider incentives in social protection and health. Rand Europe: Working Paper WR-799-WB.
— Xochellis, P., and A. Kesidou (2007): Greece. In: W. Hörner, H. Döbert, B. Von Korp, and W. Mitter (eds.): The Education Systems of Europe, 326–340.
— Zaracostas, J. (2011): Rise in user fees in Greece could reduce access to healthcare, charity warns. British Medical Journal, 11 Jan 2011.
— Zmas, A. (2015): Financial crisis and higher education policies in Greece: between intra— and super national pressures. Higher Education, 69, 495–508.

The Greek Tragedy in the Health Sector: Social and Health Implications

PLATON YFANTOPOULOS AND JOHN YFANTOPOULOS*

Platon Yfantopoulos, University of York, U. K., e-mail: py535@york.ac.uk
John Yfantopoulos, Health Economics University of Athens, e-mail: Yfantopoulos@gmail.com

Summary: Greece went into recession in 2009, after a decade of flourishing economic growth fluctuating annually around 4 percent; over the same period the average growth for the EU-27 was just about 2 percent. The economic downturn had a series of adverse effects on the economy and the health sector. More specifically, over the 2008–2015 period, GDP was reduced by 29.5 percent, wages were reduced by 35–45 percent, private consumption dropped by 30 percent and health expenditure declined by 41 percent. At the same time income inequality (shares S80/S20) increased by 11 percent and the unemployment rate reached 27.1 percent (an increase of 276.4 percent). The share of population at risk of poverty increased from 27.6 percent in 2009 to 36 percent in 2014. While life expectancy stabilized at about 80 years, infant mortality increased from 2.7 in 2008 to 3.8 in 2010, with a subsequent marginal reduction. The Eurozone countries and the IMF provided three rescue packages to Greece. The first economic adjustment program was signed in May 2010 between Greece and Troika (the European Commission, The European Central and the IMF) was worth 110 billion euro. The second adjustment program was signed in February 2012 and worth 130 billion euro, while the third one in June 2015 amounted to 86 billion euro. The terms of these bailouts included a series of required reforms, such as the liberalization of several protected economic and employment sectors, the reduction of public expenditures, the fight against corruption and the underground economy, the control of health expenditures, and the implementation of an austerity package. Consequently, the economic crisis has brought a significant deterioration to the health status and quality of life of the Greek Population. A set

→ JEL Classification: G01, G28, I10, L88
→ Keywords: Austerity, economic crisis, health expenditure, health sector, Greece

* We wish to thank Prof. Alexander Kritikos at the German Institute for Economic Research (DIW Berlin), University of Potsdam, Potsdam, Germany, and three anonymous referees for their constructive comments and valuable suggestions.

of quality of life instruments is used to assess the impact of the crisis on a Visual Analogue Scale (VAS). The quality of life mean scores indicated a significant deterioration of subjective health by 10 points. The VAS before the crisis was VAS_{Before} = 86.06 (st.d. =15.14) and the corresponding value during the crisis was VAS_{During} = 76.72 (st.d. = 20.51). The significant reduction in VAS was also associated with greater inequalities in the distribution of health. In addition low-income individuals declared losses of jobs, fears of long unemployment, and a significant deterioration of their psychological and emotional status. The findings will help develop better targeted health policies that seek to improvement of the health of the Greek population.

1 Introduction

Greece has gone bankrupt five times in its economic history through the 19th and 20th centuries. The milestones of crises are as follows: The first bankruptcy took place in 1827, four years after the Greek Revolution against the Ottoman State. Similar economic hardships leading to bankruptcy were recorded in 1832, 1843, 1893, and during the great crisis of 1932. It is worth mentioning the historic speech of then Prime Minister Charles Trikoupis, who declared on December 10, 1893, in the Greek Parliament the infamous phrase, "regretfully, we are bankrupt." At the end of the 19th century lender countries established an "International Audit Committee" to examine the economic situation in Greece in an effort to determine possible economic development paths that would ensure the repayment of the foreign loan. The committee examined the evolution of the macroeconomic aggregates in Greece and noted an important 1859 study conducted by the so called "Economic Commission"; which was composed of diplomatic representatives from Britain, Russia, and France. This study highlighted three important issues related to the functioning and efficiency of the Greek Economy: 1) the lack of reliable public financial management; 2) the voting but non implementation of the anticipated reforms revealing non-compliance with laws; and 3) the shortage of qualified civil servants, with the consequential inability of the government to effectively manage public administration initiatives to exit the crisis. It is striking how appropriate, even today, the 1859 proposal remains more than 160 years later. That May 2010 strongly resembles May 1859 is also rather worrying.[1]

The Greek bailout, later noted as the first "Greek Tragedy", was followed by a memorandum of understanding (MOU) signed between Greece and the so-called "Troika", which consists of three major international institutions: the European Central Bank, the European Commission, and the International Monetary Fund. Time passed and after three MOU agreements, Greece's economy is still in an ongoing recessionary trend that began in 2009. The prolonged economic depression has led to a grave reduction in social and health expenditures, resulting in a social and humanitarian crisis. Social and health spending in most European countries follows a "counter-cyclical trend", with and increased tendency toward satisfying the health and social needs of the populations, as is typically required during crisis periods. Greece, in the initial face of crisis and over the 2009–2012 period followed a similar expansionary trend in social spending, increasing its share to GDP from 24.4 percent in 2009 to 26.1 percent in 2012. However, cost containment measures imposed by troika led to a reduction by two percentage points over the 2012–2014 period, thereby generating considerable economic and social pressures in the middle and lower income

1 For a comprehensive review of two centuries (1829-2015) of debt crisis in Greece and its dependence on foreign financing, see Carmen Reinhart and Trebesch (2015).

classes, with large groups of people falling into poverty. The share of population at risk of poverty increased from 27.6 percent in 2009 to 36 percent in 2014 (European Commission 2015a).

2 Chronicle of the modern crisis

At first glance the economic crisis of 1929 compared to the crisis of 2009 to 2015, shows substantial differences attributable to both its "depth" and "duration", as well as the range of its impact on society and the health of citizens. A brief reference to the facts could shed more light on the differences between the 1929 crisis and the current situation. The financial crisis of 1929 began in the United States, spreading rapidly around the world, including Europe, as it infected economies and social systems. At that time, the economies of Germany, Greece, Hungary, Romania, Poland, and Austria underwent payment failure and an immediate restructuring of their debt. The financial crisis led to a dramatic increase in unemployment and uncertainty, paving the way to subsequent political instability and dictatorships in many European countries (notably, Germany, Italy, and Greece). In Greece one of the most important reasons behind the crisis was the Asia-minor disaster and the need it created for extended policy measures providing housing, health and social protection. In March 1927, Greece requested a loan from the Financial Committee of the League of Nations, which sent a four-member committee to Greece in order to study the economic situation. The commission concluded that a loan prerequisite would be a reform of the financial system with the creation of a central financial institution, the Bank of Greece. In September 1927 the Geneva Protocol was signed, establishing the creation of the central bank, which came with a grant, in the form of a loan, of 9 million Sterling. From its inception, the Bank of Greece maintained close cooperation with the Financial Committee of the League of Nations until 1940, when the Second World War completely inhibited the development programs for the creation of technological infrastructure, or any further agricultural and industrial development in Greece.

The features of the recent financial crisis are different in many facets: the geopolitical field, its emergence, and in its duration. The economic crisis broke out in September 2008 in the US where several factors (complex financial entities emerging, the housing bubble burst, shadow banking system, and inadequate financial risk assessment, to name a few reasons) led to economic chaos with many bank runs and, ultimately, giant corporations like the Lehman Brothers declaring bankruptcy. At this point it was realized that the global market was highly interconnected with the failure of specific institutions influencing corporations in other parts of the world due to high systemic financial interdependence. Ultimately the U. S. crisis led to the "infection" of several European countries, including Iceland (2008), Latvia (2008), Hungary (2008), Serbia (2009) and Romania (2009). On April 23, 2010, Greece resorted to the Troika (European Central Bank, European Union and the International Monetary Fund) requesting a loan of 110 billion euro and then, in March 2011, for an additional loan of 130 billion euro. Bailouts were also granted to Ireland (November 2010), Portugal (May 2011), and Cyprus (March 2013).

3 Macroeconomic fluctuations

After a period of economic growth and prosperity, when the average annual economic growth rate in Greece fluctuated in double the levels of the respective indices of the average European Union countries (IMF 2013a-d, EU 2013, Herrmann and Kritikos 2013), Greece experienced an unexpected financial crisis that completely reversed the economic models and expectations of Greek citizens. After experiencing an average annual GDP growth rate in Greece of 4 percent per annum from 2000 through 2008, when it was around 2 percent in the EU-28, GDP was –3.6 percent in 2009. A year later, in 2010, it was –4.7 percent. In 2011 initial expectations were busted and the recession worsened, with GDP shrinking by –8.2 percent, the worst recorded in EU history (Figure 1). This decrease is attributable to consumer demand of negative 7.1 percent, of public consumption of negative 9.1 percent, and a –20.7 percent fall in investments. The first sight recovery from the recession was observed with a GDP decrease of –6.5 percent in 2012 and –6.1 percent in 2013 (Figure 1). Despite "previous expectations" for a recovery, the recession continues. European Commission and Central Bank of Greece forecasts that the recession will continue through at least 2016. (Figure 1) Economic forecasts predict neither the "depth" – meaning the size reduction of GDP—nor the "duration" of the economic crisis. Greek GDP lost 30 percentage points over a period of only six years. Figure 1 portrays the "depth" and the "duration" of the "Greek tragedy" in comparison with the EU average. The greatest crisis "depth" was in 2011. Regarding the duration, it lasted six years and is the longest crisis for any European country.

Figure 1

Annual rate of GDP growth in Greece and the EU average
2001-2016

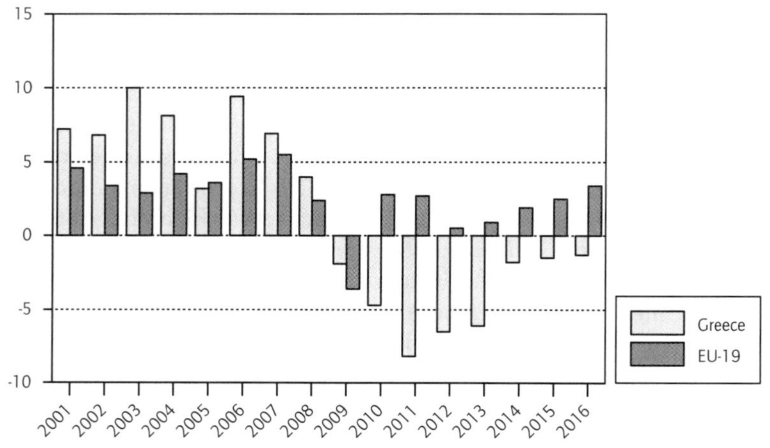

Source: Statistical Annex of European Economy Spring 2015.

4 Social expenditure

Reviewing the facts of the economic crisis raises the question about how far the extent of the crisis was felt, including whether or not the Greek social sector was at all affected. Difficult times often call for empowering measures, with many European economies employing a "counter-cyclical" economic policy, where social spending is not allowed to fall faster than the rate of GDP decrease. The main reason is that social needs dramatically increase during crisis times, when people are forced out of jobs and income levels fall. Hence the logical step for state planners rushing to meet the increased social needs, as an increasing number of people are vulnerable, is to increase funding. The reality for Greece is different, as recorded in Figure 2. For purposes of analysis, we examine the comparative picture of the crisis in OECD countries, showing change in GDP on the x-axis and the corresponding change in social expenditure on the y-axis, comparing 2007/08 to 2012/13.

In most EU countries, the decline in GDP did not result in reduced social expenditure, but rather an increase. This is also true for most OECD countries—including a majority of EU countries—as shown in Figure 2: these countries are found in the upper half, reflecting a policy of increasing social expenditure whether the countries experienced a recession (upper left quadrant, with falling GDP), or a boom (upper right quadrant, with rising GDP). Greece and Hungary are the

Figure 2

Change in social expenditure in relation to change in GDP

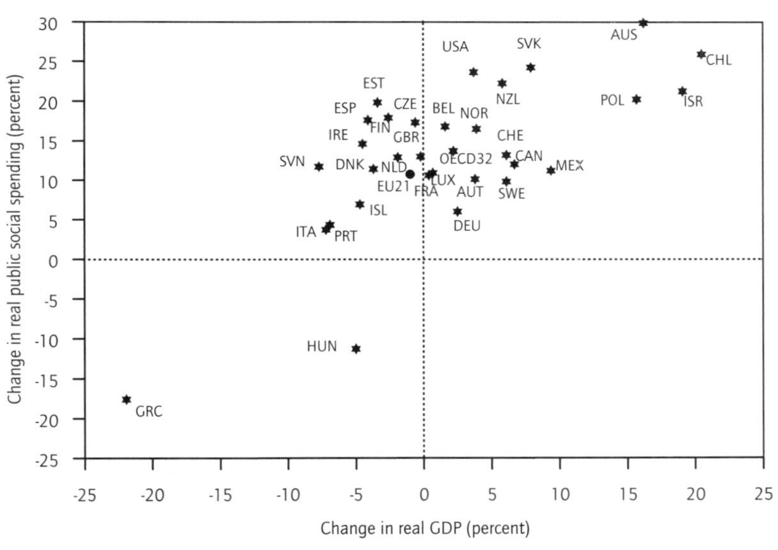

Note: AUS = Australia, CHL = Chile, SVK = Slowakia, USA = United States of America, NZL = New Zealand, POL = Poland, ISR = Israel, EST = Estonia , ESP = Spain, CZE = Czech Republic, BEL = Belgium, NOR = Norway, FIN = Finland, GBR = United Kingdom, CHE = Switzerland, CAN = Canada, MEX = Mexico, SVN = Slovenia, DNK = Denmark, NLD = Netherlands, LUX = Luxembourg, SWE = Sweden, ISL = Iceland, ITA = Italy, PRT = Portugal, DEU = Germany, GRC = Greece, HUN = Hungary.
Source: OECD Social Expenditure Data Base.

Figure 3

Social expenditure as percentage of GDP in Greece and OECD average
1980-2014

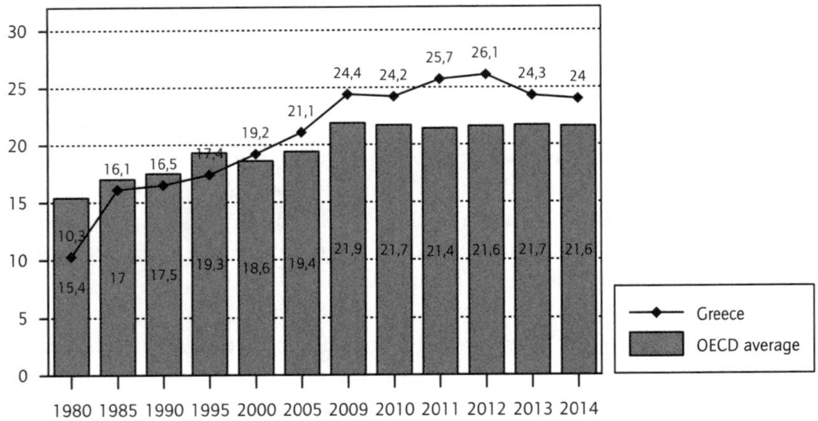

Source: OECD social expenditure data base.

exceptions: the decline in GDP is accompanied by a dramatic reduction in social spending. As noted earlier, this has a catastrophic social effect because a recession is precisely when it is crucial for governments to spend on social welfare to address increasing societal needs.

To gain a wider perspective on the matter, a dynamic view of social spending should be considered. It should be noted that Greece, like other European countries, initially expanded social expenditures during the early stages of the crisis. Figure 3 portrays the evolution of social expenditure as percentage of GDP in Greece and the OECD average from 1980 through 2014. Early in the crisis, the Greek percentage of social spending increased from 24.4 percent of GDP in 2009 to 26.1 percent in 2012.

After 2012, the second memorandum agreements imposed desperate cost containment measures to control public and social spending in order to save money that would reduce Greek debt. Hence social spending was significantly cut, a reduction of two percentage points (see Figure 3), which is how Greece ended up with the extreme counter-cyclical social spending decrease observed between 2012 and 2014.

Further investigation is needed to determine the impact of this crisis on the satisfaction of Greek citizens' "social rights." Combining the evidence of Figure 2 with the corresponding data in Figure 4, where the results of 2012 Eurobarometer study on satisfaction with welfare state performance across the OECD are presented, we find that Greeks have the lowest satisfaction with regard to welfare benefits, including the provision of health care, pensions, unemployment benefits, as well as the way in which inequality and poverty are addressed (see Figure 4).

Historically, the Greek welfare system has been fragmented and mismanaged with low levels of effectiveness and efficiency. Despite the fact that social expenditure, as percentage of GDP, in-

Figure 4

Satisfaction with welfare state performance varies across European countries

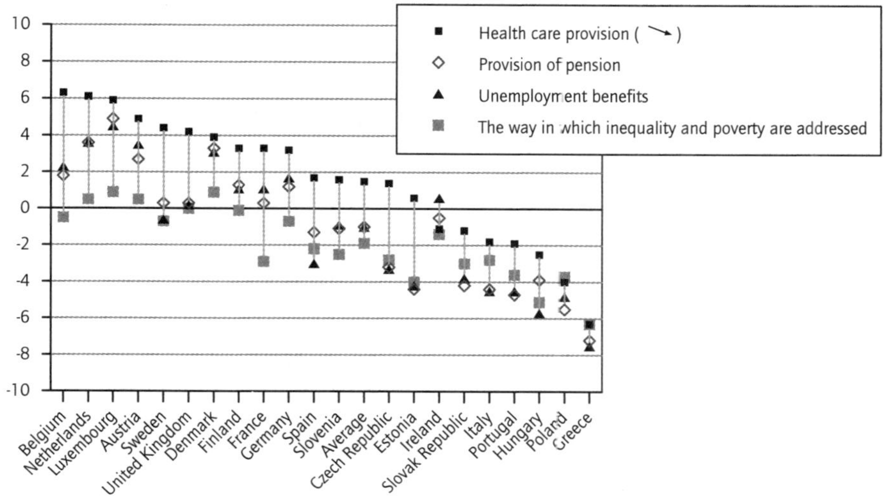

Source: OECD 2014 Society at a Glance Note: Eurobarometer index on satisfaction 2012.

creased by 14 percentage points between 1980 and 2014 (i. e from 10.3 percent in 1980 to 24 percent in 2014), at a time when the corresponding average OECD increase was 6 percent, the Greek welfare state has been less effective at achieving social objectives. According to 2014 EU statistics (European Commission 2015), social transfers (excluding pensions) only reduced poverty by 17.5 percent in Greece, compared to the EU average of 36 percent. The social protection system in Greece is not well targeted and does not cover adequately the vulnerable groups (European Commission 2015). Policy reforms aim at restructuring and widening the health and unemployment benefits for people suffering from the crisis. Under the 2014–2020 Fund for European Aid to the Most Deprived (FEAD) program, Greece received more than 280 million euro in assistance to alleviate extreme poverty. In addition the European Social Fund provided Greece with an additional 800 million euro (European Commission 2015) to reduce poverty, tackle discrimination, and increase social inclusion.

5 Health expenditures

The reduction of social expenditures triggered a significant decline in health expenditure. Before the crisis, from 1993 through 2008, health expenditure had been growing faster than GDP, in almost all the OECD Countries, ensuring income elasticity greater than 1. The largest increase in health expenditure was observed during the ten years just before the crisis, when the annual rate of health expenditure growth was 5.6 percent, while GDP increased annually by 3.6 percent (higher than one income elasticity). Health spending declined to a near zero growth rate in 2010

Figure 5

Annual growth in per capita health spending
2007-2014

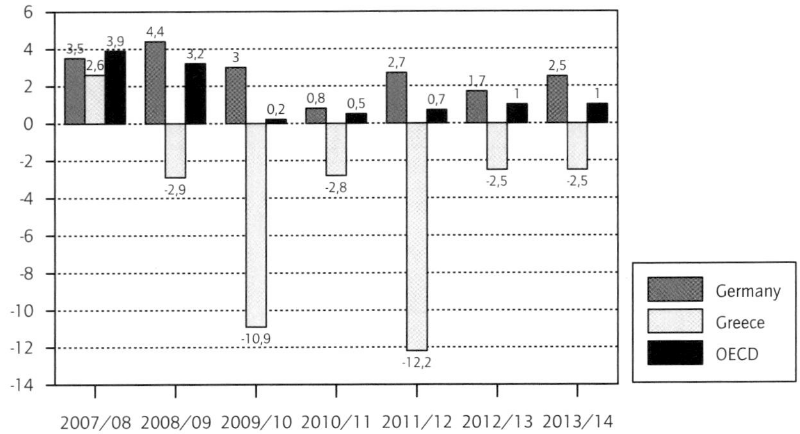

Source: OECD Health Data Base 2015.

followed by a slight increase at rate around 1 percent for the period 2011 to 2014 across northern European Countries (see Figure 5).

The Greek economic crisis led to a major setback in the social sector, especially in healthcare (Kousoulis et al. 2013, Kondilis et al. 2012, Tsiacharistas et al. 2015). The upward trend in healthcare spending witnessed over the 1993–2008 period was completely reversed by drastic cuts, which proved severe for Greece, especially compared to both other OECD and European Union countries. Figure 5 portrays the rate of increase for health expenditures over the 2007–2014 period for Greece, Germany, and the OECD average. Greece appears to be the only OECD country exhibiting devastating reductions in health expenditures: –2.9 percent in 2009, –11.4 percent in 2010, and –12.2 percent in 2012. During the 2009 to 2014 crisis period, Greek health spending was cut by 34 percent on aggregate, while the corresponding decrease in other OECD countries was almost insignificant. Even in other Memorandum Countries, such as Ireland and Portugal, healthcare expenditure reductions were more modest, around 5–10 percent. The economic recession significantly affected Greece's health sector. During the crisis, life expectancy stabilized at about 80 years, while infant mortality increased from 2.7 in 2008 to 3.8 in 2010, with a subsequent marginal reduction to 3.7 in 2013. The remaining southern EU countries recorded declining infant mortality trends throughout the crisis. However, further investigation explore the possibility that the crisis is a "window opportunity", as the OECD argues, to generate structural reforms aimed at reorganizing the health sector, fighting corruption and the underground economy, as well as improving the equity and efficiency of resources (Androutsou et al. 2011, OECD 2015).

6 The Chronicle of health reforms

In the Greek pre-crisis period, there were three major reforms attempting to reorganize and restructure the health sector. The first was the 1983 passage of Law Act 1397 that established a National Health System (NHS) following the tradition of the British NHS. The second is the effort to regionalize and decentralize the bureaucratic administration by dividing Greece into 17 regional health authorities (PESYPs) (Law Act 2889 passed in 2001 and Law Act 3106 passed in 2003). The third reform was the Kalikratis Plan (Law Act 3852 passed in 2010) promoting the establishment of 13 independent administrative regions and 370 municipalities. It was planned that primary health care and public health programs would operate at the jurisdictional level under the establishment of seven health authorities called DYPEs. However, despite the good intentions of the reformers, bureaucratic delays and political party involvement in the decision making contributed to the fragmentation in the provision and financing of services of the health care system.

In 2010s, early on during the crisis, the Greek Government signed an agreement with troika to implement reforms in the economy and in the health sector. Within the framework of the economic adjustment program (Occasional Paper 72, December 2010) the European Commission assessed the need for reforms and invited the Greek Government to, "start preparing and implementing a comprehensive reform of the health care system". The overall objectives were to improve efficiency, control, and keep the public health expenditure at a level below 6 percent of GDP, while ensuring universal access and quality of services. The first "most promising reform" was the establishment of a unified health system called EOPYY (National Organization for Health Care Provision; Law Act 3918 passed in 2011). The previous four largest insurance funds (IKA, OAEE, OPAD and OGA) were unified under a self-managed organization covering more than 95 percent of the Greek population. In addition to EOPYY, several reforms were implemented in the hospital management and pharmaceutical sectors.

In the hospital sector, the Diagnosis Related Groups (DRG's KEN) framework was used in 2011 as a tool for reimbursing hospitals (Law Act 1702 passed in 2011). In addition, since 2014, internal auditing and cost accounting systems have been progressively introduced. The adoption of a centralized procurement system, named Central Committee for Health Supplies (EPY) and covering around 25 percent of hospital buys, produced substantial savings for the hospital sector. Further extending the procurement system to cover a wider range of hospital purchasing would produce even greater savings.

The reforms implemented in the pharmaceutical sector are delivering significant results. Electronic prescription and prescription by active substance nowadays covers more than 90 percent of the EOPYY's outpatient pharmaceutical prescriptions. The effective changes in the external reference pricing system introduced since 2012, the increase in generic drugs, the adoption of the positive list, and the launching of a claw-back system have jointly contributed to a substantial decrease in pharmaceutical expenditures from 5.1 billion euro in 2009 to 2.2 billion euro in 2014. At the same time, the efficiency in the pharmaceutical sector increased substantially. However, despite the success of these reforms, efforts should continue in order to increase the competitiveness and making the pricing system more transparent.

Nonetheless, the reduction of the pharmaceutical expenditures ought to be more than a savings policy (Yfantopoulos 2008). It should be accompanied by a series of measures and incentives leading to the development of an export-oriented pharmaceutical industry. Studies at the University of Athens and other research centers indicate the export potential of the sector and investment opportunities concerning pharmaceutical products. Exports, research and innovation should be the main pillars developing the Greek pharmaceutical sector and should serve as an incentive for a more efficient and competitive Greek drug industry (Yfantopoulos 2008).

7 Unemployment and health

Unemployment is also a major social and health factor (Milner et al. 2013, Drydakis 2015). According to ELSTAT evidence, Greek unemployment reached 27.6 percent in 2014, while prior to the crisis it fluctuated around 7.6 percent. During the crisis the number of unemployed increased by 1,000 to 1,200 individuals per week. It should be noted that those most affected by unemployment are young people and women. Considering the long-term growth potential of Greek GDP, the long term prospects of reducing Greek unemployment rates are not promising (Vlachadis et al. 2014). The weighted average GDP growth for the 2013 to 2060 period is projected to fluctuate around 0.7 percent. Such small growth in GDP is not particularly conducive to employment. Therefore, unemployment is expected to remain high until 2025 (from 28 percent in 2013 to 22.1 percent in 2020 and 17.2 percent in 2025). An easing in unemployment rates is expected after 2030, with a gradual decline that will reach 7.5 percent in 2060. The most worrying fact for Greece is the phenomenon of hysteresis, whereby the current large values of short-term unemployment permanently affect long-term unemployment. In other words the vastly increased rate of unemployment in Greece today may lead many workers to gradually lose their skills, thus being driven out of the market permanently, thereby reducing the labour force, leaving an enduring effect that will lead to increased unemployment rates being observed in the Greek economy for decades.

The relationship between the economic crisis, unemployment and healthcare is widely discussed in the literature (Tapia Granados 2005, Ruhm 2008, Kentikelenis et al. 2011, Karatzanis et al. 2012, Karanikolos et al. 2013). Dr. Margaret Chan, WHO Director-General warned member states at the 2009 WHO Assembly about the effects of the crisis:

> *"The potential impact of the financial crisis and its upheavals are not to be underestimated. We should not be surprised if there is a rise in suicide rates and mental disorders"* (Stuckler et al. 2009),

in a Lancet publication, argues that a 1 percent increase in unemployment is closely associated to an increase of 0.8 percent in suicide rates and a corresponding increase of 0.8 percent in alcoholism.

Numerous studies show this relationship, some even using dynamic econometric models based on up to 10-year lags. However establishing causality in this case is very tricky from an econometric perspective. Examining the current literature on Greece we may distinguish between: 1) political statements like the one from Minister of Health who reported a 40 percent rise in suicides during the first half of 2011 compared to the same period on 2010; 2) simple descriptive statements indicating a suicide rate increase of 17 percent over the period 2007–2009 (Kentikelenis et al. 2011: 3) statistical trend analysis revealing a statistically significant reduction in the standardized suicide rates of –0.84 percent (95 percent CI –1.6 percent, –0.1 percent) from 1992 to 2008, with a subsequent statistically significant increase of 9.25 percent (95 percent CI 2.7 percent –16.3 percent) in SSR; and, lastly, 4) more rigorous and robust econometric modeling, controlling for various socio-economic, gender and demographic effects reaching the conclusion that,

> *"fiscal austerity, higher unemployment rates, negative economic growth and reduced fertility rates lead to a significant increase in overall suicide rates in Greece"* (Antonakakis and Colins 2014).

The results these studies have important policy implications for prevention programs, calling out for more targeted social and health policies.

Recent studies conducted at the University of Athens show that people left outside the labour market have multiple physical and psychological problems related to anxiety, stress, and chronic depression. Moreover, unemployed individuals make more use of drugs due to chronic diseases. Unemployment is, therefore, closely linked to the so-called "iceberg of illness". Typically unemployment measurements refer to the visible side of the iceberg that is associated with the "apparent" health of the patient. However, the hidden part of the iceberg is of social and cultural interest because unemployment is associated with psychological, cultural and physical dimensions that are not easily detectable and have a long-term nature, significantly impacting public healthcare systems and social security.

8 Health inequalities

Recording, measuring and combating social inequalities in the health sector is a major challenge for modern healthcare systems (Borrell et al. 2007). The European Commission, World Health Organization, and World Bank have developed coordinated programs to study the social factors influencing health inequalities (European Commission 2013b, OECD 2013, 2014, WHO 2009 a and b). The 19th century studies of Villerme, Chadwick, and Virchow point out that life and death are directly related to social welfare (Wilkinson and Pickett 2010). In the 1930s, following the "movement of social medicine", health inequalities were systematically investigated, only to languish in terms of scientific interest in the 1950s and 60s. However, interest again intensified in the early 1980s and is now a significant scientific endeavor achieved by using advanced forms of statistical monitoring and documentation. Research results have substantially impacted state policies, especially as governments appear to be interested in initiatives and actions aimed at reducing inequalities. Several European countries, including Finland, France, Italy, Lithuania, the Netherlands, Sweden and the United Kingdom, have already taken similar initiatives on a national level or by setting up special committees that aim to implement "targeted" reforms. European Union institutions (the Parliament, Council, and Commission), in collaboration with the WHO, have produced a large number of studies, expressing the need to address health disparities taking into account the Commission's White Paper, "Together for Health: A Strategic Approach for the EU 2008–2013". It is stated that where necessary, policy actions to reduce health inequalities across the European Member States should be pursued. Moreover, the European Commission in an initiative entitled, "Solidarity in health", started a preliminary consultation process with the aim of reducing health inequalities. An essential dimension of the European Healthcare Model is to ensure equality and social justice in the European healthcare systems. Eurostat investiga-

Figure 6

Health inequalities in subjective health across EU

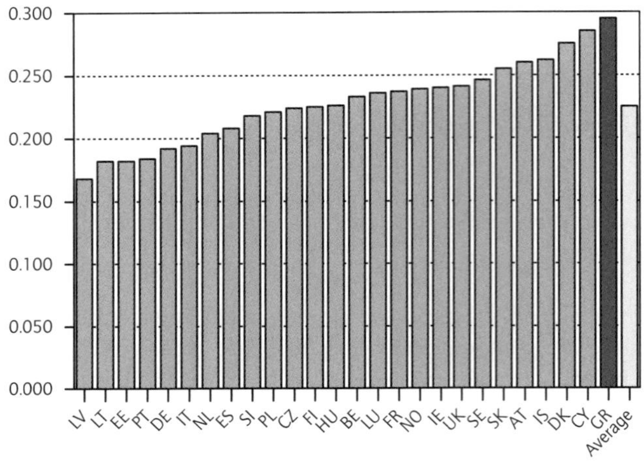

Note: LV = Latvia, LT = Lithuania, EE = Estonia, PT = Portugal, DE = Germany, IT = Italy, NL = Netherlands, ES = Spain, SI = Slovenia, PL = Poland, CZ = Czech Republic, FI = Finland, HU = Hungary, BE = Belgium, LU = Luxembourg, FR = France, NO = Norway, IE = Ireland, UK = United Kingdom, SE = Sweden, SK = Slowakia, AT = Austria, IS = Iceland, DK = Denmark, CY = Cyprus, GR = Greece.
Source: Authors' estimates of Gini Coefficients based on a University of Athens Study.

tions find that a substantial weakness of the European Healthcare Model is the satisfaction of the equality objectives, since it reveals a challenging inequality in life expectancy among men—a gap of 14 years. These inequalities are directly linked to socio-economic factors related to the history of social and healthcare systems as well as the effectiveness of the health system in reaching all citizens needing primary and secondary care services (Galbraith 2012, Gravelle 2002). However it should be noted that despite the continuous efforts of the EU and WHO for greater social justice and equality in the health sector, many studies show that health inequalities remain unbridgeable between social classes, between regions, and between EU countries (Mackenbach 2008, Mackenbach et al. 2013). A study undertaken at the University of Athens using the EU-SILC data for 26 European Union countries concludes that health disparities remain high, with Greece having the greatest inequality among EU countries (see Figure 6). Inequality in health is measured using GINI coefficients, which take values from zero to one ($0 < \text{Gini} < 1$). Small values of the Gini coefficient show little disparity while high values indicate high inequality existent. Athens University measurements find the Greek Gini coefficient is $G = 0.2947$, while the EU average is $G = 0.2248$. The study suggests that Greece and Cyprus have the greatest health disparities.

It is striking that with the 1983 enactment of Law 1397, entitled, "On the establishment of a National Health System", Greece adopted a Beveridge type of a public health system primarily aimed at ensuring the principles of equality and social justice. Following the European Social Model, Greece adopted, along with other southern European countries, a "National Health Service" under the principle of equal access to health services for all citizens regardless of income or social status. Under the European Health Model (European Commission 2013b), equality, social justice and financial sustainability should be the key objectives of any health system. Paradoxically after

30 years of the Greek NHS and the continuing reforms for greater equality, Greece appears to be the European country with the greatest inequality. Although there has been much rhetoric for greater equality, actions on the ground have not lead to a more equal and just redistribution of health resources. It should be highlighted that during the crisis, inequalities increased, affecting an increasing number of low income families, poor and vulnerable. More and more Greek citizens are unable to pay the increased charges for medicine and medical examinations. There is already research finding that the middle and low-income are less able access health care services. The sluggish growth of the public sector, combined with mismanagement and corruption, are contributing to increased health inequalities. In several Eurobarometer studies it is pointed out that the public perceives that the health sector is one of the most corrupt sectors in Greece (Special Eurobarometer 325).

9 Impact of crisis in health status and quality of life

The economic crisis has caused many adverse economic effects for all European countries causing some of them, including Greece, to implement severe fiscal austerity measures. According to existing literature (Stuckler et al. 2009, 2011, 2012, Tsiacharistas et al. 2015, Maresso et al. 2015), economic crises can have immediate effects like deterioration of health status as measured by self-reported measures and worsening of mental health status, as well as health behaviour changes. Other health effects, like changes in mortality, may take longer time to manifest. Financial crisis and economic recession are associated with increases in mental disorders, suicides, addiction problems and substance abuse, adoption of less healthy behaviours regarding nutrition and exercise, as well as in general poorer health status. The effect of crisis is not the same across all population groups. The most vulnerable groups, including the elderly, the unemployed, chronic patients, and migrants, face a greater risk of being affected. Thus, as the economic recession deepens, health inequalities are likely to widen.

At the University of Athens Health Economics Unit, we developed methodologies (Yfantopoulos and Yfantopoulos 2013, 2015) to assess, track, and mitigate the effect of the economic downturns on healthcare systems of the memorandum countries (Greece, Portugal, Ireland, Spain and Cyprus). The general objective is to fill the knowledge gap on the preparedness and operational responses of the health sector to economic shocks. In this section we report the evidence from our research on the impact of the crisis on living standards, and the quality of life of the Greek population both "before" and "during" the crisis. A set of quality of Life instruments (EuroQol 1990) is used to assess the impact of the crisis on a Visual Analogue Scale (VAS). Face to face interviews were conducted to a randomly selected sample of 5,500 individuals (53.3 percent women, 46.7 percent men) living in the Athens area. The survey was conducted by trained interviewers. The sampling was random at an individual level and stratified by gender, age group, education, and municipality. The selection of the subjects was based on the last available census at the time (2011) of the Hellenic Statistical Authority (El.Stat). The major purpose was to obtain representation of diverse population groups that may have different levels of health and quality of life profiles. The subjects were acquainted with the purpose of the study, which was previously approved by the University of Athens Committee for Ethics and Research.

Greek citizens were asked to assess their subjective health, before and during the current crisis using a Visual Analogue Scale (VAS) taking the values: 0 = worst imaginable health and 100 =

perfect imaginable health. Health related quality of life indices were assessed across: gender, age, education, employment status, income, and living conditions. The economic crisis resulted in a significant deterioration of both the perceived health status and the quality of life for the Greek population. The quality of life mean scores indicated a significant deterioration of subjective health by 10 points. The VAS before the crisis was VAS_{Before}= 86.06 (st.d. =15.14) and the corresponding value during the crisis was VAS_{During} = 76.72 (st.d. = 20.51) (see Figure 7).

The significant reduction in VAS was also associated with greater inequalities in the distribution of health. The VAS gap among the poor is much greater in comparison to richer classes. Indicatively the gap among the poor is $VAS\text{-}GAP_{poor}$ = 14.9, {VAS_{Before}= 82.2 minus VAS_{During} = 67.9} and the corresponding $VAS\text{-}GAP_{rich}$ is only 4.9 {VAS_{Before}= 88.7 minus VAS_{During} =83.8} (see Figure 8).

In addition, low-income individuals declared job losses, fears of long unemployment, as well as a significant deterioration of their psychological and emotional status, as depicted in the dimensions of Anxiety-Depression and Pain-Discomfort. Low income people faced greater difficulties

Figure 7

Visual analogue values for the state of health before and during the crisis

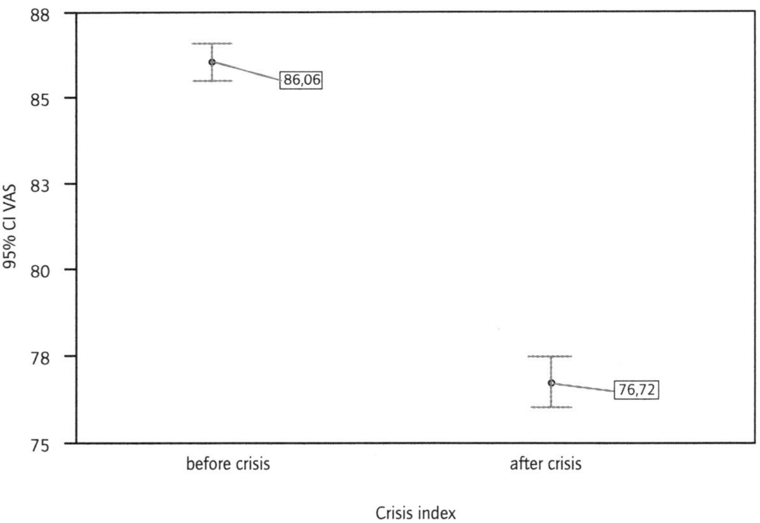

Source: Yfantopoulos, J. (2015), University of Athens.

Figure8

Distribution of health (visual analogue values) across economic groups

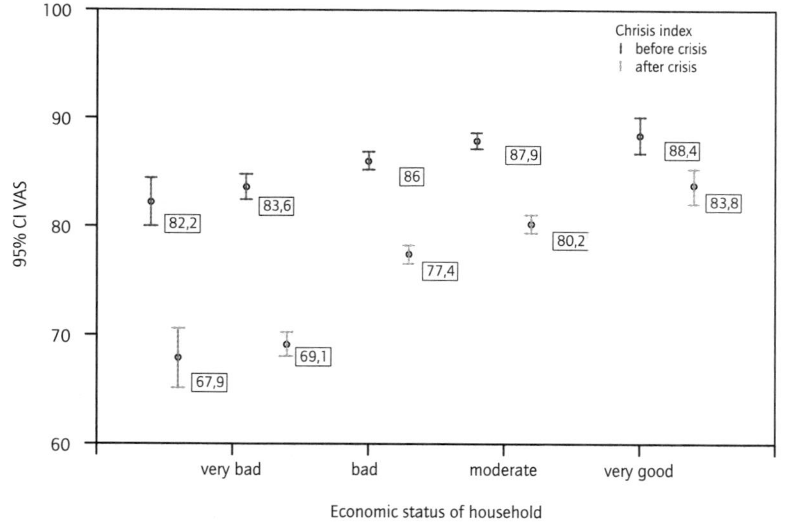

Source: Yfantopoulos (2015), University of Athens.

accessing health services and expressed greater mistrust of politicians. The finding of this research will help develop more effective health policies seeking to improve the health of the Greek population.

10 Conclusions

More than thirty years have passed since the establishment of the Greek National Health System in 1983, and yet the situation is still critical. Although there was a boom period following entrance into the Eurozone, Greece used significant borrowing to finance the economic growth observed over the 2000s. However, the instigation of the global economic crisis, initially appearing in the U. S., the major western economies faced a shock to their finances. The situation was no different for Greece, where the borrowing finally caught up with the country, with massive amounts of debt revealed and the country forced to seek assistance from the troika. In order to receive new loans, the new measures were required: With the troika seeking to save every possible penny from the Greek economy, difficult decisions were made, including the cutting of social and health expenditures by two percentage points of the GDP. This came with severe impacts for the Greek population, leading many analysts call it a "humanitarian crisis" in order to describe how the current crisis extends beyond simple financial hardships. The reduction in social and health spending has led to adverse effects on the health of the Greek population. While life expectancy stabilized at about 80 years, infant mortality increased from 2.7 in 2008 to 3.8 in 2010, although there was a subsequent marginal reduction. The quality of life mean scores indicated a significant deterioration of subjective health by 10 points. The Visual Analogue Scale (VAS) before the crisis was VAS_{Before} = 86.06 and during the crisis VAS_{During} = 76.72. Moreover the reduced overall economic activity drove many people into unemployment, which is associated with mental illness and increasing suicide rates. Historically, the Greek healthcare system has always been associated with corruption and clientelistic policies, with many reforms failing to address these important issues. In public perception surveys, Greek people express major distrust in public healthcare, characterizing it as the most corrupt societal institution. The crisis has only made things worse, with Greeks declaring rising distrust in the welfare system and the politicians representing them. However some optimists view the crisis as an opportunity for Greece to assume responsibility and address the inefficiencies that are deeply rooted in its social welfare system. In the case of health, it is vitally important that inefficiency is tackled, keeping equity in mind. Greece, in its biggest crisis of its life, both in depth and duration, needs to implement reforms and it is a gruesome paradox that the most vulnerable members of society are the ones hit hardest by the crisis. The state most do its utmost to provide a "social net" for those in need, implementing incentive systems that will effectively promote the long-term improvement of its population's health status.

References

— Androutsou, L., M. Geitona, and J. Yfantopoulos (2011), Measuring Efficiency and Productivity Across Hospitals in the Regional Health Authority of Thessaly, in Greece. Journal of Health Management, 13 (2), 121–140.
— Antonakakis, N., and A. Collins (2014): The impact of fiscal austerity on suicide: On the empirics of a modern Greek tragedy. Social Science & Medicine, (12) July, 39–50.
— Borrell, C. I. et al. (2007) Explaining variations between political traditions in the magnitude of socio-economic inequalities in self-perceived health, in Tackling Health inequalities in Europe: an integrated approach Eurothine Final report, Department of Public Health, Erasmus University Medical Centre, Rotterdam, 2007. Available from http://ec.europa.eu/health/ph_projects/2003/action1/docs/2003_1_16_frep_ en.pdf
— Drydakis, N. (2015): The effect of unemployment on self-reported health and mental health in Greece from 2008 to 2013: a longitudinal study before and during the financial crisis. Soc Sci Med 1982, 128.
— Eurobarometer (2009): Special Eurobarometer 325 Attitudes of Europeans towards corruption European Commission.
— European Commission (2013a): Health inequalities in the EU. Final report of a consortium. Consortium lead by Sir Michael Marmot.
— European Commission (2013b): The Second Economic Adjustment Programme for Greece: Second Review May 2013. European Economy Occasional Papers, No. 148. Brussels, Directorate-General for Economic and Financial Affairs. May.
— European Commission (2014): The Social Situation Report in the European Union European Commission and Eurostat. Luxembourg.
— European Commission (2015a): Commission Staff Working Document Assessment of the Social Impact of the new Stability Support Programme for Greece. Brussels, 19.8.2015 SWD(2015) 162 final.
— European Commission (2015b): Commission Staff Working Document Assessment of the Social Impact of the new Stability Support Programme for Greece. Brussels.
— EuroQol Group (1990): EuroQol—a new facility for the measurement of health-related quality of life. Health Policy, 16 (3), 199–208.

- Galbraith, J. K. (2012): Inequality and Instability: A Study of the World Economy Just Before the Great Crisis. New York, NY, Oxford University Press.
- Gool, K., M. Pearson (2014): Health, Austerity and Economic Crisis: Assessing the Short-term Impact in OECD countries. OECD Health Working Papers, No. 76, 2014 OECD. DOI: http://dx.doi.org/10.1787/5jxx71lt1zg6-en
- Gravelle, H., J. Wildman, and M. Sutton (2002): Income, income inequality and health: what can we learn from aggregate data? Soc. Sci. & Med., 54, 577–589.
- Herrmann, B., and A. Kritikos (2013): Growing out of the crisis: hidden assets to Greece's transition to an innovation economy. IZA Journal of European Labor Studies, (2), 14. www.izajoels.com/content/2/1/14
- IMF (International Monetary Fund) (2013a): World Economic Outlook: Hopes, Realities, and Risks. April. IMF, Washington, D.C.
- IMF (2013b): Greece: Ex post Evaluation of Exceptional Access under the 2010 Stand-by Arrangement. Country Report No. 13/156. IMF, Washington, D.C.
- IMF (2013c): Greece: Third Review under the Extended Arrangement under the Extended Fund Facility. Country Report No. 13/153. IMF, Washington, D.C.
- IMF (2013d): Greece: Selected Issues. Country Report No. 13/155. Washington, D.C., IMF.
- Karanikolos, M., P. Mladovsky, J. Cylus, S. Thomson, S. Basu, and D. Stuckler (2013): Financial crisis, austerity, and health in Europe. Lancet, 381 (9874), 1323–1331.
- Karatzanis, A. D., E. K. Symvoulakis, V. Nikolaou, and G. A. Velegrakis (2012): Potential impact of the financial crisis on outpatient hospital visits due to otorhinolaryngologic disorders in Crete, Greece. International Journal of Medical Science, 9, 126–128. [28].
- Kentikelenis, A., M. Karanikolos, I. Papanicolas, S. Basu, M. McKee, and D. Stuckler (2011): Health effects of financial crisis: omens of a Greek tragedy. Lancet, 378 (9801), 1457–1458.
- Kondilis, E., E. Smyrnakis, M. Gavana, S. Giannakopoulos, T. Zdoukos, and S. Iliffe (2012): Economic crisis and primary care reform in Greece: driving the wrong way? British Journal of General Practice, 62 (598), 264–265.
- Kousoulis, A. A., K. E. Angelopoulou, and C. Lionis (2013): Exploring health care reform in a changing Europe: lessons from Greece. European Journal of General Practice, 19 (3), 194–199.
- Lionis, C., E. K. Symvoulakis, A. Markaki, C. Vardavas, M. Papadakaki, and N. Daniilidou (2009): Integrated primary health care in Greece, a missing issue in the current health policy agenda: a systematic review. International Journal of Integrated Care, 9, e88.
- Mackenbach, J. P., et al. (2008): Socioeconomic inequalities in health in 22 European countries. The New England Journal of Medicine, 358, 2468–2481.
- Mackenbach, J. P., M. Karanikolos, and M. McKee (2013): The unequal health of Europeans: successes and failures of policies. Lancet, 381 (9872), 1125–1134.
- Maresso, A., P. Mladovsky, S. Thomson, A. Sagan, M. Karanikolos, E. Richardson, J. Cylus, T. Evetovits, M. Jowett, J. Figueras, and H. Kluge (2015): Economic crisis, health systems and health in Europe: country experiences. WHO EUROPE.
- Milner, A., A. Page, and A. D. LaMontagne (2013): Long-term unemployment and suicide: a systematic review and meta-analysis. PLoSOne, 8, 1932-6203 (Electronic), e51333.
- OECD (2013): OECD guidelines on measuring subjective well-being. 2013 Report. OECD, Paris.
- OECD (2014): Society at a glance 2014: OECD social indicators. OECD, Paris.
- OECD (2015): OECD Health at a Glance 2015. OECD, Paris.

— Polyzos, N., et al. (2012): Reforming reimbursement of public hospitals in Greece during the economic crisis: Implementation of a DRG system. Health Policy, 109 (1), 14–22.
— Reinhart, C., and C. Trebesch (2015): The pitfalls of external dependence: Greece. 1829-2015. Brooking Papers on Economic Activity. BPEA Conference Draft, September 10–11, 2015.
— Ruhm, C. (2008) A healthy economy can break your heart. Demography, 44, 829–848.
— Stuckler, D., S. Basu, M. Suhrcke, A. Coutts, and M. McKee (2009): The public health effect of economic crises and alternative policy responses in Europe: an empirical analysis. Lancet, 374 (9686), 315–323.
— Stuckler, D., S. Basu, M. Suhrcke, A. Coutts, and M. McKee (2011) Effects of the 2008 recession on health: a first look at European data. Lancet, [27] 378, 124–125.
— Stuckler, D., and M. McKee (2012): There is an alternative: public health professionals must not remain silent at a time of financial crisis. European Journal of Public Health, [24] 22, 2–3.
— Stuckler, D., C. Meissner, and L. King (2008): Can a bank crisis break your heart? Global Health, 4, 1–12.
— Tapia Granados, J. A. (2005): Recessions and mortality in Spain, 1980–1997. Eur J Popul, 21 (4), 393–422.
— Tsiachristas, A., Ch. Lionis, and J. Yfantopoulos (2015): Bridging knowledge to develop an action plan for integrated care for chronic diseases in Greece. International Journal of Integrated Care, 15, 22 October 2015.
— Vlachadis, N., M. Vlachadi, Z. Iliodromiti, E. Kornarou, and N. Vrachnis (2014): Greece's economic crisis and suicide rates: overview and outlook. J Epidemiol Community Health, 68 (12), 204–205.
— WHO (2009a): Financial crisis and global health: report of a high-level consultation. World Health Organization, Geneva.
— WHO (2009b): Health amid a financial crisis: a complex diagnosis. Bull World Health Organ, 87, 1–80.
— Wilkinson, R., and K. Pickett (2010): The Spirit Level: Why equality is better for everyone. London, Penguin Books.
— World Economic Outlook Database (2015): International Monetary Fund. [cited 2015 Aug 15]. Available from: www.imf.org/external/pubs/ft/weo/data/changes.htm
— Yfantopoulos, J. (2008): Pharmaceutical pricing and reimbursement reforms in Greece. European Journal of Health Economics, 9, 87–97.
— Yfantopoulos, J. (2013): Dynamic aspects of the underground economy in Greece. Journal of Economic and Social Measurement, 38 (1), 97–112.
— Yfantopoulos, J., D. Balourdos, and K. Nikolopoulos (2009): Economic and Social Dimensions of the Welfare State. Gutenberg Edition (In Greek).
— Yfantopoulos, J., and P. Yfantopoulos (2013): The psychometric properties of the EQ-5D-5L in a population-based study in Greece. In: J. Busschbach (ed.): 29th Proceedings: Scientific Plenary Meeting of the EuroQol Group. Rotterdam, EuroQol Group, 188–193.
— Yfantopoulos, J., and P. Yfantopoulos (2015): The Validity of the EQ-5D-5L instrument in assessing the impact of Economic Crisis on Population's Health. Paper presented in the 32nd Plenary Meeting of the EQ-5D Conference in Krakow, Poland.

The Impact of Public Investment on Private Investment in the Euro Area*

CHRISTIAN DREGER AND HANS-EGGERT REIMERS

Christian Dreger (corresponding author), DIW Berlin – German Institute for Economic Research, e-mail: cdreger@diw.de
Hans-Eggert Reimers, University of Wismar, e-mail: hans-eggert.reimers@hs-wismar.de

Summary: This paper explores the long-term relationship between public and private investment in the euro area. A stock-flow approach is proposed to control for the integration properties of the variables. Panel econometric techniques including international spillovers are employed. Private and public capital stocks are cointegrated. However, the residuals from the stock equilibrium are not (trend) stationary, but rather include a random walk component. Nonetheless, they can be exploited to improve the model for private investment flows. In fact, standard models that include private investment flows, GDP, and the real interest rate are only valid if the deviations from the stock equilibrium are considered. The corresponding error correction equation is well behaved, as deviations from the stock relationship are crucial for explaining the changes in private investment. Thus, the lack of public investment may have been restricting private investment and GDP growth in the euro area.

→ JEL Classification: C23, E22, E62
→ Keywords: Public and private investment, capital stocks, fiscal austerity

* This paper is a policy-oriented version of C. Dreger and H.-E. Reimers (2014): On the relationship between public and private investment in the euro area. DIW Discussion Paper No. 1365.

1 Introduction

The Stability and Growth Pact introduces upper ceilings for public debt that are usually seen as a precondition for higher and sustainable GDPs in the Economic and Monetary Union. According to the pact, annual budget deficits should not exceed 3 percent, and debt-to-GDP ratios should not exceed 60 percent. If a member state breaches these limits, corrective actions and even economic sanctions can be implemented. While the pact was initially routinely broken and watered down, particularly at the request of large member states before the crisis, it has since become more stringent in order to restore confidence in international financial markets. To foster the sustainability of public finances, austerity measures have been implemented. They are part of the restructuring process, particularly within countries in emergency. Several euro area countries (Greece, Spain, Portugal, and Ireland) were unable to refinance their debt or bail out over-indebted banks under their supervision without supranational assistance. Greece still receives conditional support from the European Stabilization Mechanism (ESM) in exchange for structural reforms and progress in the consolidation of government finances. Lower deficits enabled Ireland, Portugal, and Spain to leave the ESM umbrella.

While fiscal austerity can be beneficial to foster GDP growth in the long term, the impacts in the short and medium term are often negative (Perotti 2011). The consolidation of public finances through a reduction of fiscal expenditures and an increase in taxes hav depressed the economy in many countries (Auerbach and Gorodnichenko 2012, Dreger and Reimers 2013). Unemployment rates exceed 25 percent in Greece and Spain, and unemployment among youth is even higher. As the recovery will likely be modest, this job crisis could persist for many years. Public investment is *de facto* exposed to a reduction in spending. Cuts in investment are easier to implement than is a reduction in social transfers. While the share of public investment in overall public spending in Greece exceeded 12 percent before the crisis, it has since dropped by more than half. Although there has been some recovery in the past few years, the share is still far below the pre-crisis level. Public investment expenditures have displayed more stability in the large euro area countries over the past two decades, but the ratios are still quite low, especially in the German economy. The small levels are the result of previous consolidation efforts. In fact, the ratio was just under 10 percent in the early 1980s (Figure 1).

The low-inflation environment makes fiscal consolidation even harder. With low inflation rates, nominal GDP growth declines, thereby raising the debt-to-GDP ratios. In addition, a fall in inflation leads to higher real interest rates if nominal interest rates are fixed at the zero lower bound. Increasing real interest rates can crowd out private consumption and investment. Fostering economic growth in times of debt is a main challenge for policymakers. The modest investment performance is one of the main reasons why the economic recovery in Europe has so far been rather weak despite still-favorable financial conditions. In fact, cuts in public investment might be responsible for this development, as lower public investment might undermine private investment activities. Therefore, this study looks at the relationship between public and private investment for the euro area.

From a theoretical perspective, evidence for positive and negative effects should be expected. If public and private sectors compete for the same resources in the economy, an acceleration of public investment will raise the user costs of capital, implying a decline in private investment. Public investment needs to be financed, which can lead to a higher tax burden or higher demand of governments for capital market funding, causing real interest rates to rise. Therefore, private

Figure 1

Public investment in several euro area countries

In percent of total public expenditures

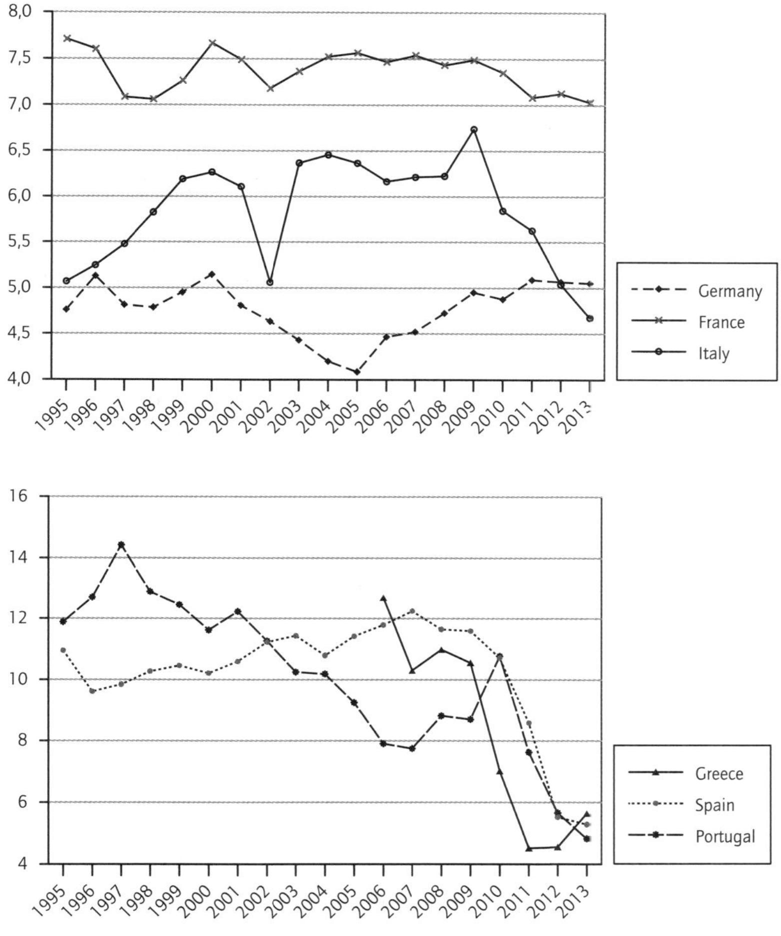

Source: AMECO database.

investment's crowding-out effects are to be expected and tend to be reinforced in times of crisis, as higher government debt can increase country-specific risk premia and interest rates. This argument would be even more valid for highly indebted countries. However, public investment may also create more favorable conditions for private investment: for example, by providing better infrastructure. The existence of facilities and the availability of common public goods can raise the productivity of private investment, which might take advantage of improved business conditions. For example, public investment in energy, telecommunications, or other network industries may have stimulated private investment (Pereira and Andraz 2013).

Because of the opposite effects, the net impact of public investment on private investment cannot be determined in advance, and must be examined on empirical grounds. Previous studies have delivered inconclusive results. As the net impact comprises both static and dynamic effects, any analysis should distinguish between the short run and the long-run. While crowding-out is mainly a short-run effect related to restrictions on available resources, crowding-in is long-lasting and can be traced to the higher productivity of private capital.

Using a neoclassical production function approach, Aschauer (1989) emphasized the possibility that public investment may induce private investment. Although higher public capital accumulation tends to raise overall investment above the level chosen by rational agents, crowding-in effects will dominate in the end. An expansion of public capital is expected to increase the rate of return to private capital, thereby leading to higher private capital accumulation and economic growth. Similarly, Baxter and King (1993) argued that public investment could stimulate private investment and output. Research based on regional production functions, disaggregated public capital, and industries arrived at similar results, particularly for roads and highways. Argimón, González-Páramo, and Roldán (1997) reported significant crowding-in effects of public investment on private investment for OECD countries due to the positive impact of infrastructure on productivity. In contrast, government consumption will crowd out private investment.

The positive view of public investment lacks robustness, as the empirical methodology plays a crucial role. The aforementioned studies take the time series in levels, thereby ignoring their non-stationarity. In addition, fixed effects are neglected in pooled models. If production functions are estimated using differenced data instead of the level series, or if pooled regressions are carried out with fixed effects, crowding-in findings seem to diminish. Even negative marginal products of public capital are detected in some cases (Perotti 2007). According to Afonso und Aubyn (2009), the effects are heterogeneous across countries. The estimated elasticities are also biased due to simultaneity. An acceleration of private investment raises the GDP and increases tax revenues that can be used for public investment.

This paper provides new evidence on the relationship between private and public investment. An approach encompassing stocks and flows is proposed. Although the distinction between stocks and flows is justified from the theoretical perspective, it has been largely ignored in the aforementioned studies. In fact, deviations from the equilibrium between the capital stocks can be relevant to drive private investment flows. Indeed, there is strong evidence for an equilibrium between the stocks, but the deviations are not stationary. Nonetheless, their inclusion in flow models can substantially improve the performance of standard investment equations. The corresponding error correction equation is well behaved and can explain the changes in private investment flows.

The rest of the paper is structured as follows: The next section (Section 2) motivates a long-run equilibrium between private and public capital stocks. While Section 3 reviews the econometric methodology, Section 4 holds the empirical results. Finally, Section 5 concludes with some policy recommendations.

2 Long-term equilibrium between private and public capital

To address the possible existence of crowding-in effects of public investment spending, it is necessary to investigate the relationship between private and public capital. Assuming a Cobb-Douglas production function with constant returns to scale, output Y is related to technical progress A, labor L, private capital K, and public capital G, i. e.

$$Y_t = A_t L_t^{\alpha} K_t^{\beta} G_t^{\gamma} \tag{1}$$

The parameters α, β, and γ denote production elasticities, while the marginal product of private capital is $\beta Y/K$, and the marginal product of public capital is $\gamma Y/G$. In equilibrium, the marginal products should be equal to the real interest rates

$$\beta Y_t / K_t = rp_t, \quad \gamma Y_t / G_t = rg_t \tag{2}$$

in the private (*rp*) and public sector (*rg*). As the interest rates are subject to arbitrage, they will move in parallel, despite possible differences related to risk premia (Hatano 2010). In the case of a constant ratio between the interest rates, $rp = \lambda rg$, one can obtain

$$K_t = \frac{\beta}{\lambda \gamma} G_t \tag{3}$$

implying that private and public capital stocks are well connected in the long-run. If the marginal products are equalized, the cointegration parameter will reflect the ratio of the production elasticities. Note that a direction of causality is not assumed by the argument. However, if public investment can be considered as exogenous, private investment will react to deviations from the long-run, implying that deviations from the cointegrating relationship can be seen as a driver for private investment. The potential equilibrium between the capital stocks might be crucial for driving private investment flows apart from the standard determinants such as economic activity and user costs of capital.

3 Panel integration and cointegration

Because the variables involved are non-stationary, an integration and cointegration analysis is the way to proceed. This is done within a panel framework, where the euro area countries constitute the cross section. Since the time series dimension is extended by the cross section, the panel environment will increase the power of tests compared to time series alternatives. For this reason, the panel evidence should be more reliable. However, no country-specific evidence can be extracted. A further problem arises if the panel members are not independent, as cross-sectional correlation can distort the test statistics. Dependencies are rather likely for the current application, as the euro area countries are exposed to common shocks. Therefore, tests to check the integration and cointegration properties should take potential international spillovers into account.

The CADF test suggested by Pesaran (2007) is applied to check for the non-stationarity of the variables in the study. It extends the standard IPS test with a factor controlling for cross-sectional correlation. The cointegration properties are examined using the panel and group mean statistics suggested by Westerlund (2007). These tests do not rely on inappropriate common factor restrictions such as tests based on residuals obtained from static relationships; see Kremers, Ericsson, and Dolado (1992). The null hypothesis of no cointegration between *y* and *x* is evaluated by testing whether the feedback parameter in a conditional panel error-correction model is equal to zero. Error-correction models are estimated separately for the panel members. Thus, heterogeneity between countries can be embedded, but it is restricted to the deterministic components like constant and trends, and to the short-run dynamics. Afterwards, the statistics for the feedback parameter are pooled along different principles. Testing can be done under two variants of the alternative. If the null hypothesis is rejected, cointegration is assumed to hold for all countries in the case of the panel statistic, and at least for one country in the group statistic. Since the cross sections are not independent, critical values are obtained using bootstrap methods.

Note that panel cointegration tests do not reveal the long-run parameters. Their aim is to identify reliable empirical models of nonstationary variables to avoid spurious regressions. Therefore, after testing for cointegration, the long-run is estimated via panel regression with fixed effects and contemporaneous correlation in the residuals. This approach is valid if cointegration is confirmed in the previous step. While the intercept, short-run coefficients, and error variances can differ across the panel members, the long-run coefficients are kept the same over the cross section.

4 Data issues and empirical evidence

Evidence on the link between public and private investment is based on annual data for the 1991–2012 period. The panel is based on twelve euro area member states, including Germany, France, Italy, Spain, Portugal, Greece, Ireland, Austria, Finland, Netherlands, Belgium, and Luxembourg. Countries that only recently joined the monetary union are excluded due to the lack of data. All series are taken from the AMECO database, which is provided by the European Commission.

While net investment flows are available at the sectoral level, capital stock data refer to the entire economy. To construct private and public capital stocks, net investment flows are cumulated. Starting values result from a decomposition of the total capital stock in an initial period (1990). In fact, the share of public capital is assumed to be equal to the ratio of cumulated net public investment to cumulated net overall investment, where the 1980s are taken as the reference period. The variables are divided by the appropriate deflator (2005 = 100) to obtain series in real terms.

Fundamental determinants of investment are also considered to ensure the robustness of the results. Real GDP and real interest rates are included as a proxy for overall demand and for financing costs to invest, respectively. To obtain real GDP, the nominal series are deflated by the GDP deflator (2005 = 100). Real interest rates are defined in an ex post manner as the difference between the long-term nominal interest rate and inflation, i.e. the annual change in the GDP deflator. Furthermore, Brautzsch and Dreger (1999) noted that the government debt ratio could potentially explain private investment in Germany. An increase in the debt ratio worsens the financial conditions via higher real interest rates and could restrict future demand, as investors might fear stronger efforts towards fiscal consolidation in later periods. Mehrotra and Välilä (2005) reported a negative effect of high public debt on public investment in a panel cointegration model for EU member states. According to the Maastricht criteria, the debt ratio is the ratio be-

Table 1

Tests for integration properties

	Levels	First differences	Decision
CS_PRI	0.695 (0.756)	0.624 (0.734)	*I* (2)
CS_PUB	0.215 (0.585)	-1.402 (0.080)	*I* (2)
PRI	0.341 (0.633)	-2.859 (0.002)	*I* (1)
PUB	-0.245 (0.403)	-3.561 (0.000)	*I* (1)
Y	0.205 (0.581)	-2.264 (0.012)	*I* (1)
R	1.203 (0.886)	-3.105 (0.001)	*I* (1)
DEBT	1.000 (0.841)	-3.418 (0.000)	*I*(1)

Note: Test according to Pesaran (2007). 12 euro area countries (Germany, France, Italy, Spain, Portugal, Ireland, Austria, Finland, Nether-lands, Belgium, Luxembourg and Greece, 1991–2012). Variables are private investment (*PRI*), public investment (*PUB*), GDP (*Y*), real interest rate (*R*), government debt to GDP ratio (*DEBT*). *CS_PRIV* and *CS_PUB* refer to the private and public capital stock, respectively. Selection of lags and deterministic terms are based on Akaike criterion. Entries are test statistics, *p*-values in parentheses.

Source: Own calculations.

tween gross government debt and GDP. All variables are measured in logs except for real interest rates, which are measured in percent.

The non-stationarity properties of the variables are exhibited in Table 1. According to the evidence, capital stocks include two unit roots. This stands in contrast to results obtained by Calderón, Moral-Benito, and Servén (2014), who find that the capital stock includes only one unit root in a panel of 88 countries that includes both rich and developing countries. All other variables are nonstationary in levels and stationary in their first differences, i. e. integrated of order one, $I(1)$. As real interest rates and government debt ratios cannot move without bounds, the outcome for these variables may be dubious from a theoretical standpoint. However, they appear to be integrated in a statistical sense and should be treated as such in the empirical analysis.

While private and public capital stocks are both $I(2)$, they are connected in the long-run. In fact they are cointegrated, according to both the panel and group statistics (Table 2). The deviations from the cointegrating relationship are non-stationary (test statistic –0.108, *p*-value 0.457), but due to the cointegration result, they possess only one unit root, as their difference is clearly stationary (test statistic –2.820, *p*-value 0.002). Apart from country fixed effects, the deviations from the stock relationship evolve according to

$$DEV_t = CS\_PRI_t - \underset{(0.002)}{0.604} CS\_PUB_t \quad \sim \quad I(1) \tag{4}$$

where the cointegrating vector has been normalized to the coefficient of the private capital stock, and standard errors are displayed in parentheses. A one percent increase in the public capital

Table 2

Tests for cointegration properties

	Panel statistic	Group statistic
CS_PRI, CS_PUB	-5.522 (0.000)	-3.768 (0.002)
PRI, Y, R	-2.513 (0.030)	-1.097 (0.110)
PRI, Y, DEBT	0.079 (0.445)	0.493 (0.445)
PRI, PUB, Y, R	-0.401 (0.195)	0.311 (0.285)
PRI, Y, R, DEV	-3.344 (0.000)	-4.182 (0.005)

Note: See Table 1. Tests according to Westerlund (2007). Selection of lags and deterministic terms are based on Akaike criterion. Entries are test statistics, *p*-values in parentheses. The *p*-values are based on bootstrap methods, where 200 replications are used. See Persyn and Westerlund (2008) for details.

Source: Own calculations.

stock is associated with a 0.6 percent rise in the private capital stock. The deviations can extend the set of $I(1)$ variables to improve standard models for private investment demand. Note that the capital stocks can enter these models only implicitly through their linear combination.

Table 2 holds the cointegration properties for several subsets of variables. The aim is to identify suitable environments for cointegration. The standard determinants for private investment are related to economic activity and user costs of capital. While the former is usually measured by GDP, the latter is proxied by the real interest rate (Eklund, 2013). This defines the benchmark model, which is subsequently enlarged. If the government debt to GDP ratio or public investment are added to the variables, the cointegration property is lost. Although government debt might be relevant for private investment in Germany, as emphasized by Brautzsch and Dreger (1999), this result does not generalize to the entire euro area. Despite the fact that the capital stocks are related in the long-run, gross investment flows are definitely not. This explains why many authors, such as Afonso and Aubyn (2009), preferred models in first differences to study the linkages between private and public investment. Evidence for cointegration is mixed even in the benchmark specification comprising private investment, GDP, and the real interest rate, as panel and group statistics point to the opposite direction. However, if deviations from the stock equilibrium are added, cointegration holds in every case. Overall, the model that includes private investment flows, GDP, the real interest rate, and the deviations from the capital stock relationship is superior. Apart from country fixed effects, the long-run equation is given by

$$PRI_t = \underset{(0.044)}{1.058}\, Y_t - \underset{(0.002)}{0.027}\, R_t - \underset{(0.023)}{0.384}\, DEV_{t-1} \qquad (5)$$

All variables are correctly signed and highly significant, where standard errors are given in parentheses. As expected, private investment flows will be stimulated by GDP in the long-run. In contrast, a rise in the real interest rate will trigger a decline in private investment activities. Note that the lagged deviations from the stock equilibrium enter with a negative sign. If the private

Table 3

Error correction models for private investment

	ΔPRI	ΔPRI
ΔPUB		0.008 (0.016)
ΔY		0.631 (0.062)
ΔR		-0.009 (0.001)
ECM (-1)	-0.215 (0.027)	-0.326 (0.036)
R-Squared	0.213	0.493
F-Statistic	6.384 (0.000)	16.467 (0.000)

Note: See Table 1. Panel regression with country fixed effects and cross-sectional correlation in the residuals. Figures in parentheses denote standard errors, and *p*-values in case of the *F*-statistic. R-Squared is the adjusted coefficient of determination.

Source: Own calculations.

capital stock increases relative to the public capital stock, private investment will consequently be reduced.

Two error correction specifications are run to explain private investment growth (Table 3). The first one includes only the error correction term, i.e. the lagged deviations from equation (5). The other one accounts for additional short-run effects. An error correction mechanism is highly significant and correctly signed, and the coefficient is of similar size in both specifications. While fluctuations in GDP and the real interest rate are also relevant to explain private investment growth, there is no short-run effect of public investment. Nevertheless, there is a crowding-in of public investment in the long-run due to the cointegration property between the capital stocks.

5 Conclusions

This paper explores the long-term relationship between public and private investment in the euro area. In contrast to previous studies, a stock-flow approach is employed to control for the different stochastic trends embedded in stock and flow variables. Panel econometric techniques are employed. Private and public capital stocks are cointegrated, but the deviations from the stock equilibrium are not (trend) stationary. However, utilizing them in a model for investment demand improves the cointegration evidence between the flows. In fact, private investment flows, GDP, and the real interest rate appear to be cointegrated only if the deviations from the stock equilibrium are included. The corresponding error correction equation is well behaved.

Overall, the lack of public capital as a result of weak public investment might have restricted private investment and GDP growth in the euro area. The results have strong implications for the proper design of future fiscal austerity programs to combat the euro area debt crisis. In particular, economic growth in the euro area could benefit from further fiscal reforms. Excluding national co-funding of EU-supported investment programs from the fiscal indicators covered by the Stability and Growth Pact could be a sensible strategy for supporting the investment performance and overall economic development in the euro area (Barbiero and Darvas 2014). The recently introduced European Semester, created to better monitor fiscal planning for individual countries, should encourage higher investment activities in member states, especially among those with rather healthy public finances and low public investment rates. This could be part of an integrated approach to overcome the crisis and achieve a path of stronger GDP growth in the future.

References

- Afonso, A, and M. Aubyn (2009): Macroeconomic rates of return of public and private investment: Crowding-in and crowding-out effects. Manchester School, 77, 21–39.
- Argimón, I., J. M., González-Páramo, and J. M. Roldán (1997): Evidence of public spending crowding-out from a panel of OECD Countries. Applied Economics, 29, 1001–1010.
- Aschauer, D. A. (1989): Does public capital crowd out private capital? Journal of Monetary Economics, 24, 171–188.
- Auerbach, A., and Y. Gorodnichenko (2012): Measuring the output responses to fiscal policy. American Economic Journal: Economic Policy, 4, 1–27.
- Barbiero, F., and Z. Darvas (2014): In sickness and health: Protecting and supporting public investment in Europe, Bruegel Policy Contribution 2014/02.
- Baxter, M., and R. G. King (1993): Fiscal policy in general equilibrium. American Economic Review, 83, 315–334.
- Calderón, C., E. Moral-Benito, and L. Servén (2014): Is infrastructure capital productive? A dynamic heterogeneous approach. Journal of Applied Econometrics, DOI: 10.1002/jae.2373.
- Dreger, C., and H.-U. Brautzsch (1999): Die Entwicklung der Unternehmensinvestitionen in Deutschland (Firm investment behaviour in the German economy). Journal of Economics and Statistics, 219, 284–297.
- Dreger, C., and H.-E. Reimers (2013): Does euro area membership affect the relation between GDP growth and debt? Journal of Macroeconomics, 38, 481–486.
- Eklund, J. E. (2013): Theories of investment: A theoretical review with empirical applications. Working Paper 2013:22. Swedish entrepreneurship forum. www.entreprenorskapsforum.se
- Hatano, T. (2010): Crowding-in effect of public investment on private investment. Japan Public Policy Review, 6, 105–119.
- Kremers, J. M., N. R. Ericsson, and J. J. Dolado (1992): The power of cointegration tests. Oxford Bulletin of Economics and Statistics, 54, 325–348.
- Mehrotra, A., and T. Välilä (2005): Evolution and determinants of public investment in Europe. Economic and Financial Reports 2005/1. European Investment Bank, Luxembourg.
- Pereira, A. M., and J. M. Andraz (2013): On the economic effects of public infrastructure investment: A survey of the international evidence. Journal of Economic Development, 38, 1–37.
- Perotti, R. (2007): In search of the transmission mechanism of fiscal policy. NBER Working Paper 13143. London.
- Perotti, R. (2011): The “Austerity Myth”: Gain without pain? NBER Working Paper 17571. London.

— Persyn, D., and J. Westerlund (2008): Error correction based cointegration tests for panel data. Stata Journal, 8, 232–241.
— Pesaran, M. H. (2007): A simple panel unit root test in the presence of cross section dependence. Journal of Applied Econometrics, 22, 265–312.
— Westerlund, J. (2007): Testing for error correction in panel data. Oxford Bulletin of Economics and Statistics, 69, 709–748.

The Greek Crisis, a Tragedy without Catharsis?

ALEXANDER S. KRITIKOS AND MARIAN HAFENSTEIN

Alexander S. Kritikos, DIW Berlin–German Institute for Economic Research, University of Potsdam, e-mail: akritikos@diw.de
Marian Hafenstein, DIW Berlin–German Institute for Economic Research, e-mail: hafenstein.marian@gmail.com

> *"The drive to define and create a public domain free from the incursion of familial and clientelistic networks in the nation's life has been less successful. [...] Modernizing Greece may be a task resembling that of Sisyphus, but with the difference that upward progress is greater than downward tumbles."*

John Koliopoulos and Thanos Veremis (2002: 363) conclude this regarding the development of Greece since 1821. To further understand the reasons for the current Greek crisis, we need to analyze the inherent weaknesses of the country that have existed since joining the European Communities (EC) in 1981.

Greek membership in the EC was not without controversy. Greece could not compete economically, given the large weight of the agricultural sector (*Neubäumer* in this issue). Further problems were linked to inflation, unemployment, and a trade deficit (Stergiou 2012). Joining the EU has not immediately resulted in economic growth. Instead a 15-year period of low economic growth followed, with a yearly real GDP increase of 0.9 percent on average. Investment contracted by an average of 2.2 percent per annum, while labor productivity languished. Unit labor costs—driven by wage indexation—increased more than a tenfold, while excessive product and labor market regulations deterred foreign investment. Although this lead to lower tax revenues and social security contributions, the government continued to increase health and pension spending as well as the number of civil servants and their wages. The result was predictable: public deficits and high inflation with negative spillovers affecting the private sector. And despite Greece's access to the common European market, it did not take advantage of it; instead its export quota fell from 19 percent of GDP in 1981 to a disastrous level of less than 9 percent in 1995.

The 1993 Maastricht Treaty gave Greece the opportunity to enter the European Monetary Union (EMU), if it could fulfill the convergence criteria. Thus, the government of Konstantinos Simitis in 1996 was induced to introduce a long list of serious and thorough reforms, including the abolishment of automatic wage indexation, the reshaping of collective bargaining, and a more restrictive monetary policy. At the turn of the century the only criterion that Greece did not meet was a maximum public debt of 60 percent of the GDP. Along with several other countries failing to meet this criterion, Greece entered the Euro zone.

During the 1996–2000 reform period, GDP growth averaged 3.7 percent annually. Housing investments showed a strong growth of 20.5 percent between 1996 and 1999, jumping by another 50 percent in 2000. Similarly, investments by companies in plants and equipment increased during the same time period by about 30 percent (*Neubäumer*). However, only investment in property continued to expand sharply after Greece joined the Euro in 2000, spurred by low interest rates due to foreign capital inflows. The housing boom led to the creation of a large number of jobs in construction and steep wage increases. Due to the rise in income, the demand for consumer goods increased, which was further stimulated by the use of credit cards and consumer loans.

Not only did private households live beyond their means, the government also took advantage of low interest rates and relied on loans to cover increasing expenditure on pensions and the growing public administration. At the same time, wide-spread tax evasion and a reduced tax quota did not allow revenues to keep up. This resulted in an average fiscal deficit of 6 percent of GDP. But Greece's growth prospects improved when it joined the Euro. Given the widespread findings on convergence of per capita income, Greeks expected higher growth rates and higher permanent incomes.

The housing boom in combination with increases in private consumption and government spending led to a rising GDP. Thus the economic growth was not due to innovation or expansion of capital stock and production capacities. The high growth, based on foreign credit, lasted until the beginning of the financial crisis, when capital inflows ran dry and the Greek economy dove into a depression.

1 Structural deficits of the Greek economy

Due to its enduring structural weakness, the Greek economy shows low levels of productivity relative to other EU member states and lacks a sustainable basis for economic growth. During the period of rather fast economic growth prior to the crisis, Greece in particular under the government of Kostas Karamanlis, failed to continue introducing further reforms that would have modernized its economic structures or to direct investment flows toward innovation. Hence, Greece was unable to take advantage of its EU membership and when the inflow of foreign capital came to a halt and the economic upswing ended abruptly, it—unlike its northern European neighbors—could not rely on exports to sustain its economic growth. Although the current account deficit decreased from 35 billion euro (2008) to about 4 billion euro (2014), this was more due to a drop in imports, caused by lower demand, than rising exports.

Overall, Greece's export intensity, with exports of goods and services constituting about 30 percent of GDP in 2014, remains low compared to countries like Hungary, Slovakia and Ireland, which have export intensities three times higher than Greece (see *Schrader*, *Benček* and *Laaser* in this issue). In the services sector, Greece relies heavily on sea transport and tourism, while business related services are underrepresented. Exports of goods center on agricultural products, raw materials, and labor-intensive products. Not even 17 percent of Greek exports originated from high or medium-high technology industries (OECD 2015), which limits opportunities for growth and hints at exactly how far away from Greece the technological frontier lies.

Manufacturing industries in Greece continue to remain underdeveloped, with a share of 8.5 percent in gross value added, as opposed to an EU-28 average of more than 15 percent. In Germany, for instance, the share exceeds 22 percent. These industries are crucial for R&D, innovation and economic growth (Hausmann and Hidalgo 2012). Greek manufacturing productivity amounted to slightly more than half of the EU-28 average. The focus in Greece is on labor intensive industries. In contrast, industries requiring skilled workers, leading to higher value-added, account for a comparatively small share of the manufacturing jobs (see Schrader et al. 2013).

In 2014, services generated 83 percent of the value added, in comparison to 74 percent in the EU-28. The composition of the service industries presents a bleak picture, as well: retail trade and tourism, both requiring low-skilled, low-paid workers, represent more than a quarter. The public sector and real estate together account for more than one fourth (see Schrader, et al. 2015).

Greece has rather fundamental institutional and structural problems, and not so much of a cost problem anymore, after cost disadvantages had been reduced over the last five years. Cutting costs will make Greece more competitive, but at a wage level far below European standards. If only the bare minimum, Troika-required, institutional reforms are made, Greece will have limited growth in sectors with low added value. Tourism, agriculture, and basic commodities are not enough to create sustainable, growing wealth for all Greeks.

2 Government revenues and expenditures

2.1 Bailout programs and reforms

In 2010 the Papandreou government signed the First Economic Adjustment Program for Greece, in which the country committed itself to a three-year program that aimed to stabilize the economy with a reduction of benefits and wages, as well as structural reforms that were supposed to enable a transformation toward an investment- and export- led growth model. Although some improvements were made, many underlying issues persist (Herrmann and Kritikos 2014).

In 2012 two actions were taken to restore debt sustainability: a haircut on privately held government bonds and a debt repayment. This has helped to reduce secondary market interest rates of government bonds and to lower the risk premium. However, since late 2014 interest rates have surged due to political struggles between the Greek government and its lenders. As a result, reform processes halted.

In August 2015 the Tsipras government signed a third bailout program, which provides liquidity up to a maximum of 86 billion euro. It will significantly increase public debt, even though part is intended to repay existing loans. *Schrader, Benček* and *Laaser* argue that Greece is unable to outgrow the accumulated public debt and that financing via capital markets is not an option.

Assuming an average long-term growth rate of 3 percent per annum, they argue that debt relief in the form of a haircut or debt restructuring of 17 to 30 percent is necessary for the country to return to more sustainable debt levels in the long term. Similarly, Belke and Dreger (2013) argue that another haircut could not only support the return to sustainable economic growth in Greece, but it would be also less expensive for European taxpayers in the medium and long run.

To achieve this growth, *Schrader, Benček* and *Laaser* consider implementing supply-oriented structural reforms to be indispensable in order to overcome the inherent structural weaknesses and foster investment- and export-led growth. However, the authors note that this is a medium- to long-term task, which comes at the cost of again lower incomes, wealth, privileges and social security in the short term. The Memorandum of Understanding between Greece and its creditors stipulates extensive reforms addressing labor and product markets, the educational system, the business environment, privatization, and reorganization of state institutions. *Schrader, Benček* and *Laaser* point out that the third bailout program includes many of the reforms that were part of the previous two, but have not yet been implemented. Considering the slow progress of reforms until now, it is doubtful that the current Greek government has the willingness or ability to implement and enforce a majority of these changes. But this is not new: the capacity of Greek public administration to carry out far-reaching reforms has long been questioned (OECD 2011b). To ensure progress in the future, *Schrader, Benček* and *Laaser* recommend the outsourcing of the implementation of reform measures to external experts, originating from European institutions or from other EU countries' public administration.

2.2 Austerity and its effects

Austerity measures constitute a key component of the bailout programs. These were introduced at a point when Greek price competitiveness had eroded; the country had an enormous current account deficit and was experiencing high capital outflows. The third of these bailout programs, passed in 2015, stipulates additional cuts in government expenditure and imposes tax increases. European finance ministers repudiate the opposition of the newly elected Syriza government to the reforms.

Gechert and *Rannenberg* estimate the effects of fiscal austerity in Greece since the crisis and find that government expenditure cuts have led to a stronger decline in economic activity during the recession than in normal times. If the austerity measures had been delayed and implemented after the recovery of the Greek economy, the negative impact on GDP could have been weaker. They also highlight that the Troika has underestimated the negative effects of austerity measures, although research on the subject was available at that time (Eggertsson 2009, Christiano, Eichenbaum and Rebelo 2011). *Gechert* and *Rannenberg* conclude that the decision to impose far-reaching austerity measures on Greece right from the outset has hampered the country's ability to repay its debt and to do so in a timely manner.

2.3 Wealth taxation of real estate

Another measure the Troika has pushed for is a substantial rise of the wealth tax on real estate (WTRE), to increase government revenues. The most recent program specifies that the tax revenue generated by the WTRE can amount to 2.7 billion euro annually, independent of overall changes to cadastral values (*Christelis* in this issue). The tax is levied on the total cadastral value of all real estate property that an individual owns. Thus it cannot easily be evaded, as opposed to other taxes in the current system. As policymakers have postponed adjustments to cadastral values until 2017, the tax base for the WTRE is now distorted, leaving some households worse off than others. Further, the WTRE does not take into account any loans, like mortgages. Hence, it especially hurts those households that have very limited liquidity, e. g. the elderly, for whom property is part of retirement provisions. *Christelis* explains that the tax scheme is designed in a way so that individuals with real estate with a nominal value of more than 600,000 euro will have to pay a disproportionately higher WTRE despite sharp drops in market values which discourages additional acquisitions and cools down the property market. As recurrent taxes on immobile property as a percentage of GDP quadrupled since the crisis, real estate prices plummeted and the property market virtually froze. For instance, in Athens the number and value of transactions have declined by about 95 percent since 2007. Due to the frozen market, households are unable to make use of the savings they have accumulated as real estate.

Christelis estimates the negative effects on tax proceeds originating from reduced disposable income and investment in dwellings, as well as a decline of consumption that is due to (perceived) financial insecurity. Further, he takes into account the decline in transaction tax revenue due to the frozen property market, which shows a drastically reduced number of real estate transactions and lower value of property sold. While the WTRE itself generates impressive gross tax receipts, *Christelis* estimates that the harm it does to the economy lets the revenue from other taxes shrink to such an extent that the effect on overall tax receipts is at best negligible, but most likely negative. This implies that the WTRE in its current form fails to achieve the government's aim to increase revenues and presents an obstacle to Greece's way out of the crisis. Therefore, *Christelis* argues that policymakers should lower the tax significantly, or abolish it altogether. This would help to revitalize the real estate market and to increase investment, both contributing to economic recovery.

2.4 Taxing wealth and only wealth?

As a way to address the inefficiency of the Greek tax system, *Papanikos* (in this issue) proposes a radically different tax scheme based on a flat tax on overall wealth—not only real estate—as the only source of government revenues. Such a tax would then be levied on real estate property, bank deposits, durable consumption goods, etc. and implemented together with the abolishment of all other taxes that do not exist for the purpose of correcting market failures and externalities.

At present, the Greek shadow economy and widespread corruption are the main reasons for large-scale tax evasion that results in unequal treatment of tax payers and unfair competition. Income tax, VAT and social security contributions are avoided by the large numbers of self-employed workers and SMEs, as well as those who bribe officials. This in turn leads to production inefficiencies.

Papanikos argues that a tax on overall wealth could not be avoided, that it would ensure fair treatment of taxpayers and through equal treatment of firms it could intensify competition and promote competitiveness of Greek firms. Abolishing all other taxes (unless they are used to correct market failures) would lead, according to *Papanikos*, to increased investment and a rise in wealth accumulation, as there would be no tax on inheritance. If this tax scheme is implemented, GDP should increase, as the wealth originating from the shadow economy can no longer be hidden. The simplification of the tax collection could lead to further economic growth.

In practice, such a tax would find strong resistance from those who currently avoid taxes, especially those who are extremely wealthy and have power to exert influence on the media and politicians. It remains subject to discussion whether wealth taxes are more suitable to establish a fairer horizontal distribution than consumption and income taxes.

3 Product market reforms in Greece beyond austerity measures

For decades product market regulations in Greece have discouraged investment and exports, thus impeding economic growth and productivity (*Richter, Giudice* and *Cozzi* in this issue). Business activity is hampered by complex regulations, time- and cost-intensive procedures that are subject to uncertainty, price rigidity, entry restrictions and an ineffective special planning system (Herrmann and Kritikos, 2014). With the economic crisis the pressure to overcome these regulatory hurdles has increased and reforms implemented by previous Greek governments are still underway. Improvements have been achieved in different areas, but many reforms face strong resistance from vested interests and are, thus, experiencing delays and are not yet fully implemented. The business environment has improved, as witnessed by the Doing Business indicators of the World Bank (2015), but Greece is still below EU average. *Richter, Giudice* and *Cozzi* report in this issue that restrictions on practicing professions as well as minimum fees and fixed prices have been abolished, which had previously kept prices for professional services at exceedingly high levels. Some legislative barriers to competition that led to inefficient production and higher prices have been removed. A successful example is the case of milk formulas for infants, for which the restriction to pharmacies as the only retail channel was lifted; prices in supermarkets were 12 percent lower than what pharmacies offered. The long-standing issue of a weak export performance is now being addressed, as the national trade facilitation strategy initiated in 2012 helped to simplify customs procedures.

Richter, Giudice and *Cozzi* as well as Herrmann and Kritikos (2014) emphasize that it is essential that Greece consistently follows through the reform process according to a comprehensive approach, as bottlenecks will otherwise restrict economic growth: e.g. investment is blocked by complicated licensing procedures and by the ineffective geographical planning system. Greece still needs to consolidate 400 land registry offices into 16 cadastral offices, of which merely two are so far operational. It is the only EU country without a computerized land registry, and although the digitalization project is long underway, full implementation is nowhere in sight. *Richter, Giudice* and *Cozzi* point out that in order for product market reforms in Greece to be successful, the country needs to coordinate the reforms centrally, and should support its implementation, closely monitoring its reform progress.

They stress that in addition to product market reforms, Greece needs the recovery of the financial sector, a functioning judicial system and an efficient public administration in order to succeed. There is the general need for higher trust in the public authorities and the Greek government.

4 Labor markets, SME policies, and investments

Driven by the economic recession, unemployment rose to rates exceeding 25 percent; with youth unemployment exceeding 50 percent (*Bozani* and *Drydakis* in this issue). At the same time Greek labor market legislation has been subject to a range of reforms with the aim of improving employment (ILO, 2014). Regulatory changes geared toward enhanced labor market flexibility and better matching between labor demand and supply (Immervoll and Scarpetta 2012). *Bozani* and *Drydakis* find that labor market legislation has undergone a sustained reform process under previous governments. Most of the reforms addressed labor taxation in order to limit tax dodging. Legislation on flexible contracts and working-hours programs has been put in place and regulations regarding severance payments and collective dismissals have been loosened. In order to induce decreased labor costs, wages of state employees as well as the minimum wage have been reduced. Labor cost in Greece declined by 11.8 percent in the 2010–2013 period, while the decrease amounted to 0.1 percent in the other member states of the euro area. Disincentives to early retirement and stricter conditions for social benefits have been introduced.

While these initiatives have helped to make Greece more competitive, the Greek government needs to continue the reform process in order to shape an environment that fosters job creation and economic growth. Still, there is the need for far-reaching reforms, e.g. to better targeted support for groups with specific labor market risks, to tie wages closer to productivity (European Commission 2015) and to reform the tax system in such a way that companies are encouraged to move from the informal to the formal economy and to grow within the country.

Bozani and *Drydakis* recommend that reforms should also address labor demand, e.g. by improving the competitiveness of the tourism industry and the agricultural sector (ILO 2014). Further, they suggest that the government should encourage investment in innovative SMEs in order to foster long-term growth and to create jobs. Access to funding is currently a major impediment, which can be improved, e.g. if Greece makes better use of the European Structural and Investment Funds (European Commission 2015). The funds could be used to finance support programs for start-ups (OECD 2015) and to strengthen ties between research institutions and businesses in order to promote innovation (Herrmann and Kritikos 2013, ILO 2014). Collaborative research with public institutions can help SMEs to introduce innovative and competitive products, which in turn supports large companies through their supply chains. According to *Bozani* and *Drydakis*, the decision of the European Commission (2015) to create a Structural Reform Support Service is an important step to improve the absorption of those financial resources. In addition, they suggest that Greece should found an institution that grants loans to SMEs and engages private investors (European Commission 2015, OECD 2015, ILO 2014). However, the current Greek government is rolling back some of the structural reforms in labor markets that previous Greek parliaments had approved.

Using a stock-flow approach, *Dreger* and *Reimers* reveal an important impact of public investment on private investment from a different angle. To analyze this link, they examined 12 European countries, finding that public investment leads to higher private investment in the long run, as the returns of private investment projects will increase. Argimón, González-Páramo and Roldán (1997) find that an increase in public investment in infrastructure can raise productivity and private investment. For instance, improved telecommunication networks may make private investment more worthwhile (Pereira and Andraz 2013). However, in Greece we observe an opposing development: Given the low investments in the pre-crisis period, in the course of the economic crisis the share of public investment to overall public spending dropped from 12 percent to less than 6 percent; recovering only slightly in 2015. As a consequence, private investment and GDP growth continues to suffer in Greece.

5 Health and education in the economic crisis

Currently, the education and the health system are characterized by unequal treatment of Greek citizens with regard to provision, coverage, accessibility, affordability and equal opportunities for all (*Dassiou* in this issue). Both sectors operate without proper mechanisms for quality assurance and cost containment. As a consequence of the financial crisis and the austerity measures, lower government spending led to a decline in service quality.

Dassiou argues that the country has experienced frequent changes of health and education policy in past decades. Greek ministers had little opportunity to oversee the implementation of a specific policy during their short tenures. The financial crisis further compounded this situation with various implementations of poorly designed policies as well as frequent reversals of previous changes by new governments or even new ministers within the same governments. Also, there is high resistance to reforms and enforcement of legislation lags. In the health and education sectors, the establishment of an independent regulator is recommended to safeguard the consistent implementation of policies and guarantee continuity.

5.1 The education system

The education system in Greece is bloated and suffers from cost inefficiency, although there are some initiatives to improve it (*Dassiou*). Part of the inefficiency arises from the geography of the country: nearly half of elementary school pupils attend small schools that are scattered across islands and mountainous regions. As many schools in Greece have very few pupils, 1,933 schools were merged into 877 in 2011. Nevertheless, pupil to teacher rates and net teaching time in Greece remain comparatively low (OECD 2011a), which leads to relatively high expenditure on teachers' salaries. The author reports that further issues arise from the tight regulations that do not give schools the ability to hire and fire teachers or to determine their salaries. Progression rules favor senior teachers rather than effective ones, even though younger and less experienced teachers currently have to teach more hours. Many reforms have not been implemented or have been reversed.

Dassiou highlights that tertiary education is characterized by inefficiency as well: while Greece has the highest number of tertiary education enrolments per 100,000 people (OECD 2011a), graduation rates are low. The performance of Greek universities continues to be meager, with low ranks in league tables of research institutions. The unemployment rate among graduates is nearly 20 percent. *Dassiou* sees glimmers of hope, e.g., in merging university departments and sharpening their research focus, as required by the 2011 bailout program and enforced under the Papademos government in 2012. In addition, Greek universities have harmonized their degree programs and adopted quality assurance (Mattheou 2004) under the Bologna Process, thus opening the flow of research funding from the EU. Through the Operational Programme of Education and Initial Vocational Training (OPEIVT) university departments and technological education institutes have been founded throughout Greece. However, as *Dassiou* reports this primarily contributed to local government's prestige and was realized with subsidized plane tickets for "flying professors". Moreover, at the beginning of 2016, the government decided to roll back reforms that had brought the Greek universities closer to European standards.

5.2 The health system

Health coverage in Greece consists of a compulsory social insurance (SSF), a National Health System (ESY) and co-payments (*Dassiou*). When the crisis struck, coverage and health benefits depended significantly on employment. As unemployment surged, many people were left without coverage. Non-coverage, in turn, exerts negative externalities to the society: as the health status of the workforce decreases, labor productivity and living standards decline. As Greece's economy crashed, few Greeks could afford private healthcare.

Furthermore, inefficiencies in the Greek health system arise e.g. from disincentives for physicians: As they receive modest salaries, and as there is no clear evaluation system that provides opportunities for promotion, bribes for preferential treatment and operating a private practice to bolster their salaries are commonplace.

As the Greek healthcare system is fragmented and mismanaged, and thus ineffective and inefficient, the bailout program included health reforms, to ensure broader provision and better quality of healthcare services while cutting costs (*Yfantopoulos* and *Yfantopoulos* in this issue). A series of measures were successfully implemented, such as merging the four largest insurance funds that cover 95 percent of the Greek citizens (Economou 2010), introducing internal auditing and cost accounting systems in hospitals as well as the implementation of a centralized procurement system. Electronic prescriptions, increased generic drugs usage and the introduction of a claw-back system have helped to significantly cut pharmaceutical costs. After 2010, benefits were standardized for all citizens (Economou et al. 2014). However, reforms must continue: while centralized procurement has led to reduced expenses, it only covers a quarter of hospital's purchases.

Among OECD countries Greece has experienced the steepest cuts in health expenditure as a percentage of GDP: 34 percent from 2009 to 2014. Along with expenditures, the satisfaction of Greek people with healthcare (and other welfare benefits) has declined and is now lower than in any other EU country (OECD 2014: 117). In that direction, *Yfantopoulos* and *Yfantopoulos* present the results of 5,500 face-to-face interviews in the Athens area that used quality of life instruments to measure the subjective health status before and during the crisis. Individuals report a decline in subjective health, which is especially pronounced for vulnerable groups with low income, signifying a need for targeted health policies. Moreover, persistent inefficiencies and corruption in healthcare provision must be addressed. To coherently implement and enforce reforms, as well as to set incentives that facilitate efficient resources usage, *Dassiou* suggests introducing an independent health regulator.

6 Is there a way out of the crisis?

The future looks bleak: there are no obvious signs that the Greek economic crisis will come to an end. Unemployment, in particular youth unemployment, remains exceptionally high. How bad the actual income situation for the Greek working population is, is revealed by the following relation: As of today, the main source of income for over half of Greek households is a pension, while only about 37 percent mainly rely on wages (see MacroPolis 2016).

Greece is facing continual institutional and structural deficits in combination with a small industrial basis, low export ratio, few large businesses, and many closed professions. If decreasing labor costs and the bare minimally necessary institutional reforms remain to be the only active policy, then Greeks are doomed to providing other, innovative, economies a low wage factory workbench. The existing tourism, agriculture and trade are not a strong enough foundation to build sustainable, growing wealth for the whole country. If Greece is to grow while a Euro-zone member, it must move beyond institutional reforms and make better use of its hidden assets that are substantially underappreciated and otherwise overlooked in analyses of its economic prospects.

6.1 Greek assets

The first asset is the small number of basic research institutes producing considerable research (Grant et al. 2011). Unfortunately, knowledge transfer is lacking: the valuable research results are trapped inside the gates, often unapplied and unexploited or used by firms in other countries. Without a way to transfer this new knowledge, the scientists remain isolated and unappreciated —with top researchers moving to places beyond the Greek borders, where they are rewarded for their work.

This hints at the second hidden asset: the large number of top Greek scientists. Although Greeks make up a mere 0.2 percent of the world's population, more than 3 percent of all researchers are Greek (Ioannidis 2014). But 85 percent of these researchers have already self-exported to other EU or US research institutions. If this "brain power" could be unleashed in Greece instead, Greece would quickly become an innovation driven economy.

Third, Greece retains a few innovative companies despite the adverse innovation environment. Many are in the IT business, typically based in Athens. These firms sporadically work with the existing research institutes, but they are neither clustered nor co-located, despite the obvious potential for mutually beneficial cooperation. But while a few have stayed, many others have left the country and developed their innovations abroad. The response to the capital controls introduced in July 2015 and the mere plans for increasing tax and social security payments should be unnerving: not only innovative firms but more and more regular businesses are exiting at an even higher pace. And it is not only the US and Western Europe anymore, now they are moving even to Albania and Bulgaria (The Economist 2016).

This brings us to the fourth "hidden asset" of Greece: Its attractiveness in terms of climate and quality of life. In an increasingly global race for the best talents, quality of life outside labs is crucial. So far, Europe lacks a place where high-level academic research and entrepreneurial activities are matched with an attractive climate. Thus, Greece could take advantage of its inherent climate, add investments into research, and gain a competitive advantage, while simultaneously resolving a collective EU conundrum where these two components have remained mutually exclusive. Once quality of life is matched with excellent research and public administration, Greece will go beyond attracting tourists to also attracting global talents (see Herrmann and Kritikos 2013). At the moment these hidden assets are, at best, ignored; at worst they are held in contempt.

6.2 The reform agenda for Greece: A growth strategy for the future

Combining the insights from this volume on the Greek crisis, allows us to derive a number of significant additional reforms that need to be implemented in order to create the necessary structure and a business and innovation friendly environment. Moreover, while these reforms and policy changes are ultimately the responsibility of the Greek government, Greek investors, company owners, and citizens must support, endorse, and even lobby for them.

Thus, while Greece currently has

- unsustainable public debt;
- a badly working tax system and a non-viable real estate tax;
- fundamental institutional and structural problems in labor and product markets;
- overregulation, with too many civil servants and a bureaucracy that acts arbitrarily; and
- badly functioning public services that are worsening with time,

we recommend the following specific policy measures designed to stimulate economic growth processes in Greece and to accelerate its transformation process to a modern, innovation-driven economy.

1) The Greek public debt must be made sustainable. There are two ways of realizing this target, either by debt restructuring or by introducing GDP—linked loans. Restructuring would induce lower interest rates, longer maturities, and a temporary suspension of interest payments. Under the second solution, interest payments would be linked to the development of Greece's GDP.[1]

In doing so, markets, investors, Greek citizens and its European partners will start regaining trust in the Greek government. Only then can capital controls be cancelled; these controls are strongly and negatively affecting the Greek economy. Ceasing capital controls will also stop if not turn around, the exodus of Greek and foreign capital, and Greek companies, once public debt is sustainable.

2) To support the regaining of trust into the Greek government, it must continue the otherwise incomplete structural and institutional reforms. This not only includes the further opening of closed professions and liberal trades. In addition, Greek regulation remains excessive, especially for new firms: hindering them and imposing substantial costs. Administrative efforts for business activities need to be massively reduced and codified. This should include reducing the efforts needed to register new businesses, as well as reducing the number of regulations, fees and reporting duties for existing businesses and for closing down businesses (Kritikos 2014). Moreover, courts must support the reforms, while all administrative officials must be appropriately trained. Reducing the daily bureaucratic hurdles confronting Greek citizens, entrepreneurs,

1 See Fratzscher et al. (2014) for a discussion on the advantages of GDP-linked loans.

business owners and managers is also critical. Thus, the still oversized and inefficient public administration must be reformed.

3) Despite six years of reform process, the most important structural reforms have not been implemented and efforts to do so through existing structures appear futile. Greece remains nearly as overregulated in 2016 as before the crisis. This clarifies that the reform process needs to be organized in a different way in the future. So, this third point relates to how reforms should be organized, rather than what reforms need to be done. The Greek government should commission outside experts, for instance strengthening institutions like the EU Task Force for Greece, to redesign the system and how the public interacts with it. Careful attention to ensure that the modern, reformist part of the Greek society has a voice in the process is critical. Reforms "against" the society, as often stipulated by the Troika, do not work and will be not lead to effective changes of the overregulated system (Kritikos 2015).

Moreover, the use of professional regulators will help improve public services like the health and the education system to overcome the failures of the past. These regulators will need to make sure that no unreasonable changes are executed with the change of every government or even of every minister, persons who were sometimes replaced four times a year. These regulators will need to make sure that changes in these systems are implemented consistently, despite changes of governments or ministers.

4) Expanding Greece's industrial base requires actively investing in a better innovation system. The country can only become prosperous if it uses its comparative advantages and lays the groundwork for higher value-added goods production. R&D investments are critical because these investments yield innovative, exportable goods, while simultaneously creating jobs and prosperity. The institutional reforms under way are not enough: R&D needs an innovation-oriented industrial structure and a well-functioning innovation system. This is a considerable challenge: Other Euro-zone economies invest around 3 percent of their gross domestic product in R&D. Greece invests 0.67 percent. Another major difference is that governments elsewhere are committed to R&D, no matter which party is in control. The budget is set and the scientists are given wide latitude to do their work. As a result, their economies are driven by innovation and continual refinement, with new products and technologies regularly introduced.

Thus, Greece must close this investment gap by increasing its expenditure in R&D, by investing in new, additional cutting-edge applied research centers, and by ensuring that high-quality science supports and serves entrepreneurs developing new technologies. To unleash this potential, Greece also needs to encourage strong ties and knowledge transfer between its universities, research institutions and private companies. Building scientifically competitive research clusters, with co-located participants, will help close the gaps in the innovation chain and attract talent, both Greek and non-Greek.[2]

---

2 This investment in people and research can be partly financed through the EU's Horizon 2020 program, which is designed to strengthen both European and national research systems. Of particular importance for Greece are the programs to develop cutting-edge research centers. Horizon 2020 could be the foundation underlying an integrated and comprehensive Greek investment strategy for creating scientific excellence in the country if public expenditures are shifted from consumption to investments into research and development.

Moreover, this approach will only work if universities and research institutes are independent of political influence. Ministers and MPs need to provide an overall budget and then get out of the way, leaving, for instance, the selection of new researchers to internationally recognized scientists. Of course, whether or not Greece actually becomes an innovation hub depends not just on investments in R&D and research centers, but also on establishing a partnership between the spheres of research, business and entrepreneurship, where ideas can be freely exchanged. Creating an environment that brings both Greek researchers and entrepreneurs back to Greece, and that also supports the local innovation chain, is critical for the country's future.

5) Last but not least, Greece needs to reorganize its public finances. The dysfunctional tax system needs to be reformed to become a tool that helps Greece move forward instead of stagnate (Börsch-Supan and Tinios 2001). In general, future Greek governments should avoid seeking their salvation in ever-increasing taxes as the current government does. The better way is to improve the enforcement of existing taxes (like income or value-added taxes) while rather decreasing tax rates and simultaneously broadening the tax base. This includes the creation of a business friendly tax system at the local and federal level, which will give incentives to businesses to become legally recognized, and to those business owners who aim to grow their companies to stay in Greece. This further includes a complete reform of real estate taxes, which would bring back life into this otherwise frozen market.

Potential alternatives include the introduction of a flat tax (see Peichl 2014) or of a wealth tax as discussed by *Papanikos*. In any case, taxes need to be designed in a way that enforcement is possible and that the private sector gets positive incentives.

Put in a nutshell, Greece's economic recovery will only start once it is able to produce products with higher value-added, thus making its economy more competitive in international markets. This recovery requires simultaneously addressing several key issues. Making the Greek public debt sustainable, while substantially improving the tax base is one decisive part within the public sector, improving public services like health and education is another. Fundamental institutional and structural reforms in labor and product markets are a third. At the same time, red tape must be cut and bureaucracy streamlined in order to make the business environment attractive, while investing in the Greek innovation system is crucial.

But such substantial reforms will only come about if familial and clientelistic approaches stop being the main driving force behind political decisions; the same forces underlying the Greek crisis. Greek statesmen are wanted who make decisions that look beyond vested interests, instead focusing on those that benefit all of Greece. This is the core reform required to engender a fundamental change to Greek society. For that Catharsis is needed.

References

- Argimón, I., J. M. González-Páramo, and J. M. Roldán (1997): Evidence of public spending crowding-out from a panel of OECD Countries. Applied Economics, 29 (8), 1001–1010.
- Belke A., and C. Dreger (2011): Ramifications of debt restructuring on the euro area—The exposure of large European economies to Greece. Intereconomics, 46, 188–196.
- Börsch-Supan, A., and P. Tinios (2001): The Greek pension system: Strategic framework for reform. In: R. C. Bryant, N. C. Garganas, and G. S. Tavlas, (eds.) (2001): Greece's economic performance and prospects. Bank of Greece and Brookings Institution, 361–442.
- Christiano, L. J., M. Eichenbaum, and S. Rebelo. (2011): When is the Government Spending Multiplier Large? Journal of Political Economy, 119 (1), 78–121.
- Economou, C. (2010): Greece: Health system review. Health Systems in Transition, 12 (7), 1–180.
- Economou, C., D. Kaitelidou, A. Kentikelenis, A. Sissouras, and A. Maresso (2014): The impact of the financial crisis on the health system and health in Greece. World Health Organization for the European Observatory on Health Systems and Policies.
- Eggertsson, G. B. (2009): What Fiscal Policy Is Effective at Zero Interest Rates? Federal Reserve Bank of New York Staff Reports, Nr. 402.
- European Commission (2015): Communication From the Commission to the European Parliament, The Council, The European Economic and Social Committee and the Committee of the Regions. A New Start for Jobs and Growth in Greece.
- Fratzscher, M., C. Große Steffen, and M. Rieth (2014): GDP-Linked Loans for Greece. DIW Economic Bulletin 9, 40–49.
- Grant, J., T. Ling, D. Potoglou, and D. M. Culley (2011): A rapid review of the Greek research and development system, Rand Europe. Discussion Paper, September 2011.
- Hausmann, R., and C. A. Hidalgo (2012): Economic Complexity and The Future of Manufacturing. In: J. Moavenzadeh, P. Philip, C. A. Giffi, and A. Thakker (eds.): The Future of Manufacturing. Opportunities to Drive Economic Growth. A World Economic Forum Report.
- Herrmann, B., and A. S. Kritikos (2013): Growing out of the Crisis: Hidden Assets to Greece's Transition to an Innovation Economy. IZA Journal of European Labor Studies, 2 (1), 1–23.
- Immervoll, H., and S. Scarpetta (2012): Activation and Employment Support Policies in OECD Countries. An Overview of Current Approaches. IZA Journal of Labor Policy, 1 (1), 1–20.
- International Labor Office (2014): Productive Jobs for Greece. Geneva, International Labor Office.
- Ioannidis, J. (2014): The Best Greek Scientists Exiled from Greece, available at http://greece.greekreporter.com/2014/08/01/the-best-greek-scientists-exiled-from-greece.
- Koliopoulos, J. S., and T. M. Veremis (2002): Greece, the Modern Sequel. New York, New York University Press.
- Kritikos, A. S. (2014): Entrepreneurs and their Impact on Jobs and Economic Growth. IZA World of Labor, 2014 (8).
- Kritikos, A. S. (2015): Das Scheitern der Troika. Cicero, 3, 80–81.
- MacroPolis Bulletin (2016): More than half of Greek households rely mainly on pensions, January 28, 2016. www.macropolis.gr/?i=portal.en.society.3589.

— Mattheou, D. (2004): Marketing a new institutional identity for the University in Europe. The Bologna Process and the national context. In: E. Bulk-Berge, S. Holm-Larsen, and S. Wiborg (eds.): Education across borders- comparative studies. Oslo, Didakta, 57–72.
— OECD (2011a): Education policy advice for Greece; strong reformers and successful reformers in education. OECD publishing.
— OECD (2011b): Greece: Review of the Central Administration. OECD Public Governance Reviews. OECD Publishing.
— OECD (2014): Society at a Glance 2014: OECD Social Indicators. OECD Publishing.
— OECD (2015): Financing SMEs and Entrepreneurs 2015: An OECD Scoreboard. OECD Publishing.
— Peichl, A. (2014): Flat-rate tax systems and their effect on labor markets. IZA World of Labor, 2014 (61).
— Pereira, A. M., and J. M. Andraz (2013): On the Economic Effects of Public Infrastructure Investment: A Survey of the International Evidence. Journal of Economic Development, 38 (4), 1–37.
— Schrader, K., D. Benček, and C.-F. Laaser (2013): IfW-Krisencheck: Alles wieder gut in Griechenland? Kieler Diskussionsbeiträge 522/523. Kiel Institute for the World Economy, Kiel.
— Schrader, K., D. Benček, and C.-F. Laaser (2015): Greece: How to Take a Turn for the Better. Kiel Policy Brief 83. Kiel Institute for the World Economy, January.
— Stergiou, A. (2012): Anatomie eines Niedergangs? Griechenland und die Europäische Union. Bundeszentrale für politische Bildung, December 23. www.bpb.de/apuz/142837/griechenland-und-die-europaeische-union?p=all (in German).
— The Economist (2016): An actual Grexit. Big tax rises are driving companies out of the country. The Economist, February 20. www.economist.com/node/21693213.
— World Bank (2015): Doing Business 2015: Measuring Regulatory Quality and Efficiency. Washington, D.C.

AUTHORS

David Benček, born 1984, is an economist at the Kiel Institute for the World Economy and member of its Economic Policy Center. His current research focuses on debt sustainability, the political economy of institutional change and the application of agent-based computational models.

Vasiliki Bozani is currently a research fellow at the Economic Research Centre of the University of Cyprus, working on the EU-funded programme of "Employment in Europe". Her main research interests include Macroeconomic Theory and Policy, Monetary Theory and Policy, Political Economy, while the main concern of her research is concentrated on the problem of unemployment and the policies that can manage it. Prior to this position, she participated in the "Macroeconomic Analysis Unit and Economic Transformation" as a member of the research team of the Centre for Economic and Social Developments in Labour Institute (INE)-GSEE (Greece), where she contributed to the research field relative to the Greek Co-Operative Banks. She also worked as a Scientific and Laboratory Assistant at the Department of Accounting of the Technological Educational Institute (TEI) of Epirus, Greece. She holds a BSc in Economics, MSc in Economic Theory and Policy and a PhD in Economics, all acquired at the University of Crete (Greece).

Dimitris Christelis is a Research Fellow of the Centre for Studies in Economics and Finance at the University of Naples Federico II. He has also worked as a senior economist in the Directorate General Research of the European Central Bank, and consults with various institutions on issues related to micro data surveys. He holds a PhD in Economics from the University of Pennsylvania. His research interests include household saving and portfolio choice, microeconometrics, and health economics. His work has appeared in journals such as the Review of Economics and Statistics, the Journal of Monetary Economics, the European Economic Review, the Journal of Health Economics, and the Journal of Banking and Finance. He has also been involved with the production of micro data, as he participated in the design of the questionnaire and implemented the imputation of missing data for the first two waves of the Survey of Health, Ageing and Retirement in Europe.

Angelo Cozzi, Master in Economics, Finance and International Integration, Università degli Studi di Pavia, Italy and Eberhard Karls Universität Tübingen, works currently with the European Commission (DG ECFIN, Unit F2: Greece). Previously Cozzi worked as research and teaching assistent at Eberhard Karls Universität Tübingen and as an intern at the German Cartel Office. Research interests: Policy Analysis and Political Economics in the European Union, Competition Policy and Market Regulation.

Xeni Dassiou, Dr., has been a Reader in Economics at City University of London since 2009. She is also a founding member and director of the Research Centre for Competition and Regulatory Policy (CCRP) (www.city.ac.uk/arts-social-sciences/economics/research/centre-for-competition-and-regulatory-policy) in the School of Arts & Social Sciences at City. The Centre commenced its operation in June 2005 and Xeni has led the Centre since June 2008. During her directorship, she has organised/co-organised and participated in over 30 CCRP workshops and annual competition policy roundtables both at City as well as in domestic and overseas universities and regulatory bodies hosting panellists from the academic world and leading regulatory institutions including the National Audit Office, Ofwat, the Competition and Markets Authority, the Institute for Government, Which? She has edited/co-edited journals and books on topics such as the regulation of infrastructure utilities, competition in modern market structures, and advances in the analysis of competition policy and regulation. Xeni Dassiou is an experienced leader, education and research strategist, teaching & research director, and an excellent communicator with strong connections in the regulatory world. She has a 25 years-long established reputation as a rigorous, objective, systematic, clear- headed and objective analyst using economic theory and evidence-based analysis in her teaching, research, and professional work in industrial organisation, competition economics and regulatory economics. She also has a long experience in training both the regulators and the regulated on the practice and complexities of regulation and competition policy and is regularly exposed to the types of issues raised in this type of training both in her role as a lecturer, a programme director of the MSc in Economic Regulation and Competition (MSc ERC), and as part of her custom-made professional training and consultancy work. Her ability to explain and analyse very complex economic issues to different audiences with different educational backgrounds is exceptional. Xeni Dassiou has given numerous invited talks on behavioural issues in regulation and competition, as well as on the competition and oversight issues surrounding public service markets, including health and education. Her research and professional work as an academic researcher, independent consultant, expert speaker and professional trainer in competition and regulation has been commissioned by competition and regulation bodies, policy think-tanks, commercial and academic organisations including: BBC Trust, The Institute of Economic Affairs, The Competition and Markets Authority, Centre for Analysis of Risk and Regulation—London School of Economics, LSE Enterprise, National Audit Office, The Office of Fair Trading (now merged into CMA), The Financial Ombudsman, The Centre for Parliamentary Studies, The European Public Law Organisation (EPLO), Rand Europe, Regulatory Policy Committee (RPC), The Regulators' Forum, Ofgem, SINOPEC, British Gas etc.

Christian Dreger, Prof. Dr., is Professor for Macroeconomics at the European University Viadrina in Frankfurt/Oder and Research Director International Economics at the German Institute for Economics (DIW Berlin). Formerly, he acted as the Head of the Departments for Business Cycle analysis and Macroeconomics. Before 2005, he worked as a senior researcher at the Institute for Economic Research in Halle in the Departments for Labour Markets and Business Cycles. He studied economics at the Freie Universität Berlin and holds a doctoral and habilitation degree in Economics from the University of Kassel. He has conducted many national and international research projects and published extensively in leading international journals in the relevant fields. His main areas of expertise are international business cycle analysis, monetary policy and financial markets, integration of emerging markets into the world economy and macroeconometric modelling.

Nick Drydakis is a Reader in Economics at Anglia Ruskin University in the UK, and Research Fellow at the Institute for the Study of Labor in Germany. Nick's research interests include labour economics. He has published sole author articles in leading journals such as: Social Science and Medicine, Industrial Relations: A Journal for Economy and Society, Labour Economics, Journal of Population Economics, Review of the Economics of the Household, European Journal of Health Economics, Feminist Economics and International Journal of Intercultural Relations. His research activity has contributed in several domains in evaluating among others the negative effect of economic crisis on health and mental health, health-impaired employees' job satisfaction adjustments, the positive effects of assimilation and integration on immigrants' employment and wages, and negative transmission mechanisms between bullying, human capital, mental health and labour market outcomes. Nick is the founding director of the Scientific Centre for the

Study of Discrimination in Greece and has worked on European Union and World Bank research programmes.

Sebastian Gechert, Dr., is a senior economist at the Macroeconomic Policy Institute (IMK) of the Hans-Böckler-Foundation in Düsseldorf (Germany). He received his PhD (Dr. rer. pol.) from Chemnitz University of Technology in 2014 with a dissertation on fiscal multipliers. From 2008 to 2012 he worked as teaching and research assistant at Chemnitz University of Technology before joining the IMK in October 2012. Several research and study visits at IWH Halle, IMK and Levy Economics Institute of Bard College.

Gabriele Giudice, Head of Unit and deputy Mission Chief for Greece in the Directorate General for Economic and Financial Affairs, at the European Commission where he has been working since 1994. He is in charge of the team which monitors the Greek economy, and—on behalf of the Euro Area Member States and the European Stability Mechanism—the implementation of the economic adjustment programme of Greece. Previously, he was in charge of the units carrying out the surveillance of the UK, Estonia, Latvia, Lithuania and Sweden, including as EU Mission Chief for the Balance of Payments assistance provided to Latvia (2009–2012), and in charge of cyclical analysis and the management of the EU Business Surveys programme (2008–2009). He has been advising Joaquin Almunia, Commissioner for economic and monetary affairs in 2004–2008, on economic, budgetary and monetary issues in the EU and the euro area, including the functioning of EMU and the design and implementation of the Stability and Growth Pact and economic policy coordination. He was educated as an international economist at Bocconi University, Milan and at the Institute for International Policy Studies, Milan. He has written extensively on budgetary policies, in relation to the design and implementation of the Stability and Growth Pact and, more recently, on country specific matters. The latter include, as author/co-editor, the books „EU Balance-of-payments assistance for Latvia. Foundations of success", European Economy, Occasional Paper, No. 120/2012, and The UK Economy: The Crisis in Perspective, 2011, Routledge.

Marian Hafenstein is a Research Assistant for Entrepreneurship Research at the German Institute for Economic Research (DIW Berlin). His main research interests are innovation economics, entrepreneurship and policy evaluation.

Alexander S. Kritikos is Research Director at the DIW Berlin. At the same time, he is Full Professor for Industrial and Institutional Economics at the University of Potsdam and Research Fellow at the IZA Bonn. His research interests are Innovation and Entrepreneurship Research, and Experimental and Behavioral Economics.

Claus-Friedrich Laaser, Dr. sc. pol., born 1955, is a senior economist at the Kiel Institute for the World Economy. He is member of the institute's Policy Coordination Unit, its Economic Policy Center and its Communication Center. His current research topics are trade integration in the EU and the role of infrastructure in the course of economic integration.

Renate Neubäumer is full professor of economics and economic policy and chief of the institute of social sciences at the University of Koblenz-Landau, Germany. She is research fellow of the IAB (Nuremberg) and of the IZA (Bonn). Her main research interests are in the fields of economic policy, economics of education, and empirical labor economics. She has published several articles in refereed journals, including Journal for Labour Market Research, Industrial Relations Journal,

Applied Economics Quarterly, Journal of Economics and Statistics, Review of Economics, International Journal of Manpower.

Gregory T. Papanikos, Dr., has studied economics at the Aristotelian University of Thessaloniki and did his postgraduate studies at the University of Ottawa and Carleton University in Canada. He has taught at: University of Ottawa (Canada); Ryerson Polytechnic University (Canada); York University (Canada); University of Patras (Greece); University of Crete (Greece); National Technological University of Athens (Greece); University of Ioannina (Greece); Athens University of Economics and Business (Greece), Technological Educational Institute (Greece). His papers have appeared in Applied Economics, Journal of Policy Modelling, Economic Modeling, Agricultural Economics, International Review of Regional Science, Technological Forecasting, International Journal of Social Economics, Singapore Economic Review (invited contribution), Romanian Journal of Fiscal Policy (invited contribution) etc. He published more than 50 papers in Greek "academic" journals and 14 books-monographs; edited 40 books and conference proceedings. Published over 120 articles in the Greek and International press. He has undertaken more than 25 research projects financed by the European Union, OECD, Governments, Professional Associations, and Private Companies in addition to 250 research "opinions" to the Greek Government (1997-2011). He was an institutional member of the National Operation Committee of the Strategic Development Plan of the Greek Structural Funds and a Member of the National Committee for the Organization of the Olympic Games of 2004. His commissioned research projects included the euro impact on the Greek economy in 1996, the Tourism Impact of the Olympic Games in 1999 and the Post Olympic Use of Venues in 2003. In 2014 he wrote a book on the Greek Economic Crisis subtitled a Class Analysis in Support of Austerity Measures. He is the President of the Athens Institute for Education and Research since 1995 and Honorary Professor of Economics at the University of Stirling since 2013.

Ansgar Rannenberg, Dr., is a macroeconomist at the Central Bank of Ireland. He holds a PhD from the University of St. Andrews (United Kingdom). Prior to joining the Central Bank of Ireland, he worked at the Macroeconomic Policy Institute (IMK) of the Hans-Boeckler Foundation in Düsseldorf (Germany), from which he is currently on leave. He has previously worked at the Deutsche Bundesbank and the National Bank of Belgium.

Hans-Eggert Reimers has been Professor of Macroeconomics at the Hochschule Wismar University of Applied Sciences, Technology, Business and Design since 1995. He studied economics at the Christian-Albrechts-University of Kiel. After his Master degree he worked at the University of Konstanz and at the Institute of Statistic and Econometrics of the Christian-Albrechts-University of Kiel. In 1991 he obtained his doctoral degree in Economics. Then he was economist at the Deutsche Bundesbank in the econometric division. He published articles, for example, in Journal of Economic Dynamics and Control, Macroeconomic Dynamics, Spanish Economic Review and Portuguese Economic Journal. His main research interests include time series econometrics, testing long-run macroeconomic hypotheses applying panel time series methods and the development of early warning systems of financial markets.

Kaspar Richter heads the growth and business climate entity for the structural reform service of the European Commission. From 2013 to 2015 he was responsible for product market reforms in the Greece department of the EU Directorate General for Economics and Finance. Prior to that Kaspar Richter has worked for 13 years for the World Bank in Africa, Asia and Europe. He holds a

PhD and MsC in Economics from the London School of Economics and diplomas in economics and political science from the Freie Universität Berlin.

Klaus Schrader, Dr. rer. pol., born 1962, is a senior economist at the Kiel Institute for the World Economy. He is deputy head of the institute's Economic Policy Center. His present research focuses on EU trade integration and the international competitiveness of South and Eastern European countries.

Platon Yfantopoulos, M. A., York UK, holds an Honours Degree in Economics from the School of Management and Economics of the University of Lancaster and a Master Degree in Health Economics from the University of York UK. He participated in several Research Projects undertaken by the National Centre for Social Research for the Greek Government and the European Commission. He had been working in the Department of Public Health in the World Health Organization, in the Centre for Health Economics at the University of York, and currently in the European Commission in the area of health reforms across Europe. He has been the author and co-author of several publications.

John Yfantopoulos, Prof., D. Phil., York UK., Professor of Health Economics at the University of Athens, former President of the National Centre for Social Research and key note Speaker in several Ministerial meetings during the 2014th Greek Presidency in the European Commission and the European Parliament. He received his Doctor of Philosophy in Health Economics from the University of York, UK. Professor Yfantopoulos has extensive teaching and research experience in Health Economics, Health Technology Assessment (HTA) and Health Inequalities. He collaborated with several Universities in Europe, and USA. He has been working and advising the European Commission, (Eurostat), the W.H.O., the OECD, the ILO, and the World Bank. He was the elected Rapporteur of the 23rd WHO Regional Office for Europe and the elected Chair of the 11th European Congress of ISPOR. He is currently the president of the ISPOR Greek Chapter. He has extensive research experience with the Eurostat data sources (HBS, LFS, ECHP, SILC, EHIS) as well as with the EU Research Projects. Recent activities in a number of Eastern European countries include studies in the evaluation of economic efficiency and implementing effective health reforms. He has published 31 books, as well as more than 280 articles in international journals.

PROOFREADERS

Adam Lederer is DIW Berlin Academic Editor, where he spends his days helping scientists improve their written communications. Prior to joining DIW Berlin, he was with the Max Planck Institute of Economics. He studied at the University of Wyoming, in Laramie, Wyoming.

Miranda Siegel is an American author and journalist who is currently working as a translator and English-language editor in the Communication Department at the German Institute for Economic Research. For five years, she worked as an editor in the Culture section of New York magazine, during which she took part in panel discussions and served on film festival juries.

HINWEISE FÜR AUTOREN DER VIERTELJAHRSHEFTE

Die Vierteljahrshefte zur Wirtschaftsforschung werden seit 1927 vom DIW Berlin herausgegeben. Sie veröffentlichen Aufsätze zu aktuellen wirtschaftspolitischen Fragestellungen und wenden sich an Wissenschaft, Politik und Wirtschaft.

Zwischen Abgabetermin des Manuskripts und Erscheinen des Beitrags in den Vierteljahrsheften liegen im Allgemeinen weniger als drei Monate. Alle Beiträge werden begutachtet. Die Themen der nächsten Schwerpunkthefte und ausführliche Hinweise für Autoren können der DIW-Internetseite entnommen werden (www.diw.de).

Beiträge sind an die Redaktion, an das jeweils zuständige Redaktionsmitglied oder zu Händen Ellen Müller-Gödtel einzusenden. Berücksichtigt werden nur Originalbeiträge, die im Falle der Annahme auch tatsächlich zur Veröffentlichung in den Vierteljahrsheften zur Verfügung stehen.

Die Beiträge sind in deutscher Sprache zu verfassen. Beiträge von englischsprachigen Autoren können in deutschsprachige Hefte nur Eingang finden, wenn sie vorher übersetzt wurden. Es gilt die neue deutsche Rechtschreibung. Eine Zusammenfassung des Beitrags ist in deutscher und in englischer Sprache gesondert zu erstellen. Diese soll jeweils nicht mehr als 150 Wörter umfassen. Außerdem müssen dem Manuskript mindestens drei Begriffe der JEL-Klassifikation (www.aeaweb.org/journal/jel_class_system.html) und mindestens drei englischsprachige Keywords beigefügt werden. Neben dem Regelfall des deutschsprachigen Heftes sind auch Vierteljahrshefte in englischer Sprache möglich, wenn die Themenstellung dies nahelegt.

Das Manuskript ist in Schriftgröße 12 pt im Zeilenabstand von 1,5 zu erstellen und mit einem linken und rechten Rand von 2,5 cm zu versehen. Der Umfang des Manuskripts sollte 15 Seiten (circa 30 000 Zeichen, ohne Tabellen und Abbildungen) nicht überschreiten. Die Zitierweise ist den Aufsätzen des Vierteljahrsheftes beziehungsweise der oben genannten Internetseite zu entnehmen.

Der Textteil ist in MS Word zu liefern. Tabellen und Abbildungen sind als separate Dateien (Tabellen in MS Excel, Abbildungen zusammen mit den zugrunde liegenden Daten – entweder ebenfalls in Excel oder einem anderen gängigen Grafikprogramm) zu liefern. Die Stellen, an denen sie im Text erscheinen sollen, müssen im Manuskript markiert werden. Die maximale Breite von Tabellen und Abbildungen beträgt 12,6 cm. Bei Tabellen die Zeilen- und Spaltenmerkmale bitte übersichtlich aufteilen. Anmerkungen und Fußnoten sowie Quellenangabe(n) bitte unter dem Tabellenfeld beziehungsweise der Grafik positionieren.

Wichtiger Hinweis: Falls Sie Abbildungen oder Ähnliches aus dem Internet entnehmen, bitten wir um Mitlieferung einer Kopie der Druckgenehmigung.